NOTES
ON THE STATE
OF VIRGINIA

harper ☙ torchbooks

EDITORS' NOTE: *A check-list of Harper Torchbooks, classified by subjects, is printed at the end of this volume.*

AMERICAN PERSPECTIVES
edited by BERNARD WISHY *and*
WILLIAM E. LEUCHTENBURG

* in preparation

NOTES
ON THE STATE
OF VIRGINIA

Thomas Jefferson

INTRODUCTION TO THE TORCHBOOK EDITION BY
THOMAS PERKINS ABERNETHY

HARPER TORCHBOOKS
THE UNIVERSITY LIBRARY

HARPER & ROW, PUBLISHERS
NEW YORK, EVANSTON, AND LONDON

NOTES ON THE STATE OF VIRGINIA

Introduction to the Torchbook edition copyright © 1964 by
Thomas Perkins Abernethy.

Printed in the United States of America.

This book was originally published in 1861 by H. W. Derby,
New York, as part of Volume VIII of *The Writings of Thomas
Jefferson*, edited by H. A. Washington.

First HARPER TORCHBOOK edition published 1964 by
Harper & Row, Publishers, Incorporated
49 East 33rd Street
New York 16, N. Y.

CONTENTS

INTRODUCTION TO THE
TORCHBOOK EDITION

by Thomas Perkins Abernethy

———— ··◆·· ————

Most men in this country who achieve high public office do so by using their tongues. Only a few, notably Thomas Jefferson and Woodrow Wilson, have used their pens to reach the top, and now television, along with ghost writing, perhaps, has foreclosed the probability of another literary President. Wilson wrote a number of scholarly volumes; Jefferson produced only one, and that was not intended for publication. It was, in fact, motivated only by love of his native state and a desire to furnish European scholars with accurate information concerning Virginia.

When, toward the end of 1780, the fortunes of war were running strongly against the embattled British colonies, and their Gallic ally was becoming nervous about the outcome of the conflict, François Barbé-Marbois, secretary to the French legation at Philadelphia, sent a semi-official questionnaire concerning the American states to certain influential members of the Continental Congress. One copy went to Joseph Jones of the Virginia delegation, an uncle of James Monroe. Realizing that Thomas Jefferson, who had drafted the Declaration of Independence at the age of thirty-three, and now at thirty-seven was governor of Virginia, was better qualified than any other Virginian to answer the questionnaire, Jones submitted it to him.

This document arrived at a most inopportune time. On August 16, the Virginia militia, along with other troops, had been disastrously defeated at the battle of Camden. Then, on October 20, a British fleet of fifty-four ships, bringing an invading force of several thousand men, entered Hampton Roads and immediately occupied the town of Hampton. Since the resources of the state, both in men and supplies, had been used primarily to reinforce Washington's army to the north and Gates' to the south, Jefferson was almost destitute of means for defense. But, fortunately for him and for Virginia, the British withdrew their forces on November 22, and on the 30th the Governor wrote to a friend that he was "at present busily employed for Monsr. Marbois without his knowing it."[1] But this congenial occupation was soon interrupted by the arrival of another hostile force of some 1,500 men under the traitor, Benedict Arnold. On Sunday, December 31, 1780, the Governor was notified that a British fleet had been sighted in the Bay. On the following Friday the enemy entered Richmond in triumph, but evacuated the town on Sunday January 7th, 1781, and Jefferson returned the next day. He thought that if the militia had been called two days earlier, Arnold might never have got to Richmond, where he destroyed most of the official records of colonial and revolutionary Virginia. The Governor blamed this tragedy on lack of adequate reports of the enemy's movements.[2]

This was by no means the end of Jefferson's distress. On April 15, 1781, his two-year-old daughter, Lucy Elizabeth, died, and the next day he was unable to attend a meeting of the Council because of the serious illness of his wife, who died shortly thereafter. Three days later he received word that eleven square-rigged British warships were sailing up the James. But Lafayette came in time to save the capital. The English got no closer than Manchester, across the James to the south. Jefferson and Lafayette now met for the first time; the Virginia militia joined the Continental regulars under the Marquis and the British were soon retreating down the James.[3] On March 4, the Governor had written Marbois that though "present occupations" made it impossible for him to complete his answers, he intended shortly "to be in a condition which will leave me quite at leisure to take them up."[4]

But the fates were against Jefferson. Thinking that the enemy would not return, he considered Richmond a safe place for the Legislature to meet at the scheduled time in early May. The legislators themselves did not think so and on May 10 they agreed to meet two weeks later in Charlottesville, a Piedmont town seventy miles to the west. This proved to be a wise move, for the British troops in Virginia reversed their course and planned

---

[1] William Peden (ed.), *Notes on the State of Virginia, by Thomas Jefferson* (The University of North Carolina Press, Chapel Hill, 1955), p. xiii.
[2] Dumas Malone, *Jefferson the Virginian* (Boston, 1948), pp. 339-341.
[3] *Ibid.*, 349.
[4] Peden, *op. cit.*, p. xiv.

to join Cornwallis (who was leaving a smaller force to cope with Nathanael Greene in the Carolinas) at Petersburg. Aside from local forces, the Continentals under Lafayette were now the sole defenders of Virginia. After a last conference with him and a last official meeting with the Council on May 15, Jefferson quitted his capital and rode sorrowfully westward toward Charlottesville and his beloved Monticello." Now the fortunes of war changed and on May 13 the British General Phillips lay dead in Petersburg. Soon Jefferson ceased to be governor of Virginia.[5]

On reaching Monticello the retiring governor, on May 28, penned a last appeal to General Washington. He explained that the armies of Cornwallis and Arnold had, according to plan, been united at Petersburg, and had been reinforced by troops coming by water from New York. They had now moved northward with 7,000 men and Lafayette could oppose them with less than half that number. With the object of disrupting the government of the tottering Commonwealth, Cornwallis now detached a force of 250 men to ride to Charlottesville. Counting on taking the Governor by surprise, they covered seventy miles in twenty-four hours, but at "Cuckoo Tavern," some forty miles from Charlottesville, their movements were observed and their objective surmised by a daring young Virginian, known to history as Captain Jack Jouett.[6]

Riding desperately through the night, along trails that no stranger could have found in this rugged country, Jouett reached Monticello before sunrise on Monday, June 4. Jefferson had been unable to assemble a meeting of the Council, but the Assembly had finally achieved a quorum for a fruitless meeting on May 28. The speakers of the two houses and a few other guests were at Monticello when Jouett arrived. According to tradition, the exhausted horseman was revived with old Madeira and rode on to arouse the sleeping legislators in Charlottesville. Assembling hastily, these gentlemen agreed to adjourn to Staunton, beyond the Blue Ridge, but, in their breathless haste, they did not take time to elect a new governor to replace Jefferson, whose term had expired two days earlier.[7]

Jefferson's departure from Monticello has been described by hostile historians as a precipitate and undignified flight, but it was nothing of the sort. He and his guests ate a normal country

[5] Malone, *op. cit.*, pp. 350-351.
[6] *Ibid.*, pp. 354-355.
[7] *Ibid.*, 355-356.

breakfast, and while the delegates went to town for that brief meeting of the Legislature, he and his family moved by easy stages to his rural retreat at Poplar Forest, some ninety miles southwest of Charlottesville. With him he carried the voluminous notes from which he planned to answer Marbois' queries.[8] Despite injuries sustained in a fall from his horse, he worked rapidly and efficiently, and when he returned to Monticello early in August, he had his manuscript virtually completed. He needed only some information which he could not get until the legislature met in Richmond in December, where his conduct as governor was to be brought up for critical review. This was a humiliation which vindication did not wholly erase, but Jefferson did not let this distract him from work on his *Notes*. On December 20, 1781, he was able to write to Marbois that the task was finished. "I now do myself the honor," he said, "of inclosing you answers to the queries which Mr. Jones put into my hands—.Even now you will find them very imperfect and not worth offering but as a proof of my respect for your wishes."[9]

Originally Jefferson appears to have planned to make no further use of his work, but he retained a copy and circulated it among friends who might be able to furnish additional information. This led to a constant series of revisions during the winter of 1782-1783, and the process was continued while the author was a member of the Continental Congress during the winter of 1783-1784. The interest of his friends persuaded Jefferson to have a few copies privately printed for their benefit; then in May, 1784, Congress decided to send him to Paris on a diplomatic mission. Thus it was that when, within a short while, he sailed from Boston, he carried with him a carefully revised manuscript which was three times the length of the original.[10] Arriving at his destination in August, he soon made arrangements with a printer named Philippe-Denis Pierres to bring out an anonymous edition of two hundred copies, intended only for distribution among friends. After making a final revision and preparing numerous tables, lists of Indian tribes and other materials, Jefferson had the text ready for the press early in May, 1785. Giving his work the modest title of *Notes on the State of Viginia,* he was mainly concerned that it should not reach the public. This was primarily because he feared an unfavorable reaction to his remarks on the

[8] Peden, *op. cit.*, p. xiv.
[9] *Ibid.*, pp. xiv-xv.
[10] *Ibid.*, pp. xv-xvi.

subject of slavery and his criticisms of the 1776 Constitution of Virginia.

Jefferson's misgivings were realized when he received the unwelcome news that the bookseller, Barrois, had obtained a copy of the *Notes* and was planning to publish an unauthorized French translation. Some consolation came when the Abbé Morellet, a member of the French Academy, agreed to sponsor the translation, and the relieved American undertook to prepare a map, based largely on that made in 1751 by his father, Peter Jefferson, in collaboration with his friend and neighbor, Joshua Fry, which he said he considered more valuable than his text.[11] This edition was finally published with only the initials of the translator on the title page.

The author took no pride in this French edition, but he now decided that he would have to face the publicity which he had unwittingly called down upon himself. He accordingly opened negotiations with the London bookseller and publisher, John Stockdale, who agreed to publish an English edition. Jefferson sent him a carefully corrected copy of the 1785 Paris edition, with instructions to print his commentaries "precisely as they are, without additions, alterations, preface, or anything else but what is there." According to William Peden, "The Stockdale *Notes* represents Jefferson's idea of a 'definitive text.'" It was the first edition to carry the author's name and except for one minor alteration, all subsequent editions published during Jefferson's life followed this text to the letter.[12]

However, with his ever alert and inquiring mind, Jefferson could not possibly consider any intellectual production as "definitive." He constantly sought new information and recorded it in his personal copy of the Stockdale edition of the *Notes*, which copy is now in the collection of Alderman Library of the University of Virginia. He had thought of publishing a new edition to incorporate this additional information, but his unabated interest in national affairs and the time consumed in the founding of the University of Virginia forestalled any such effort.[13] Consequently, on December 10, 1814, he wrote to John Melish, an interested publisher, that "you propose to me the preparation of a new edition of the Notes on Virginia. I formerly entertained the idea,

---

[11] *Ibid.*, pp. xvii–xviii.
[12] *Ibid.*, pp. xix–xx.
[13] Paul Leicester Ford (ed.), *The Writings of Thomas Jefferson* (New York, 1894), III, 78–80.

and from time to time noted some new matter, which I thought I would arrange at leisure for a posthumous edition. But I now begin to see that it is impracticable for me.[14]

On his death in 1826, Jefferson's estate passed into the capable hands of his grandson, Thomas Jefferson Randolph. Since Carey and Lea of Philadelphia had recently published a new edition of the *Notes*, it was decided not to rush into print with another, but by 1853, the 1825 edition being nearly exhausted, Thomas Jefferson Randolph turned over his grandfather's revised copy to J. W. Randolph and Company, with the idea of bringing out a definitive work.[15] In preparing his copy, the editor chose to follow the text of the first, rather than the Stockdale edition, which Jefferson preferred and had used in making his emendations. However, Randolph included all of these, whether in the form of footnotes or textual changes, and those which had been written in foreign languages were translated into English. When Paul Leicester Ford brought out his edition of the *Writings of Thomas Jefferson* (New York, 1894), he included this material along with additions of his own. Many years elapsed before Professor William Peden of the University of Missouri brought out the definitive edition in 1955.

All editions of the *Notes* included several appendices as well as illustrative material, such as maps, charts, and pictures. The appendix to the first edition included: (a) Draught of a Fundamental Constitution for the Commonwealth of Virginia; (b) Notes on the establishment of a Money Unit, and of a coinage for the United States; and (c) An act for Establishing Religious Freedom, passed in the Assembly of Virginia in the beginning of the year 1786 (this was added by the author to late copies of the *Notes*). Later editions modified the contents of the appendix, but continued to include the proposed constitution for Virginia and the Virginia act establishing religious freedom in the state.

As Jefferson, who always wished to avoid controversy, fully realized, the *Notes*, if made available to the public, could not avoid inviting criticism. His argument with the famous French naturalist Buffon over the development of animal life in America as compared to that of Europe; his theories on the appearance of sea shells at high altitudes; and the classification of the mammoth bones found in Virginia, have no more than academic interest today. Nor does the question as to whether Michael

[14] *Ibid.*, III, 79-80; Peden, *op. cit.*, xxi.
[15] *Ibid.*, III, 79-80.

Cresap killed the family of the Indian chief Logan. But Jefferson's ideas concerning religious freedom, the organization of governmental institutions, and the problem of Negro slavery are as highly pertinent now as they were when he reluctantly submitted them to the public.

His proposals concerning the proper organization of civil government in a free society, and his thoughts on certain basic social questions are presented in his discussion of Query XIV (pp. 124-143) and in the proposed constitution for Virginia, which he drafted in 1783 and printed as Appendix II to the *Notes* (pp. 193-206). As a result of colonial experience, the Master of Monticello entertained a deep-seated fear of executive despotism and sought to curb this tendency by setting up a government sharply divided into executive, legislative, and judicial departments. Each was to exercise a certain restraint on the other two, and the voters were expected to exercise final restraint upon all three. The matter of the suffrage was therefore a crucial one and Jefferson had this to say: "Every government degenerates when trusted to the rulers of the people alone. The people themselves therefore are its only safe depositories. And to render them safe, their minds must be improved to a certain degree.—The influence over government must be shared among all the people." However, a citizen might, according to colonial custom, vote not only in the county of his residence, but also in any county in which he owned real property.[16]

One of Jefferson's principal objections to the Virginia Constitution of 1776, drafted chiefly by George Mason, was that it gave each county an equal number of representatives in the House of Delegates, and thus perpetuated the dominance of the older and more numerous but smaller Tidewater counties. He wished to have representation apportioned according to population, and so provided in his proposals for a new constitution. These proposals for popular rule were, however, somewhat offset by other ideas which were a denial of egalitarian democracy. Insisting that the two legislative bodies should represent different constituencies, he proposed that the state Senate should be elected by an electoral college, thus removing it to a considerable degree from the body of the people. Moreover, the governor and the judges of superior courts were to be chosen by the legislature, and all county officials appointed by the governor and Council. Thus,

[16] Thomas Jefferson, *Notes on the State of Virginia* (H. C. Carey and I. Lea, Philadelphia, 1825), p. 204.

as during colonial times, the people had no voice in the direction of their local and most intimate institutions, and all judges and justices held their offices during good behavior. It is also interesting that, though Jefferson provided for religious freedom and all basic civil rights, his system was not predicated, as was Mason's constitution of 1776, upon an enumeration of "inalienable rights" according to the principles of John Locke.

No phase of Jefferson's thinking is more interesting than his ideas upon the subject of education. Believing that democracy depended upon an educated electorate, he proposed that each county be divided into districts called "hundreds" and that an elementary school, to teach reading, writing, and arithmetic, be established in each. The teacher was to be supported by the community and every child was to be taught gratis for three years and as much longer as the parents were willing to pay. Each year the supervisor was to select the most promising boy whose parents were not able to pay for his education, and send him to one of the twenty "grammar schools" which were to be opened in different parts of the state for teaching Greek, Latin, Geography, and the higher branches of "Numerical arithmetic." It was provided that "of the boys thus sent in one year, trial is to be made at the grammar schools one or two years, and the best genius of the whole selected, and continued six years, and the residue dismissed. By this means twenty of the best geniuses will be raked from the rubbish annually, and be instructed, at the public expense, as far as the grammar schools go. At the end of six years instruction, one half are to be discontinued (from among whom the grammar schools will probably be supplied with future masters); and the other half—are to be sent and continued three years—at William and Mary College—. The general objects of this law are to provide an education adapted to the years, to the capacity, and the condition of every one, and directed to their freedom and happiness." This is a far cry from present conceptions of mass education.[17]

Even more removed from modern conceptions were Jefferson's ideas as to the Negro and slavery. He was bitterly opposed to slavery and declared that if it were not abolished as a result of philanthropy, its end would be accomplished in a holocaust of blood. He specifically recommended that all slaves born after the passage of the proposed act be emancipated, but "that they should continue with their parents to a certain age, then be

[17] *Ibid.*, pp. 200-201.

brought up at public expense—till the females should be eighteen, and the males twenty-one years of age, when they should be colonized to such place as the circumstances of the time should render most proper,—and to send vessels at the same time to other parts of the world for an equal number of white inhabitants;—It will probably be asked," he wrote, "Why not retain and incorporate the blacks into the state, and thus save the expense of supplying by importation of white settlers, the vacancies they will leave?" Jefferson follows this with nine pages of reasons explaining why he considers his impractical program desirable.[18]

Neither this discussion nor that concerning the Virginia constitution attracted as much attention as did that relating to the murder of Chief Logan's family. Though the accusation against Cresap was not justified, yet the preliminary skirmishes of Lord Dunmore's War were then being fought in the Pittsburgh area, and Cresap was involved in them. The question was scarcely as important as the controversy made it seem.[19] Much more significant, though less noticed, was the bearing of the *Notes* on Jefferson's political prospects. During the campaign of 1796 a person who signed himself "A Southern Planter" addressed a broadside "To the Citizens of the Southern States":

> At this important Crisis, *George Washington* having declined serving as *President* after the Fourth of March next, and Thomas Jefferson being held up in some of the Southern States as a Candidate for that high Office, I conceive it a duty to make known *to you his opinions and wishes* on a subject the most interesting to your tranquility, and to your very existence.

The anonymous author proceeds to quote the *Notes* on the subject of emancipation and concludes: "If this wild project succeeds, under the auspices of Thomas Jefferson, President of the United States, and *three hundred thousand* slaves are set free in Virginia, farewell to the safety, prosperity, the importance, perhaps the very existence of the Southern States."[20]

The election of 1800 brought the *Notes* once more to the attention of the public. A Baltimore printer named Pechin now

[18] *Ibid.*, pp. 189-198.
[19] Thomas Perkins Abernethy, *Western Lands and the American Revolution* (New York, 1937), pp. 105-107.
[20] Broadside addressed to "The Citizens of the Southern States," signed "A Southern Planter," (Philadelphia [?], 1796), Alderman Library, University of Virginia.

published a new edition, which carried the appendix dealing for the first time with the Logan affair. Within the year he produced a reprint, "To which is subjoined, a sublime and Argumentative Dissertation, on Mr. Jefferson's Religious Principles." This was signed by Samuel Knox and, though carrying a separate title page, was bound with the *Notes*. Thus Jefferson's only book was used both for and against him, and during 1801 five new editions were printed.[21] A philosophical treatise had unintentionally become a political document.

University of Virginia
December, 1963

[21] Coolie Verner, *A Further Checklist of the Separate Editions of Jefferson's Notes on the State of Virginia* (Charlottesville, Va., 1950), pp. 12-22.

PART I.

NOTES ON VIRGINIA.

QUERY I.

An exact description of the limits and boundaries of the State of Virginia ?

Virginia is bounded on the east by the Atlantic; on the north by a line of latitude crossing the eastern shore through Watkin's Point, being about 37° 57′ north latitude; from thence by a straight line to Cinquac, near the mouth of Potomac; thence by the Potomac, which is common to Virginia and Maryland, to the first fountain of its northern branch; thence by a meridian line, passing through that fountain till it intersects a line running east and west, in latitude 39° 43′ 42.4″ which divides Maryland from Pennsylvania, and which was marked by Messrs. Mason and Dixon; thence by that line, and a continuation of it westwardly to the completion of five degrees of longitude from the eastern boundary of Pennsylvania, in the same latitude, and thence by a meridian line to the Ohio; on the west by the Ohio and Mississippi, to latitude 36° 30′ north, and on the south by the line of latitude last mentioned. By admeasurements through nearly the whole of this last line, and supplying the unmeasured parts from good data, the Atlantic and Mississippi are found in this latitude to be seven hundred and fifty-eight miles distant, equal to 30° 38′ of longitude, reckoning fifty-five miles and three thousand one hundred and forty-four feet to the degree. This being our comprehension of longitude, that of our latitude, taken between this and Mason and Dixon's line, is 3° 13′ 42.4″ equal to two hundred and twenty-three and one-third miles, supposing a degree of a great circle to be sixty-nine miles, eight hundred and sixty-four feet, as computed by Cassina. These boundaries include an area somewhat triangular of one hundred and twenty-one thousand five hundred and twenty-five square miles, whereof seventy-nine thousand six hundred and fifty lie westward of the Alleghany mountains, and fifty-seven thousand and thirty-four westward of the meridian of the mouth of the Great Kanhaway. This State is therefore one-third larger than the islands of Great Britain and Ireland, which are reckoned at eighty-eight thousand three hundred and fifty-seven square miles.

These limits result from, 1. The ancient charters from the crown of England. 2. The grant of Maryland to the Lord Baltimore, and the subsequent determinations of the British court as to the extent of that grant. 3. The grant of Pennsylvania to William Penn, and a compact between the general assemblies of the commonwealths of Virginia and Pennsylvania as to the extent of that grant. 4. The grant of Carolina, and actual location of its northern boundary, by consent of both parties. 5. The treaty of Paris of 1763. 6. The confirmation of the charters of the neighboring States by the convention of *Virginia* at the time of constituting their commonwealth. 7. The cession made by *Virginia* to Congress of all the lands to which they had title on the north side of the Ohio.

QUERY II.

A notice of its rivers, rivulets, and how far they are navigable?

An inspection of a map of *Virginia*, will give a better idea of the geography of its rivers, than any description in writing. Their navigation may be imperfectly noted.

Roanoke, so far as it lies within the State, is nowhere navigable but for canoes, or light batteaux; and even for these in such detached parcels as to have prevented the inhabitants from availing themselves of it at all.

James River, and its waters, afford navigation as follows :

The whole of *Elizabeth River*, the lowest of those which run into James River, is a harbor, and would contain upwards of three hundred ships. The channel is from one hundred and fifty to two hundred fathoms wide, and at common flood tide affords eighteen feet water to Norfolk. The Stafford, a sixty gun ship, went there, lightening herself to cross the bar at Sowel's Point. The Fier Rodrigue, pierced for sixty-four guns, and carrying fifty, went there without lightening. Craney Island, at the mouth of this river, commands its channel tolerably well.

Nansemond River is navigable to Sleepy Hole for vessels of two hundred and fifty tons; to Suffolk for those of one hundred tons; and to Milner's for those of twenty-five.

Pagan Creek affords eight or ten feet water to Smithfield, which admits vessels of twenty tons.

Chickahominy has at its mouth a bar, on which is only twelve feet water at common flood tide. Vessels passing that, may go eight miles up the river; those of ten feet draught may go four miles further, and those of six tons burden twenty miles further.

Appamattox may be navigated as far as Broadways, by any vessel which has crossed Harrison's bar in James River; it keeps eight or ten feet water a mile or two higher up to Fisher's bar, and four feet on that and upwards to Petersburg, where all navigation ceases.

James River itself affords a harbor for vessels of any size in Hampton Road, but not in safety through the whole winter; and there is navigable water for them as far as Mulberry Island. A forty gun ship goes to Jamestown, and, lightening herself, may pass Harrison's bar; on which there is only fifteen feet water. Vessels of two hundred and fifty tons may go to Warwick; those of one hundred and twenty-five go to Rocket's, a mile below Richmond; from thence is about seven feet water to Richmond; and about the centre of the town, four feet and a half, where the navigation is interrupted by falls, which in a course of six miles, descend about eighty-eight feet perpendicular; above these it is resumed in canoes and batteaux, and is prosecuted safely and advantageously to within ten miles of the Blue Ridge and even through the Blue Ridge a ton weight has been brought and the expense would not be great, when compared with its object, to open a tolerable navigation up Jackson's river and Carpenter's creek, to within twenty-five miles of Howard's creek of Green Briar, both of which have then water enough to float vessels into the Great Kanhaway. In some future state of population I think it possible that its navigation may also be made to interlock with that of the Potomac, and through that to communicate by a short portage with the Ohio. It is to be noted that this river is called in the maps *James River*, only to its confluence with the Rivanna; thence to the Blue Ridge it is called the Fluvanna; and thence to its source Jackson's river. But in common speech, it is called James River to its source.

The *Rivanna*, a branch of James River, is navigable for canoes and batteaux to its intersection with the South-West mountains, which is about twenty-two miles; and may easily be opened to navigation through these mountains to its fork above Charlottesville.

York River, at Yorktown, affords the best harbor in the State for vessels of the largest size. The river there narrows to the width of a mile, and is contained within very high banks, close under which vessels may ride. It holds four fathom water at high tide for twenty-five miles above York to the mouth of Poropotank, where the river is a mile and a half wide, and the channel only seventy-five fathom, and passing under a high bank. At the confluence of *Pamunkey* and *Mattapony*, it is reduced to three fathom depth, which continues up Pamunkey to Cumberland, where the width is one hundred yards, and up Mattapony to within two miles of Frazier's ferry, where it becomes two and a half fathom deep, and holds that about five miles. Pamunkey is then capable of navigation for loaded flats to Brockman's bridge, fifty miles above Hanover town, and Mattapony to Downer's bridge, seventy miles above its mouth.

Piankatank, the little rivers making out of *Mobjack Bay* and those of the eastern shore, receive only very small vessels, and these can but enter them.

Rappahannock affords four fathom water to Hobb's hole, and two fathom from thence to Fredericksburg.

Potomac is seven and a half miles wide at the mouth; four and a half at Nomony bay; three at Aquia; one and a half at Hallowing point; one and a quarter at Alexandria. Its soundings are seven fathom at the mouth; five at St. George's island; four and a half at Lower Matchodic; three at Swan's point, and thence up to Alexandria; thence ten feet water to the falls, which are thirteen miles above Alexandria. These falls are fifteen miles in length, and of very great descent, and the navigation above them for batteaux and canoes is so much interrupted as to be little used. It is, however, used in a small degree up the Cohongoronta branch as far as fort Cumberland, which was at the mouth of Willis's creek; and is capable, at no great expense, of being rendered very practicable. The Shenandoah branch interlocks with James river about the Blue Ridge, and may perhaps in future be opened.

The *Mississippi* will be one of the principal channels of future commerce for the country westward of the Alleghany. From the mouth of this river to where it receives the Ohio, is one thousand miles by water, but only five hundred by land, passing through the Chickasaw country. From the mouth of the Ohio to that of the Missouri, is two hundred and thirty miles by water, and one hundred and forty by land, from thence to the mouth of the Illinois river, is about twenty-five miles. The Mississippi, below the mouth of the Missouri, is always muddy, and abounding with sand bars, which frequently change their places. However, it carries fifteen feet water to the mouth of the Ohio, to which place it is from one and a half to two miles wide, and thence to Kaskaskia from one mile to a mile and a quarter wide. Its current is so rapid, that it never can be stemmed by the force of the wind alone, acting on sails. Any vessel, however, navigated with oars, may come up at any time, and receive much aid from the wind. A batteau passes from the mouth of Ohio to the mouth of Mississippi in three weeks, and is from two to three months getting up again. During its floods, which are periodical as those of the Nile, the largest vessels may pass down it, if their steerage can be insured. These floods begin in April, and the river returns into its banks early in August. The inundation extends further on the western than eastern side, covering the lands in some places for fifty miles from its banks. Above the mouth of the Missouri it becomes much such a river as the Ohio, like it clear and gentle in its current, not quite so wide, the period of its floods nearly the same, but not rising to so great a height. The streets of the village at Cohoes are not more than ten feet above the ordinary level of the water, and yet were never overflowed. Its bed deepens every year. Cohoes, in the memory of many people now living, was insulated by every flood of the river. What was the eastern channel has now become a lake, nine miles in length and one in width, into which the river at this day never flows. This river yields turtle of a peculiar kind, perch, trout, gar, pike, mullets, herrings, carp, spatula-fish of fifty pounds weight, cat-fish of one hundred pounds weight, buffalo fish, and sturgeon. Aligators or crocodiles have been seen as high up as the Acansas. It also abounds in herons, cranes, ducks, brant, geese, and swans. Its passage is commanded by a fort established by this State, five miles below the mouth of the Ohio, and ten miles above the Carolina boundary.

The Missouri, since the treaty of Paris, the Illinois and northern branches of the Ohio, since the cession to Congress, are no longer within our limits. Yet having been so heretofore, and still opening to us channels of extensive communication with the western and north-western country, they shall be noted in their order.

The *Missouri* is, in fact, the principal river, contributing more to the common stream than does the Mississippi, even after its junction with the Illinois. It is remarkably cold, muddy, and rapid. Its overflowings are considerable. They happen during the months of June and July. Their commencement being so much later than those of the Mississippi, would induce a belief that the sources of the Missouri are northward of those of the Mississippi, unless we suppose that the cold increases again with the ascent of the land from the Mississippi westwardly. That this ascent is great, is proved by the rapidity of the river. Six miles above the mouth, it is brought within the compass of a

quarter of a mile's width ; yet the Spanish merchants at Pancore,
or St. Louis, say they go two thousand miles up it.   It heads far
westward of the Rio Norte, or North River.   There is, in the
villages of Kaskaskia, Cohoes, and St. Vincennes, no inconsider-
able quantity of plate, said to have been plundered during the
last war by the Indians from the churches and private houses of
Santa Fé, on the North river, and brought to the villages for
sale.   From the mouth of the Ohio to Sante Fé are forty days
journey, or about one thousand miles.   What is the shortest distance between the navigable waters of the Missouri, and those
of the North river, or how far this is navigable above Santa Fé,
I could never learn.   From Santa Fé to its mouth in the Gulf
of Mexico is about twelve hundred miles.   The road from New
Orleans to Mexico crosses this river at the post of Rio Norte, eight
hundred miles below Santa Fé, and from this post to New Orleans is about twelve hundred miles ; thus making two thousand
miles between Santa Fé and New Orleans, passing down the
North river, Red river, and Mississippi ; whereas it is two thousand two hundred and thirty through the Missouri and Mississippi.   From the same post of Rio Norte, passing near the mines
of La Sierra and Laiguana, which are between the North river,
and the river Salina to Sartilla, is three hundred and seventy-five
miles, and from thence, passing the mines of Charcas, Zaccatecas,
and Potosi, to the city of Mexico, is three hundred and seventy-
five miles ; in all, one thousand five hundred and fifty miles from
Santa Fé to the city of Mexico.   From New Orleans to the city
of Mexico is about one thousand nine hundred and fifty miles ;
the roads after setting out from the Red river, near Natchitoches,
keeping generally parallel with the coast, and about two hundred miles from it, till it enters the city of Mexico.

The *Illinois* is a fine river, clear, gentle, and without rapids ;
insomuch that it is navigable for batteaux to its source.   From
thence is a portage of two miles only to the Chicago, which affords a batteau navigation of sixteen miles to its entrance into
lake Michigan.   The Illinois, about ten miles above its mouth,
is three hundred yards wide.

The *Kaskaskia* is one hundred yards wide at its entrance into the Mississippi, and preserves that breadth to the Buffalo plains seventy miles above. So far, also, it is navigable for loaded bateaux, and perhaps much further. It is not rapid.

The *Ohio* is the most beautiful river on earth. Its current gentle, waters clear, and bosom smooth and unbroken by rocks and rapids, a single instance only excepted.

It is one-quarter of a mile wide at Fort Pitt, five hundred yards at the mouth of the Great Kanhaway, one mile and twenty-five poles at Louisville, one-quarter of a mile on the rapids three or four miles below Louisville, half a mile where the low country begins, which is twenty miles above Green river, a mile and a quarter at the receipt of the Tennessee, and a mile wide at the mouth.

Its length, as measured according to its meanders by Captain Hutchins, is as follows:—

From Fort Pitt

To Log's Town	18½	Little Miami	126¼
Big Beaver Creek	10¾	Licking Creek	8
Little Beaver Creek	13½	Great Miami	26¾
Yellow Creek	11¾	Big Bones	32½
Two Creeks	21¾	Kentucky	44¼
Long Reach	53¾	Rapids	77¼
End Long Reach	16½	Low Country	155¾
Muskingum	25½	Buffalo River	64½
Little Kanhaway	12¼	Wabash	97¼
Hockhocking	16	Big Cave	42¾
Great Kanhaway	82½	Shawanee River	52½
Guiandot	43¾	Cherokee River	13
Sandy Creek	14½	Massac	11
Sioto	48¼	Mississippi	46
			1188

In common winter and spring tides it affords fifteen feet water to Louisville, ten feet to Le Tarte's rapids, forty miles above the mouth of the great Kanhaway, and a sufficiency at all times for light batteaux and canoes to Fort Pitt. The rapids are in latitude 38° 8′. The inundations of this river begin about the last of March, and subside in July. During these, a first-rate man-of-war may be carried from Louisville to New Orleans, if the sudden turns of the river and the strength of its current will admit a safe steerage. The rapids at Louisville descend about thirty feet in a length of a mile and a half. The bed of the river there is a solid rock, and is divided by an island into two branches, the southern of which is about two hundred yards wide, and is dry four months in the year. The bed of the northern branch is worn into channels by the constant course of the water, and attrition of the pebble stones carried on with that, so as to be passable for batteaux through the greater part of the year. Yet it is thought that the southern arm may be the most easily opened for constant navigation. The rise of the waters in these rapids does not exceed ten or twelve feet. A part of this island is so high as to have been never overflowed, and to command the settlement at Louisville, which is opposite to it. The fort, however, is situated at the head of the falls. The ground on the south side rises very gradually.

The *Tennessee*, Cherokee, or Hogohege river, is six hundred yards wide at its mouth, a quarter of a mile at the mouth of Holston, and two hundred yards at Chotee, which is twenty miles above Holston, and three hundred miles above the mouth of the Tennessee. This river crosses the southern boundary of Virginia, fifty-eight miles from the Mississippi. Its current is moderate. It is navigable for loaded boats of any burden to the Muscle shoals, where the river passes through the Cumberland mountain. These shoals are six or eight miles long, passable downwards for loaded canoes, but not upwards, unless there be a swell in the river. Above these the navigation for loaded canoes and batteaux continues to the Long island. This river has its inundations also. Above the Chickamogga towns is a whirlpool called the Sucking-pot, which takes in trunks of trees or boats, and throws them out again half a mile below. It is avoided by keeping very close to the bank, on the south side. There are but a few miles portage between a branch of this river and the navigable waters of the river Mobile, which runs into the Gulf of Mexico.

Cumberland, or Shawanee river, intersects the boundary between Virginia and North Carolina sixty-seven miles from the Mississippi, and again one hundred and ninety-eight miles from the same river, a little above the entrance of Obey's river into the Cumberland. Its Clear fork crosses the same boundary about three hundred miles from the Mississippi. Cumberland is a very gentle stream, navigable for loaded batteaux eight hundred miles, without interruption ; then intervene some rapids of fifteen miles in length, after which it is again navigable seventy miles upwards, which brings you within ten miles of the Cumberland mountains. It is about one hundred and twenty yards wide through its whole course, from the head of its navigation to its mouth.

The *Wabash* is a very beautiful river, four hundred yards wide at the mouth, and three hundred at St. Vincennes, which is a post one hundred miles above the mouth, in a direct line. Within this space there are two small rapids, which give very little obstruction to the navigation. It is four hundred yards wide at the mouth, and navigable thirty leagues upwards for canoes and small boats. From the mouth of Maple river to that of Eel river is about eighty miles in a direct line, the river continuing navigable, and from one to two hundred yards in width. The Eel river is one hundred and fifty yards wide, and affords at all times navigation for periaguas, to within eighteen miles of the Miami of the Lake. The Wabash, from the mouth of Eel river to Little river, a distance of fifty miles direct, is interrupted with frequent rapids and shoals, which obstruct the navigation, except in a swell. Little river affords navigation during a swell to within three miles of the Miami, which thence affords a similar navigation into Lake Erie, one hundred miles distant in a direct line. The Wabash overflows periodically in correspondence with the Ohio, and in some places two leagues from its banks.

Green River is navigable for loaded batteaux at all times fifty miles upwards ; but it is then interrupted by impassable rapids, above which the navigation again commences and continues good thirty or forty miles to the mouth of Barren river.

Kentucky River is ninety yards wide at the mouth, and also at Boonsborough, eighty miles above. It affords a navigation for loaded batteaux one hundred and eighty miles in a direct line, in the winter tides.

The *Great Miami* of the Ohio, is two hundred yards wide at the mouth.   At the Piccawee towns, seventy-five miles above, it is reduced to thirty yards; it is, nevertheless, navigable for loaded canoes fifty miles above these towns.   The portage from its western branch into the Miami of Lake Erie, is five miles; that from its eastern branch into Sandusky river, is of nine miles.

Salt River is at all times navigable for loaded batteaux seventy or eighty miles.   It is eighty yards wide at its mouth, and keeps that width to its fork, twenty-five miles above.

The *Little Miami* of the Ohio, is sixty or seventy yards wide at its mouth, sixty miles to its source, and affords no navigation.

The *Sioto* is two hundred and fifty yards wide at its mouth, which is in latitude 38° 22', and at the Saltlick towns, two hundred miles above the mouth, it is yet one hundred yards wide. To these towns it is navigable for loaded batteaux, and its eastern branch affords navigation almost to its source.

Great Sandy River is about sixty yards wide, and navigable sixty miles for loaded batteaux.

Guiandot is about the width of the river last mentioned, but is more rapid.   It may be navigated by canoes sixty miles.

The *Great Kanhaway* is a river of considerable note for the fertility of its lands, and still more, as leading towards the head waters of James river.   Nevertheless, it is doubtful whether its great and numerous rapids will admit a navigation, but at an expense to which it will require ages to render its inhabitants equal.   The great obstacles begin at what are called the Great Falls, ninety miles above the mouth, below which are only five or six rapids, and these passable, with some difficulty, even at low water.   From the falls to the mouth of Greenbriar is one hundred miles, and thence to the lead mines one hundred and twenty.   It is two hundred and eighty yards wide at its mouth.

Hockbocking is eighty yards wide at its mouth, and yields navigation for loaded batteaux to the Press-place, sixty miles above its mouth.

The *Little Kanhaway* is one hundred and fifty yards wide at the mouth.   It yields a navigation of ten miles only.   Perhaps its northern branch, called Junius' creek, which interlocks with the western of Monongahela, may one day admit a shorter passage from the latter into the Ohio.

The *Muskingum* is two hundred and eighty yards wide at its mouth, and two hundred yards at the lower Indian towns, one hundred and fifty miles upwards. It is navigable for small batteaux to within one mile of a navigable part of Cuyahoga river, which runs into Lake Erie.

At Fort Pitt the river Ohio loses its name, branching into the Monongahela and Alleghany.

The *Monongahela* is four hundred yards wide at its mouth. From thence is twelve or fifteen miles to the mouth of Yohogany, where it is three hundred yards wide. Thence to Redstone by water is fifty miles, by land thirty. Then to the mouth of Cheat river by water forty miles, by land twenty-eight, the width continuing at three hundred yards, and the navigation good for boats. Thence the width is about two hundred yards to the western fork, fifty miles higher, and the navigation frequently interrupted by rapids, which, however, with a swell of two or three feet, become very passable for boats. It then admits light boats, except in dry seasons, sixty-five miles further to the head of Tygart's valley, presenting only some small rapids and falls of one or two feet perpendicular, and lessening in its width to twenty yards. The *Western fork* is navigable in the winter ten or fifteen miles towards the northern of the Little Kanhaway, and will admit a good wagon road to it. The *Yahogany* is the principal branch of this river. It passes through the Laurel mountain, about thirty miles from its mouth; is so far from three hundred to one hundred and fifty yards wide, and the navigation much obstructed in dry weather by rapids and shoals. In its passage through the mountain it makes very great falls, admitting no navigation for ten miles to the Turkey Foot. Thence to the Great Crossing, about twenty miles, it is again navigable, except in dry seasons, and at this place is two hundred yards wide. The sources of this river are divided from those of the Potomac by the Alleghany mountain. From the falls, where it intersects the Laurel mountain, to Fort Cumberland, the head of the navigation on the Potomac, is forty miles of very mountainous road. Wills' creek, at the mouth of which was Fort Cumberland, is thirty or forty yards wide, but affords no navigation as yet. *Cheat* river, another considerable branch of the Monongahela, is two hundred yards wide at its mouth, and one hundred yards at the *Dunkard's* settlement, fifty miles higher. It is navigable for boats, except in dry seasons. The boundary between Virginia and Pennsylvania crosses it about three or four miles above its mouth.

The *Alleghany* river, with a slight swell, affords navigation for light batteaux to Venango, at the mouth of French Creek, where it is two hundred yards wide, and is practised even to Le Bœuf, from whence there is a portage of fifteen miles to Presque Isle on the Lake Erie.

The country watered by the Mississippi and its eastern branches, constitutes five-eighths of the United States, two of which five-eighths are occupied by the Ohio and its waters; the residuary streams which run into the Gulf of Mexico, the Atlantic, and the St. Lawrence, water the remaining three-eighths.

Before we quit the subject of the western waters, we will take a view of their principal connections with the Atlantic. These are three ; the Hudson river, the Potomac, and the Mississippi itself. Down the last will pass all heavy commodities. But the navigation through the Gulf of Mexico is so dangerous, and that up the Mississippi so difficult and tedious, that it is thought probable that European merchandise will not return through that channel. It is most likely that flour, timber, and other heavy articles will be floated on rafts, which will themselves be an article for sale as well as their loading, the navigators returning by land, or in light batteaux. There will, therefore, be a competition between the Hudson and Potomac rivers for the residue of the commerce of all the country westward of Lake Erie, on the waters of the lakes, of the Ohio, and upper parts of the Mississippi. To go to New York, that part of the trade which comes from the lakes or their waters, must first be brought into Lake Erie. Between Lake Superior and its waters and Huron, are the rapids of St. Mary, which will permit boats to pass, but not larger vessels. Lakes Huron and Michigan afford communication with

Lake Erie by vessels of eight feet draught. That part of the trade which comes from the waters of the Mississippi must pass from them through some portage into the waters of the lakes. The portage from the Illinois river into a water of Michigan is of one mile only. From the Wabash, Miami, Muskingum, or Alleghany, are portages into the waters of Lake Erie, of from one to fifteen miles. When the commodities are brought into, and have passed through Lake Erie, there is between that and Ontario an interruption by the falls 'of Niagara, where the portage is of eight miles; and between Ontario and the Hudson river are portages at the falls of Onondago, a little above Oswego, of a quarter of a mile; from Wood creek to the Mohawks river two miles; at the little falls of the Mohawks river half a mile; and from Schenectady to Albany sixteen miles. Besides the increase of expense occasioned by frequent change of carriage, there is an increased risk of pillage produced by committing merchandise to a greater number of hands successively. The Potomac offers itself under the following circumstances: For the trade of the lakes and their waters westward of Lake Erie, when it shall have entered that lake, it must coast along its southern shore, on account of the number and excellence of its harbors; the northern, though shortest, having few harbors, and these unsafe. Having reached Cuyahoga, to proceed on to New York it will have eight hundred and twenty-five miles and five portages; whereas it is but four hundred and twenty-five miles to Alexandria, its emporium on the Potomac, if it turns into the Cuyahoga, and passes through that, Big Beaver, Ohio, Yohogany, (or Monongahela and Cheat,) and Potomac, and there are but two portages; the first of which, between Cuyahoga and Beaver, may be removed by uniting the sources of these waters, which are lakes in the neighborhood of each other, and in a champaign country; the other from the waters of Ohio to Potomac will be from fifteen to forty miles, according to the trouble which shall be taken to approach the two navigations. For the trade of the Ohio, or that which shall come into it from its own waters or the Mississippi, it is nearer through the Potomac to Alexandria than to New York by five hundred and eighty miles, and it is interrupted by one portage only.   There is another circumstance of difference too.   The lakes themselves never freeze, but the communications between them freeze, and the Hudson river is itself shut up by the ice three months in the year; whereas the channel to the Chesapeake leads directly into a warmer climate. The southern parts of it very rarely freeze at all, and whenever the northern do, it is so near the sources of the rivers, that the frequent floods to which they are there liable, break up the ice immediately, so that vessels may pass through the whole winter, subject only to accidental and short delays.   Add to all this, that in case of war with our neighbors, the Anglo-Americans or the Indians, the route to New York becomes a frontier through almost its whole length, and all commerce through it ceases from that moment.   But the channel to New York is already known to practice, whereas the upper waters of the Ohio and the Potomac, and the great falls of the latter, are yet to be cleared of their fixed obstructions. (A.)

QUERY III.

A notice of the best Seaports of the State, and how big are the vessels they can receive ?

Having no ports but our rivers and creeks, this *Query* has been answered under the preceding one.

QUERY IV.

A notice of its Mountains ?

For the particular geography of our mountains I must refer to Fry and Jefferson's map of Virginia ; and to Evans' analysis of this map of America, for a more philosophical view of them than is to be found in any other work.   It is worthy of notice, that our mountains are not solitary and scattered confusedly over the face of the country ; but that they commence at about one hundred and fifty miles from the sea-coast, are disposed in ridges, one behind another, running nearly parallel with the sea-coast, though rather approaching it as they advance north-east-wardly. To the south-west, as the tract of country between the sea-coast and the Mississippi becomes narrower, the mountains converge into a single ridge, which, as it approaches the Gulf of Mexico, subsides into plain country, and gives rise to some of the waters of that gulf, and particularly to a river called the Apalachicola, probably from the Apalachies, an Indian nation formerly residing on it. Hence the mountains giving rise to that river, and seen from its various parts, were called the Apalachian mountains, being in fact the end or termination only of the great ridges passing through the continent. European geographers, however, extended the name northwardly as far as the mountains extended; some giving it, after their separation into different ridges, to the Blue Ridge, others to the North Mountain, others to the Alleghany, others to the Laurel Ridge, as may be seen by their different maps. But the fact I believe is, that none of these ridges were ever known by that name to the inhabitants, either native or emigrant, but as they saw them so called in European maps. In the same direction, generally, are the veins of limestone, coal, and other minerals hitherto discovered; and so range the falls of our great rivers. But the courses of the great rivers are at right angles with these. James and Potomac penetrate through all the ridges of mountains eastward of the Alleghany; that is, broken by no water course. It is in fact the spine of the country between the Atlantic on one side, and the Mississippi and St. Lawrence on the other. The passage of the Potomac through the Blue Ridge is, perhaps, one of the most stupendous scenes in nature. You stand on a very high point of land. On your right comes up the Shenandoah, having ranged along the foot of the mountain an hundred miles to seek a vent. On your left approaches the Potomac, in quest of a passage also. In the moment of their junction, they rush together against the mountain, rend it asunder, and pass off to the sea. The first glance of this scene hurries our senses into the opinion, that this earth has been created in time, that the mountains were formed first, that the rivers began to flow afterwards, that in this place, particularly, they have been dammed up by the Blue Ridge of mountains, and have formed an ocean which filled the whole valley ; that continuing to rise they have at length broken over at this spot, and have torn the mountain down from its summit to its base. The piles of rock on each hand, but particularly on the Shenandoah, the evident marks of their disrupture and avulsion from their beds by the most powerful agents of nature, corroborate the impression. But the distant finishing which nature has given to the picture, is of a very different character. It is a true contrast to the foreground. It is as placid and delightful as that is wild and tremendous. For the mountain being cloven asunder, she presents to your eye, through the cleft, a small catch of smooth blue horizon, at an infinite distance in the plain country, inviting you, as it were, from the riot and tumult roaring around, to pass through the breach and participate of the calm below. Here the eye ultimately composes itself ; and that way, too, the road happens actually to lead. You cross the Potomac above the junction, pass along its side through the base of the mountain for three miles, its terrible precipices hanging in fragments over you, and within about twenty miles reach Fredericktown, and the fine country round that. This scene is worth a voyage across the Atlantic. Yet here, as in the neighborhood of the Natural Bridge, are people who have passed their lives within half a dozen miles, and have never been to survey these monuments of a war between rivers and mountains, which must have shaken the earth itself to its centre. (B.)

The height of our mountains has not yet been estimated with any degree of exactness. The Alleghany being the great ridge which divides the waters of the Atlantic from those of the Mississippi, its summit is doubtless more elevated above the ocean than that of any other mountain.' But its relative height, compared with the base on which it stands, is not so great as that of some others, the country rising behind the successive ridges like the steps of stairs. The mountains of the Blue Ridge, and of these the Peaks of Otter, are thought to be of a greater height, measured from their base, than any others in our country, and perhaps

in North America.   From data, which may found a tolerable
conjecture, we suppose the highest peak to be about four thousand
feet perpendicular, which is not a fifth part of the height of the
mountains of South America, nor one-third of the height which
would be necessary in our latitude to preserve ice in the open
air unmelted through the year.   The ridge of mountains next
beyond the Blue Ridge, called by us the North mountain, is of
the greatest extent ; for which reason they were named by the
Indians the endless mountains.

A substance supposed to be Pumice, found floating on the
Mississippi, has induced a conjecture that there is a volcano on
some of its waters ; and as these are mostly known to their
sources, except the Missouri, our expectations of verifying the conjecture would of course be led to the mountains which divide
the waters of the Mexican Gulf from those of the South Sea ;
but no volcano having ever yet been known at such a distance
from the sea, we must rather suppose that this floating substance
has been erroneously deemed Pumice.

QUERY V.

Its Cascades and Caverns ?

The only remarkable cascade in this country is that of the
Falling Spring in Augusta.   It is a water of James' river where
it is called Jackson's river, rising in the warm spring mountains,
about twenty miles south west of the warm spring, and flowing
into that valley.   About three-quarters of a mile from its source
it falls over a rock two hundred feet into the valley below.   The
sheet of water is broken in its breadth by the rock, in two or
three places, but not at all in its height.   Between the sheet and
the rock, at the bottom, you may walk across dry.   This cata-
ract will bear no comparison with that of Niagara as to the
quantity of water composing it ; the sheet being only twelve or
fifteen feet wide above and somewhat more spread below ; but
it is half as high again, the latter being only one hundred and

fifty-six feet, according to the mensuration made by order of
M. Vaudreuil, Governor of Canada, and one hundred and thirty
according to a more recent account.

In the lime-stone country
there are many caverns of
very considerable extent.
The most noted is called
Madison's Cave, and is on
the north side of the Blue
Ridge, near the intersection
of the Rockingham and Au-
gusta line with the south
fork of the southern river of
Shenandoah.   It is in a hill
of about two hundred feet
perpendicular height, the ascent of which, on one side,
is so steep that you may
pitch a biscuit from its summit into the river which
washes its base.   The entrance of the cave is, in this
side, about two-thirds of the
way up.   It extends into
the earth about three hundred feet, branching into
subordinate caverns, sometimes ascending a little, but
more generally descending,
and at length terminates,

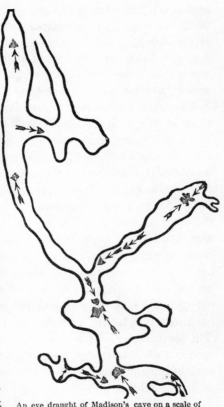

An eye draught of Madison's cave on a scale of
67 feet to the inch. The arrows show
where it descends or ascends.

in two different places, at basons of water of unknown extent, and which I should judge to be nearly on a level with
the water of the river ; however, I do not think they are
formed by refluent water from that, because they are never tur-
bid ; because they do not rise and fall in correspondence with
that in times of flood or of drought ; and because the water is
always cool.   It is probably one of the many reservoirs with

which the interior parts of the earth are supposed to abound, and yield supplies to the fountains of water, distinguished from others only by being accessible. The vault of this cave is of solid lime-stone, from twenty to forty or fifty feet high; through which water is continually percolating. This, trickling down the sides of the cave, has incrusted them over in the form of elegant drapery; and dripping from the top of the vault generates on that and on the base below, stalactites of a conical form, some of which have met and formed massive columns.

Another of these caves is near the north mountain, in the county of Frederic, on the lands of Mr. Zane. The entrance into this is on the top of an extensive ridge. You descend thirty or forty feet, as into a well, from whence the cave extends, nearly horizontally, four hundred feet into the earth, preserving a breadth of from twenty to fifty feet, and a height of from five to twelve feet. After entering this cave a few feet, the mercury, which in the open air was 50°, rose to 57° of Fahrenheit's thermometer, answering to 11° of Reaumur's, and it continued at that to the remotest parts of the cave. The uniform temperature of the cellars of the observatory of Paris, which are ninety feet deep, and of all subterraneous cavities of any depth, where no chemical agencies may be supposed to produce a factitious heat, has been found to be 10° of Reaumur, equal to 54½° of Fahrenheit. The temperature of the cave above mentioned so nearly corresponds with this, that the difference may be ascribed to a difference of instruments.

At the Panther gap, in the ridge which divides the waters of the Crow and the Calf pasture, is what is called the *Blowing Cave*. It is in the side of a hill, is of about one hundred feet diameter, and emits constantly a current of air of such force as to keep the weeds prostrate to the distance of twenty yards before it. This current is strongest in dry, frosty weather, and in long spells of rain weakest. Regular inspirations and expirations of air, by caverns and fissures, have been probably enough accounted for by supposing them combined with intermitting fountains; as they must of course inhale air while their reservoirs are emptying themselves, and again emit it while they are filling.

But a constant issue of air, only varying in its force as the weather is drier or damper, will require a new hypothesis. There is another blowing cave in the Cumberland mountain, about a mile from where it crosses the Carolina line. All we know of this is, that it is not constant, and that a fountain of water issues from it.

The *Natural Bridge*, the most sublime of nature's works, though not comprehended under the present head, must not be pretermitted. It is on the ascent of a hill, which seems to have been cloven through its length by some great convulsion. The fissure, just at the bridge, is, by some admeasurements, two hundred and seventy feet deep, by others only two hundred and five. It is about forty-five feet wide at the bottom and ninety feet at the top; this of course determines the length of the bridge, and its height from the water. Its breadth in the middle is about sixty feet, but more at the ends, and the thickness of the mass, at the summit of the arch, about forty feet. A part of this thickness is constituted by a coat of earth, which gives growth to many large trees, The residue, with the hill on both sides, is one solid rock of lime-stone. The arch approaches the semi-elliptical form; but the larger axis of the ellipsis, which would be the cord of the arch, is many times longer than the transverse. Though the sides of this bridge are provided in some parts with a parapet of fixed rocks, yet few men have resolution to walk to them, and look over into the abyss. You involuntarily fall on your hands and feet, creep to the parapet, and peep over it. Looking down from this height about a minute, gave me a violent head-ache. If the view from the top be painful and intolerable, that from below is delightful in an equal extreme. It is impossible for the emotions arising from the sublime to be felt beyond what they are here; so beautiful an arch, so elevated, so light, and springing as it were up to heaven! the rapture of the spectator is really indescribable! The fissure continuing narrow, deep, and straight, for a considerable distance above and below the bridge, opens a short but very pleasing view of the North mountain on one side and the Blue Ridge on the other, at the distance each of them of about five miles. This bridge is in the county of Rockbridge, to which it has given name, and affords a public and commodious passage over a valley which cannot be crossed elsewhere for a considerable distance. The stream passing under it is called Cedar-creek. It is a water of James' river, and sufficient in the driest seasons to turn a grist-mill, though its fountain is not more than two miles above.*

QUERY VI.

A notice of the mines and other subterraneous riches ; its trees, plants, fruits, &c.

I knew a single instance of gold found in this State. It was interspersed in small specks through a lump of ore of about four

---

* Don Ulloa mentions a break, similar to this, in the province of Angaraez, in South America. It is from sixteen to twenty-two feet wide, one hundred and eleven feet deep, and of 1.3 miles continuance, English measure. Its breadth at top is not sensibly greater than at bottom. But the following fact is remarkable, and will furnish some light for conjecturing the probable origin of our natural bridge. "Esta caxa, o cauce está cortada en péna viva con tanta precision, que las desigualdades del un lado entrantes, corresponden á las del otro lado salientes, como si aquella altura se hubiese abierto expresameute, con sus bueltas y tortuosidades, para darle transito á los aguas por entre los dos morallones que la forman ; siendo tal su igualdad, que si llegasen á juntarse se endentarian uno con otro sin dextar hueco." Not. Amer. ii. § 10. Don Ulloa inclines to the opinion that this channel has been effected by the wearing of the water which runs through it, rather than that the mountain should have been broken open by any convulsion of nature. But if it had been worn by the running of water, would not the rocks which form the sides, have been worn plain? or if, meeting in some parts with veins of harder stone, the water had left prominences on the one side, would not the same cause have sometimes, or perhaps generally, occasioned prominences on the other side also? Yet Don Ulloa tells us, that on the other side there are always corresponding cavities, and that these tally with the prominences so perfectly, that, were the two sides to come together they would fit in all their indentures, without leaving any void. I think that this does not resemble the effect of running water, but looks rather as if the two sides had parted asunder. The sides of the break, over which is the natural bridge of Virginia, consisting of a veiny rock which yields to time, the correspondence between the salient and re-entering inequalities, if it existed at all, has now disappeared. This break has the advantage of the one described by Don Ulloa in its finest circumstance; no portion in that instance having held together, during the separation of the other parts, so as to form a bridge over the abyss.

pounds weight, which yielded seventeen pennyweights of gold, of extraordinary ductility. This ore was found on the north side of Rappahanoc, about four miles below the falls. I never heard of any other indication of gold in its neighborhood.

On the Great Kanhaway, opposite to the mouth of Cripple creek, and about twenty-five miles from our southern boundary, in the county of Montgomery, are mines of lead. The metal is mixed, sometimes with earth, and sometimes with rock, which requires the force of gunpowder to open it ; and is accompanied with a portion of silver too small to be worth separation under any process hitherto attempted there. The proportion yielded is from fifty to eighty pounds of pure metal from one hundred pounds of washed ore. The most common is that of sixty to one hundred pounds. The veins are sometimes most flattering, at others they disappear suddenly and totally. They enter the side of the hill and proceed horizontally. Two of them are wrought at present by the public, the best of which is one hundred yards under the hill. These would employ about fifty laborers to advantage. We have not, however, more than thirty generally, and these cultivate their own corn. They have produced sixty tons of lead in the year; but the general quantity is from twenty to twenty-five tons. The present furnace is a mile from the ore bank and on the opposite side of the river. The ore is first wagoned to the river, a quarter of a mile, then laden on board of canoes and carried across the river, which is there about two hundred yards wide, and then again taken into wagons and carried to the furnace. This mode was originally adopted that they might avail themselves of a good situation on a creek for a pounding mill ; but it would be easy to have the furnace and pounding mill on the same side of the river, which would yield water, without any dam, by a canal of about half a mile in length. From the furnace the lead is transported one hundred and thirty miles along a good road, leading through the peaks of Otter to Lynch's ferry, or Winston's on James' river, from whence it is carried by water about the same distance to Westham. This land carriage may be greatly shortened, by delivering the lead on James' river, above the Blue Ridge, from whence a ton weight has been brought on two canoes. The Great Kanhaway has considerable falls in the neighborhood of the mines. About seven miles below are three falls, of three or four feet perpendicular each ; and three miles above is a rapid of three miles continuance, which has been compared in its descent to the great falls of James' river. Yet it is the opinion, that they may be laid open for useful navigation, so as to reduce very much the portage between the Kanhaway and James' river.

A valuable lead mine is said to have been lately discovered in Cumberland, below the mouth of Red river. The greatest, however, known in the western country, are on the Mississippi, extending from the mouth of Rock river one hundred and fifty miles upwards. These are not wrought, the lead used in that country being from the banks on the Spanish side of the Mississippi, opposite to Kaskaskia.

A mine of copper was once opened in the county of Amherst, on the north side of James' river, and another in the opposite country, on the south side. However, either from bad management or the poverty of the veins, they were discontinued. We are told of a rich mine of native copper on the Ouabache, below the upper Wiaw.

The mines of iron worked at present are Callaway's, Ross's, and Ballendine's, on the south side of James' river ; Old's on the north side, in Albemarle ; Miller's in Augusta, and Zane's in Frederic. These two last are in the valley between the Blue Ridge and North mountain. Callaway's, Ross's, Miller's, and Zane's make about one hundred and fifty tons of bar iron each, in the year. Ross's makes also about sixteen hundred tons of pig iron annually ; Ballendine's one thousand ; Callaway's, Miller's, and Zane's, about six hundred each. Besides these, a forge of Mr. Hunter's, at Fredericksburg, makes about three hundred tons a year of bar iron, from pigs imported from Maryland ; and Taylor's forge on Neapsco of Potomac, works in the same way, but to what extent I am not informed. The indications of iron in other places are numerous, and dispersed through all he middle country. The toughness of the cast iron of Ross's and Zane's furnaces is very remarkable. Pots and other utensils, cast thinner than usual, of this iron, may be safely thrown into, or out of the wagons in which they are transported. Salt-pans made of the same, and no longer wanted for that purpose, cannot be broken up, in order to be melted again, unless previously drilled in many parts.

In the western country, we are told of iron mines between the Muskingum and Ohio; of others on Kentucky, between the Cumberland and Barren rivers, between Cumberland and Tennessee, on Reedy creek, near the Long Island, and on Chesnut creek, a branch of the Great Kanhaway, near where it crosses the Carolina line. What are called the iron banks, on the Mississippi, are believed, by a good judge, to have no iron in them. In general, from what is hitherto known of that country, it seems to want iron.

Considerable quantities of black lead are taken occasionally for use from Winterham in the county of Amelia. I am not able, however, to give a particular state of the mine. There is no work established at it; those who want, going and procuring it for themselves.

The country on James' river, from fifteen to twenty miles above Richmond, and for several miles northward and southward, is replete with mineral coal of a very excellent quality. Being in the hands of many proprietors, pits have been opened, and, before the interruption of our commerce, were worked to an extent equal to the demand.

In the western country coal is known to be in so many places, as to have induced an opinion, that the whole tract between the Laurel mountain, Mississippi, and Ohio, yields coal. It is also known in many places on the north side of the Ohio. The coal at Pittsburg is of very superior quality. A bed of it at that place has been a-fire since the year 1765. Another coal-hill on the Pike-run of Monongahela has been a-fire ten years; yet it has burnt away about twenty yards only.

I have known one instance of an emerald found in this country. Amethysts have been frequent, and crystals common; yet not in such numbers any of them as to be worth seeking.

There is very good marble, and in very great abundance, on James' river, at the mouth of Rockfish. The samples I have seen, were some of them of a white as pure as one might expect to find on the surface of the earth ; but most of them were variegated with red, blue, and purple. None of it has been ever worked. It forms a very large precipice, which hangs over a navigable part of the river. It is said there is marble at Kentucky.

But one vein of limestone is known below the Blue Ridge. Its first appearance, in our country, is in Prince William, two miles below the Pignut ridge of mountains ; thence it passes on nearly parallel with that, and crosses the Rivanna about five miles below it, where it is called the South-west ridge. It then crosses Hard-ware, above the mouth of Hudson's creek, James' river at the mouth of Rockfish, at the marble quarry before spoken of, probably runs up that river to where it appears again at Ross's iron-works, and so passes off south-westwardly by Flat Creek of Otter river. It is never more than one hundred yards wide. From the Blue Ridge westwardly, the whole country seems to be founded on a rock of limestone, besides infinite quantities on the surface, both loose and fixed. This is cut into beds, which range, as the mountains and sea-coast do, from south-west to north-east, the lamina of each bed declining from the horizon towards a parallelism with the axis of the earth. Being struck with this observation, I made, with a quadrant, a great number of trials on the angles of their declination, and found them to vary from 22° to 60° ; but averaging all my trials, the result was within one-third of a degree of the elevation of the pole or latitude of the place, and much the greatest part of them taken separately were little different from that ; by which it appears, that these lamina are, in the main, parallel with the axis of the earth. In some instances, indeed, I found them perpendicular, and even reclining the other way ; but these were extremely rare, and always attended with signs of convulsion, or other circumstances of singularity, which admitted a possibility of removal from their original position. These trials were made between Madison's cave and the Potomac. We hear of limestone on the Mississippi and Ohio, and in all the mountainous country between the eastern and western waters, not on the mountains themselves, but occupying the valleys between them.

Near the eastern foot of the North mountain are immense bodies of *Schist*, containing impressions of shells in a variety of forms. I have received petrified shells of very different kinds from the first sources of Kentucky, which bear no resemblance to any I have ever seen on the tide-waters. It is said that shells are found in the Andes, in South America, fifteen thousand feet above the level of the ocean. This is considered by many, both of the learned and unlearned, as a proof of an universal deluge. To the many considerations opposing this opinion, the following may be added : The atmosphere, and all its contents, whether of water, air, or other matter, gravitate to the earth; that is to say, they have weight. Experience tells us, that the weight of all these together never exceeds that of a column of mercury of thirty-one inches height, which is equal to one of rain water of thirty-five feet high. If the whole contents of the atmosphere, then, were water, instead of what they are, it would cover the globe but thirty-five feet deep ; but as these waters, as they fell, would run into the seas, the superficial measure of which is to that of the dry parts of the globe, as two to one, the seas would be raised only fifty-two and a half feet above their present level, and of course would overflow the lands to that height only. In Virginia this would be a very small proportion even of the champaign country, the banks of our tide-waters being frequently, if not generally, of a greater height. Deluges beyond this extent, then, as for instance, to the North mountain or to Kentucky, seem out of the laws of nature. But within it they may have taken place to a greater or less degree, in proportion to the combination of natural causes which may be supposed to have produced them. History renders probably some instances of a partial deluge in the country lying round the Mediterranean sea. It has been often* supposed, and it is not unlikely, that that sea was once a lake. While such, let us admit an extraordinary collection of the waters of the atmosphere from the other parts

* 2 Buffon Epoques, 96.

of the globe to have been discharged over that and the countries whose waters run into it. Or without supposing it a lake, admit such an extraordinary collection of the waters of the atmosphere, and an influx from the Atlantic ocean, forced by long-continued western winds. The lake, or that sea, may thus have been so raised as to overflow the low lands adjacent to it, as those of Egypt and Armenia, which, according to a tradition of the Egyptians and Hebrews, were overflowed about two thousand three hundred years before the Christian era; those of Attica, said to have been overflowed in the time of Ogyges, about five hundred years later; and those of Thessaly, in the time of Deucalion, still three hundred years posterior. But such deluges as these will not account for the shells found in the higher lands. A second opinion has been entertained, which is, that in times anterior to the records either of history or tradition, the bed of the ocean, the principal residence of the shelled tribe, has, by some great convulsion of nature, been heaved to the heights at which we now find shells and other marine animals. The favorers of this opinion do well to suppose the great events on which it rests to have taken place beyond all the eras of history; for within these, certainly, none such are to be found; and we may venture to say farther, that no fact has taken place, either in our own days, or in the thousands of years recorded in history, which proves the existence of any natural agents, within or without the bowels of the earth, of force sufficient to heave, to the height of fifteen thousand feet, such masses as the Andes. The difference between the power necessary to produce such an effect, and that which shuffled together the different parts of Calabria in our days, is so immense, that from the existence of the latter, we are not authorized to infer that of the former.

M. de Voltaire has suggested a third solution of this difficulty. (Quest. Encycl. Coquilles.) He cites an instance in Touraine, where, in the space of eighty years, a particular spot of earth had been twice metamorphosed into soft stone, which had become hard when employed in building. In this stone shells of various kinds were produced, discoverable at first only with a microscope, but afterwards growing with the stone. From this fact, I suppose, he would have us infer, that, besides the usual process for generating shells by the elaboration of earth and water in animal vessels, nature may have provided an equivalent operation, by passing the same materials through the pores of calcareous earths and stones; as we see calcareous drop-stones generating every day, by the percolation of water through limestone, and new marble forming in the quarries from which the old has been taken out. And it might be asked, whether is it more difficult for nature to shoot the calcareous juice into the form of a shell, than other juices into the forms of crystals, plants, animals, according to the construction of the vessels through which they pass? There is a wonder somewhere. Is it greatest on this branch of the dilemma; on that which supposes the existence of a power, of which we have no evidence in any other case; or on the first, which requires us to believe the creation of a body of water and its subsequent annihilation? The establishment of the instance, cited by M. de Voltaire, of the growth of shells unattached to animal bodies, would have been that of his theory. But he has not established it. He has not even left it on ground so respectable as to have rendered it an object of inquiry to the *literati* of his own country. Abandoning this fact, therefore, the three hypotheses are equally unsatisfactory; and we must be contented to acknowledge, that this great phenomenon is as yet unsolved. Ignorance is preferable to error; and he is less remote from the truth who believes nothing, than he who believes what is wrong.

There is great abundance (more especially when you approach the mountains) of stone, white, blue, brown, &c., fit for the chisel, good mill-stone, such also as stands the fire, and slate stone. We are told of flint, fit for gun-flints, on the Meherrin in Brunswick, on the Mississippi between the mouth of the Ohio and Kaskaskia, and on others of the western waters. Isinglass or mica is in several places; loadstone also; and an Asbestos of a ligneous texture, is sometimes to be met with.

Marle abounds generally. A clay, of which, like the Sturbridge in England, bricks are made, which will resist long the violent action of fire, has been found on Tuckahoe creek of

James' river, and no doubt will be found in other places. Chalk is said to be in Botetourt and Bedford. In the latter county is some earth believed to be gypseous. Ochres are found in various parts.

In the lime-stone country are many caves, the earthy floors of which are impregnated with nitre. On Rich creek, a branch of the Great Kanhaway, about sixty miles below the lead mines, is a very large one, about twenty yards wide, and entering a hill a quarter or half a mile. The vault is of rock, from nine to fifteen or twenty feet above the floor. A Mr. Lynch, who gives me this account, undertook to extract the nitre. Besides a coat of the salt which had formed on the vault and floor, he found the earth highly impregnated to the depth of seven feet in some places, and generally of three, every bushel yielding on an average three pounds of nitre. Mr. Lynch having made about ten hundred pounds of the salt from it, consigned it to some others, who have since made ten thousand pounds. They have done this by pursuing the cave into the hill, never trying a second time the earth they have once exhausted, to see how far or soon it receives another impregnation. At least fifty of these caves are worked on the Greenbriar. There are many of them known on Cumberland river.

The country westward of the Alleghany abounds with springs of common salt. The most remarkable we have heard of are at Bullet's-lick, the Big-bones, the Blue-licks, and on the north fork of Holston. The area of Bullet's-lick is of many acres. Digging the earth to the depth of three feet the water begins to boil up, and the deeper you go and the drier the weather, the stronger is the brine. A thousand gallons of water yield from a bushel to a bushel and a half of salt, which is about eighty pounds of water to one pound of salt. So that sea-water is more than three times as strong as that of these springs. A salt spring has been lately discovered at the Turkey foot on Yohogany, by which river it is overflowed, except at very low water. Its merit is not yet known. Dunning's lick is also as yet untried, but it is supposed to be the best on this side the Ohio. The salt springs on the margin of the Onondago lake are said to give a saline taste to the waters of the lake.

There are several medicinal springs, some of which are indubitably efficacious, while others seem to owe their reputation as much to fancy and change of air and regimen, as to their real virtues. None of them having undergone a chemical analysis in skilful hands, nor been so far the subject of observations as to have produced a reduction into classes of the disorders which they relieve ; it is in my power to give little more than an enumeration of them.

The most efficacious of these are two springs in Augusta near the first sources of James' river, where it is called Jackson's river. They rise near the foot of the ridge of mountains generally called the Warm spring mountains, but in the maps Jackson's mountains. The one distinguished by the name of the Warm spring, and the other of the Hot spring. The Warm spring issues with a very bold stream, sufficient to work a grist mill and to keep the waters of its basin, which is thirty feet in diameter, at the vital warmth, viz. 96° of Fahrenheit's thermometer. The matter with which these waters is allied is very volatile ; its smell indicates it to be sulphureous, as also does the circumstance of its turning silver black. They relieve rheumatisms. Other complaints also of very different natures have been removed or lessened by them. It rains here four or five days in every week.

The *Hot spring* is about six miles from the Warm, is much smaller, and has been so hot as to have boiled an egg. Some believe its degree of heat to be lessened. It raises the mercury in Fahrenheit's thermometer to 112 degrees, which is fever heat. It sometimes relieves where the Warm fails. A fountain of common water, issuing within a few inches of its margin, gives it a singular appearance. Comparing the temperature of these with that of the Hot springs of Kamschatka, of which Krachininni-kow gives an account, the difference is very great, the latter raising the mercury to 200° which is within 12° of boiling water. These springs are very much resorted to in spite of a total want of accommodation for the sick. Their waters are strongest in the hottest months, which occasions their being visited in July and August principally.

The Sweet springs are in the county of Botetourt, at the eastern foot of the Aleghany, about forty-two miles from the Warm springs. They are still less known. Having been found to relieve cases in which the others had been ineffectually tried, it is probable their composition is different. They are different also in their temperature, being as cold as common water; which is not mentioned, however, as a proof of a distinct impregnation. This is among the first sources of James' river.

On Potomac river, in Berkley county, above the North mountain, are medicinal springs, much more frequented than those of Augusta. Their powers, however, are less, the waters weakly mineralized, and scarcely warm. They are more visited, because situated in a fertile, plentiful, and populous country, better provided with accommodations, always safe from the Indians, and nearest to the more populous States.

In Louisa county, on the head waters of the South Ann branch of York river, are springs of some medicinal virtue. They are not much used however. There is a weak chalybeate at Richmond; and many others in various parts of the country, which are of too little worth, or too little note, to be enumerated after those before mentioned.

We are told of a sulphur spring on Howard's creek of Greenbriar, and another at Boonsborough on Kentucky.

In the low grounds of the Great Kanhaway, seven miles above the mouth of Elk river, and sixty-seven above that of the Kanhaway itself, is a hole in the earth of the capacity of thirty or forty gallons, from which issues constantly a bituminous vapor, in so strong a current as to give to the sand about its orifice the motion which it has in a boiling spring. On presenting a lighted candle or torch within eighteen inches of the hole it flames up in a column of eighteen inches in diameter, and four or five feet height, which sometimes burns out within twenty minutes, and at other times has been known to continue three days, and then has been still left burning. The flame is unsteady, of the density of that of burning spirits, and smells like burning pit coal. Water sometimes collects in the basin, which is remarkably cold, and is kept in ebullition by the vapor issuing through it. If the vapor be fired in that state, the water soon becomes so warm that the hand cannot bear it, and evaporates wholly in a short time. This, with the circumjacent lands, is the property of His Excellency General Washington and of General Lewis.

There is a similar one on Sandy river, the flame of which is a column of about twelve inches diameter, and three feet high. General Clarke, who informs me of it, kindled the vapor, staid about an hour, and left it burning.

The mention of uncommon springs leads me to that of Syphon fountains. There is one of these near the intersection of the Lord Fairfax's boundary with the North mountain, not far from Brock's gap, on the stream of which is a grist mill, which grinds two bushel of grain at every flood of the spring ; another near Cow-pasture river, a mile and a half below its confluence with the Bull-pasture river, and sixteen or seventeen miles from Hot springs, which intermits once in every twelve hours ; one also near the mouth of the north Holston.

After these may be mentioned the *Natural Well*, on the lands of a Mr. Lewis in Frederick county. It is somewhat larger than a common well ; the water rises in it as near the surface of the earth as in the neighboring artificial wells, and is of a depth as yet unknown. It is said there is a current in it tending sensibly downwards. If this be true, it probably feeds some fountain, of which it is the natural reservoir, distinguished from others, like that of Madison's cave, by being accessible. It is used with a bucket and windlass as an ordinary well.

A complete catalogue of the trees, plants, fruits, &c., is probably not desired. I will sketch out those which would principally attract notice, as being first, Medicinal; second, Esculent; third, Ornamental; or four, useful for fabrication; adding the Linnæan to the popular names, as the latter might not convey precise information to a foreigner. I shall confine myself too to native plants.

1. Senna.   Cassia ligustrina.
   Arsmart.   Polygonum Sagittatum.
   Clivers, or goose-grass.   Galium spurium.
   Lobelia of several species.

Palma Christi. Ricinus.

(3,) Jamestown weed. Datura Stramonium.

Mallow. Malva rotundafolia.

Syrian mallow. Hibiscus moschentos.

Hibiscus Virginicus.

Indian mallow. Sida rhombifolia.

Sida abutilon.

Virginia marshmallow. Napæa hermaphrodita.

Napæa dioica.

Indian physic. Spiria trifoliata.

Euphorbia Ipecacuanhæ.

Pleurisy root. Asclepias decumbens.

Virginia snake-root. Aristolochia serpentaria.

Black snake-root. Actæ racemosa.

Seneca rattlesnake-root. Polygala Senega.

Valerian. Valeriana locusta radiata.

Gentiana, Saponaria, Villosa & Centaurium.

Ginseng. Panax quinquefolium.

Angelica. Angelica sylvestris.

Cassava. Jatropha urens.

2. Tuckahoe. Lycoperdon tuber.

Jerusalem artichoke. Helianthus tuberosus.

Long potatoes. Convolvulas batatas.

Granadillas. Maycocks, Maracocks, Passiflora incarnata.

Panic. Panicum of many species.

Indian millet. Holcus laxus.

Indian millet. Holcus striosus.

Wild oat. Zizania aquaticia.

Wild pea. Dolichos of Clayton.

Lupine. Lupinus perennis.

Wild hop. Humulus lupulus.

Wild cherry. Prunus Virginiana.

Cherokee plum. Prunus sylvestris fructu majori. Clayton.

Wild plum. Prunus sylvestris fructu minori. Clayton.

Wild crab apple. Pyrus coronaria.

Red mulberry. Morus rubra.

Persimmon. Diospiros Virginiana.

Sugar maple. Acer saccarinum.

Scaly bark hiccory. Juglans alba cortice squamoso. Clayton.

Common hiccory. Juglans alba, fructu minore rancido. Clayton.

Paccan, or Illinois nut. Not described by Linnæus, Millar, or Clayton. Were I to venture to describe this, speaking of the fruit from memory, and of the leaf from plants of two years' growth, I should specify it as Juglans alba, foliolis lanceolatis, acuminatis, serratis, tomentosis, fructu minore, ovato, compresso, vix insculpto, dulci, putamine tenerrimo. It grows on the Illinois, Wabash, Ohio, and Mississippi. It is spoken of by Don Ulloa under the name of Pacanos, in his Noticias Americanas. Entret. 6.

Black walnut   Juglans nigra.
White walnut.   Juglans alba.
Chesnut.   Fagus castanea.
Chinquapin.   Fagus pumila.
Hazlenut.   Corylus avellana.
Grapes.   Vitis.   Various kinds; though only three described by Clayton.
Scarlet strawberries.   Fragaria Virginiana of Millar
Whortleberries.   Vaccinium uliginosum.
Wild gooseberries.   Ribes grossularia.
Cranberries.   Vaccinium oxycoccos.
Black raspberries.   Rubus occidentalis.
Blackberries.   Rubus fructicosus.
Dewberries.   Rubus cæsius.
Cloudberries.   Rubus Chamæmorus.
3. Plane tree.   Platanus occidentalis.
Poplar.   Liriodendron tulipifera.
            Populus heterophylla.
Black poplar.   Populus nigra.
Aspen.   Populus tremula.
Linden, or lime.   Telia Americana.
Red flowering maple.   Acer rubrum.
Horse-chesnut, or buck's-eye.   Æsculus pavia.
Catalpa.   Bignonia catalpa.
Umbrella.   Magnolia tripetala
Swamp laurel.   Magnolia glauca.
Cucumber-tree.   Magnolia acuminata.
Portugal bay.   Laurus indica.
Red bay.   Laurus borbonia.
Dwarf-rose bay.   Rhododendron maximum.
Laurel of the western country.   Qu. species?
Wild pimento.   Laurus benzoin.
Sassafras.   Laurus sassafras.
Locust.   Robinia pseudo-acacia.
Honey-locust.   Gleditsia. 1. 6
Dogwood.   Cornus florida.
Fringe, or snow-drop tree.   Chionanthus Virginica.
Barberry.   Barberis vulgaris.
Redbud, or Judas-tree.   Cercis Canadensis.
Holly.   Ilex aquifolium.
Cockspur hawthorn.   Cratægus coccinea.
Spindle-tree.   Euonymus Europæus.
Evergreen spindle-tree.   Euonymus Americanus.
Itea Virginica.
Elder.   Sambucus nigra.
Papaw.   Annona triloba.
Candleberry myrtle.   Myrica cerifera.
Dwarf laurel.   Kalmia angustifolia } called ivy with us.
        Kalmia latifolia

Ivy.   Hedera quinquefolia.
Trumpet honeysuckle.   Lonicera sempervirens
Upright honeysuckle.   Azalea nudiflora.
Yellow jasmine.   Bignonia sempervirens.
Calycanthus floridus.
American aloe.   Agave Virginica.
Sumach.   Rhus.   Qu. species?
Poke.   Phytolacca decandra.
Long moss.   Tillandsia Usneoides.
4. Reed.   Aruudo phragmitis.
Virginia hemp.   Acnida cannabina.
Flax.   Linum Virginianum.
Black, or pitch-pine.   Pinus tæda.
White pine,   Pinus strobus.
Yellow pine.   Pinus Virginica.
Spruce pine.   Pinus foliis singularibus.   Clayton.
Hemlock spruce Fir.   Pinus Canadensis.
Abor vitæ.   Thuya occidentalis.
Juniper.   Juniperus Virginica (called cedar with us.)
Cypress.   Cupressus disticha.
White cedar.   Cupressus Thyoides.
Black oak.   Quercus nigra.
White oak.   Quercus alba.
Red oak.   Quercus rubra.
Willow oak.   Quercus phellos.
Chesnut oak.   Quercus prinus.
Black jack oak.   Quercus aquatica.   Clayton.
Ground oak.   Quercus pumila.   Clayton.
Live oak.   Quercus Virginiana.   Millar.
Black birch.   Betula nigra.
White birch.   Betula alba.
Beach.   Fagus sylvatica.
Ash.   Fraxinus Americana.
         Fraxinus Novæ Angliæ.   Millar.
Elm.   Ulmus Americana.
Willow.   Salix.   Qu. species?
Sweet gum.   Liquidambar styraciflua.

The following were found in Virginia when first visited by the English; but it is not said whether of spontaneous growth, or by cultivation only. Most probably they were natives of more southern climates, and handed along the continent from one nation to another of the savages.

Tobacco.   Nicotiana.
Maize.   Zea mays.

Round potatoes.   Solanum tuberosum.
Pumpkins.   Cucurbita pepo.
Cymlings.   Cucurbita verrucosa.
Squashes.   Cucurbita melopepo.

There is an infinitude of other plants and flowers, for an enumeration and scientific description of which I must refer to the Flora Virginica of our great botanist, Dr. Clayton, published by Gronovius at Leyden, in 1762. This accurate observer was a native and resident of this State, passed a long life in exploring and describing its plants, and is supposed to have enlarged the botanical catalogue as much as almost any man who has lived.

Besides these plants, which are native, our *farms* produce wheat, rye, barley, oats, buck-wheat, broom corn, and Indian corn. The climate suits rice well enough, wherever the lands do. Tobacco, hemp, flax, and cotton, are staple commodities. Indigo yields two cuttings. The silk-worm is a native, and the mulberry, proper for its food, grows kindly.

We cultivate, also, potatoes, both the long and the round, turnips, carrots, parsnips, pumkins, and ground nuts (Arachis.) Our grasses are lucerne, st. foin, burnet, timothy, ray, and orchard grass; red, white, and yellow clover; greensward, blue grass, and crab grass.

The *gardens* yield musk-melons, water-melons, tomatoes, okra, pomegranates, figs, and the esculant plants of Europe.

The *orchards* produce apples, pears, cherries, quinces, peaches, nectarines, apricots, almonds, and plums.

Our quadrupeds have been mostly described by Linnæus and Mons. de Buffon. Of these the mammoth, or big buffalo, as called by the Indians, must certainly have been the largest. Their tradition is, that he was carnivorous, and still exists in the northern parts of America. A delegation of warriors from the Delaware tribe having visited the Governor of Virginia, during the revolution, on matters of business, after these had been discussed and settled in council, the Governor asked them some questions relative to their country, and among others, what they knew or had heard of the animal whose bones were found at the

Saltlicks on the Ohio. Their chief speaker immediately put himself into an attitude of oratory, and with a pomp suited to what he conceived the elevation of his subject, informed him that it was a tradition handed down from their fathers, " That in ancient times a herd of these tremendous animals came to the Big-bone licks, and began an universal destruction of the bear, deer, elks, buffaloes, and other animals which had been created for the use of the Indians; that the Great Man above, looking down and seeing this, was so enraged that he seized his lightning, descended on the earth, seated himself on a neighboring mountain, on a rock of which his seat and the print of his feet are still to be seen, and hurled his bolts among them till the whole were slaughtered, except the big bull, who presenting his forehead to the shafts, shook them off as they fell; but missing one at length, it wounded him in the side; whereon, springing round, he bounded over the Ohio, over the Wabash, the Illinois, and finally over the great lakes, where he is living at this day." It is well known, that on the Ohio, and in many parts of America further north, tusks, grinders, and skeletons of unparalleled magnitude, are found in great numbers, some lying on the surface of the earth, and some a little below it. A Mr. Stanley, taken prisoner near the mouth of the Tennessee, relates, that after being transferred through several tribes, from one to another, he was at length carried over the mountains west of the Missouri to a river which runs westwardly; that these bones abounded there, and that the natives described to him the animal to which they belonged as still existing in the northern parts of their country; from which description he judged it to be an elephant. Bones of the same kind have been lately found, some feet below the surface of the earth, in salines opened on the North Holston, a branch of the Tennessee, about the latitude of $36\frac{1}{2}°$ north. From the accounts published in Europe, I suppose it to be decided that these are of the same kind with those found in Siberia. Instances are mentioned of like animal remains found in the more southern climates of both hemispheres; but they are either so loosely mentioned as to leave a doubt of the fact, so inaccurately described as not to authorize the classing them with the great northern bones, or so rare as to found a suspicion that they have been carried thither as curiosities from the northern regions. So that, on the whole, there seem to be no certain vestiges of the existence of this animal farther south than the salines just mentioned. It is remarkable that the tusks and skeletons have been ascribed by the naturalists of Europe to the elephant, while the grinders have been given to the hippopotamus, or river horse. Yet it is acknowledged, that the tusks and skeletons are much larger than those of the elephant, and the grinders many times greater than those of the hippopotamus, and essentially different in form. Wherever these grinders are found, there also we find the tusks and skeleton ; but no skeleton of the hippopotamus nor grinders of the elephant. It will not be said that the hippopotamus and elephant came always to the same spot, the former to deposit his grinders, and the latter his tusks and skeleton. For what became of the parts not deposited there ? We must agree then, that these remains belong to each other, that they are of one and the same animal, that this was not a hippopotamus, because the hippopotamus had no tusks, nor such a frame, and because the grinders differ in their size as well as in the number and form of their points. That this was not an elephant, I think ascertained by proofs equally decisive. I will not avail myself of the authority of the celebrated* anatomist, who, from an examination of the form and structure of the tusks, has declared they were essentially different from those of the elephant; because another† anatomist, equally celebrated, has declared, on a like examination, that they are precisely the same. Between two such authorities I will suppose this circumstance equivocal. But, 1. The skeleton of the mammoth (for so the incognitum has been called) bespeaks an animal of five or six times the cubic volume of the elephant, as Mons. de Buffon has admitted. 2. The grinders are five times as large, are square, and the grinding surface studded with four or five rows of blunt points ; whereas those of the elephant are broad and thin, and their grinding surface flat. 3. I have never heard an instance, and suppose there has been none, of the grinder of an elephant being found in America. 4.

* Hunter. † D'Aubenton.

From the known temperature and constitution of the elephant, he could never have existed in those regions where the remains of the mammoth have been found. The elephant is a native only of the torrid zone and its vicinities; if, with the assistance of warm apartments and warm clothing, he has been preserved in the temperate climates of Europe, it has only been for a small portion of what would have been his natural period, and no instance of his multiplication in them has ever been known. But no bones of the mammoth, as I have before observed, have been ever found further south than the salines of Holston, and they have been found as far north as the Arctic circle. Those, therefore, who are of opinion that the elephant and mammoth are the same, must believe, 1. That the elephant known to us can exist and multiply in the frozen zone; or, 2. That an eternal fire may once have warmed those regions, and since abandoned them, of which, however, the globe exhibits no unequivocal indications; or, 3. That the obliquity of the ecliptic, when these elephants lived, was so great as to include within the tropics all those regions in which the bones are found; the tropics being, as is before observed, the natural limits of habitation for the elephant. But if it be admitted that this obliquity has really decreased, and we adopt the highest rate of decrease yet pretended, that is, of one minute in a century, to transfer the northern tropic to the Arctic circle, would carry the existence of these supposed elephants two hundred and fifty thousand years back; a period far beyond our conception of the duration of animal bones less exposed to the open air than these are in many instances. Besides, though these regions would then be supposed within the tropics, yet their winters would have been too severe for the sensibility of the elephant. They would have had, too, but one day and one night in the year, a circumstance to which we have no reason to suppose the nature of the elephant fitted. However, it has been demonstrated, that, if a variation of obliquity in the ecliptic takes place at all, it is vibratory, and never exceeds the limits of nine degrees, which is not sufficient to bring these bones within the tropics. One of these hypotheses, or some other equally voluntary and inadmissible to cautious philosophy, must be adopted to support the opinion that these are the bones of the elephant. For my own part, I find it easier to believe that an animal may have existed, resembling the elephant in his tusks, and general anatomy, while his nature was in other respects extremely different. From the 30th degree of south latitude to the 30th degree of north, are nearly the limits which nature has fixed for the existence and multiplication of the elephant known to us. Proceeding thence northwardly to $36\frac{1}{2}$ degrees, we enter those assigned to the mammoth. The farther we advance north, the more their vestiges multiply as far as the earth has been explored in that direction; and it is as probable as otherwise, that this progression continues to the pole itself, if land extends so far. The centre of the frozen zone, then, may be the acmé of their vigor, as that of the torrid is of the elephant. Thus nature seems to have drawn a belt of separation between these two tremendous animals, whose breadth, indeed, is not precisely known, though at present we may suppose it about $6\frac{1}{2}$ degrees of latitude; to have assigned to the elephant the regions south of these confines, and those north to the mammoth, founding the constitution of the one in her extreme of heat, and that of the other in the extreme of cold. When the Creator has therefore separated their nature as far as the extent of the scale of animal life allowed to this planet would permit, it seems perverse to declare it the same, from a partial resemblance of their tusks and bones. But to whatever animal we ascribe these remains, it is certain such a one has existed in America, and that it has been the largest of all terrestrial beings. It should have sufficed to have rescued the earth it inhabited, and the atmosphere it breathed, from the imputation of impotence in the conception and nourishment of animal life on a large scale; to have stifled, in its birth, the opinion of a writer, the most learned, too, of all others in the science of animal history, that in the new world, "La nature vivante est beaucoup moins agissante, beaucoup moins forte:"* that nature is less active, less energetic on one side of the globe than she is on the other. As if both sides were not warmed by the same genial sun; as if a

* Buffon, xviii. 112 edit. Paris, 1764.

soil of the same chemical composition was less capable of elaboration into animal nutriment; as if the fruits and grains from that soil and sun yielded a less rich chyle, gave less extension to the solids and fluids of the body, or produced sooner in the cartilages, membranes, and fibres, that rigidity which restrains all further extension, and terminates animal growth. The truth is, that a pigmy and a Patagonian, a mouse and a mammoth, derive their dimensions from the same nutritive juices. The difference of increment depends on circumstances unsearchable to beings with our capacities. Every race of animals seems to have received from their Maker certain laws of extension at the time of their formation. Their elaborate organs were formed to produce this, while proper obstacles were opposed to its further progress. Below these limits they cannot fall, nor rise above them. What intermediate station they shall take may depend on soil, on climate, on food, on a careful choice of breeders. But all the manna of heaven would never raise the mouse to the bulk of the mammoth.

The opinion advanced by the Count de Buffon,* is 1. That the animals common both to the old and new world are smaller in the latter. 2. That those peculiar to the new are on a smaller scale. 3. That those which have been domesticated in both have degenerated in America; and 4. That on the whole it exhibits fewer species. And the reason he thinks is, that the heats of America are less; that more waters are spread over its surface by nature, and fewer of these drained off by the hand of man. In other words, that *heat* is friendly, and *moisture* adverse to the production and development of large quadrupeds. I will not meet this hypothesis on its first doubtful ground, whether the climate of America be comparatively more humid? Because we are not furnished with observations sufficient to decide this question. And though, till it be decided, we are as free to deny as others are to affirm the fact, yet for a moment let it be supposed. The hypothesis, after this supposition, proceeds to another; that *moisture* is unfriendly to animal growth. The truth of this is inscrutable to us by reasonings *à priori*. Nature has

* Buffon, xviii. 100, 156.

hidden from us her *modus agendi*. Our only appeal on such questions is to experience; and I think that experience is against the supposition. It is by the assistance of *heat* and *moisture* that vegetables are elaborated from the elements of earth, air, water, and fire. We accordingly see the more humid climates produce the greater quantity of vegetables. Vegetables are memediately or immediately the food of every animal; and in proportion to the quantity of food, we see animals not only multiplied in their numbers, but improved in their bulk, as far as the laws of their nature will admit. Of this opinion is the Count de Buffon himself in another part of his work;* " en general il paroit ques les pays un peu *froids* conviennent mieux á nos boeufs que les pays chauds, et qu'ils sont d'autant plus gross et plus grands que le climat est plus *humide* et plus abondans en paturages. Les boeufs de Danemarck, de la Podolie, de l'Ukraine et de la Tartarie qu habitent les Calmouques sont les plus grands de tous." Here then a race of animals, and one of the largest too, has been increased in its dimensions by *cold* and *moisture*, in direct opposition to the hypothesis, which supposes that these two circumstances diminish animal bulk, and that it is their contraries *heat* and *dryness* which enlarge it. But when we appeal to experience we are not to rest satisfied with a single fact. Let us, therefore, try our question on more general ground. Let us take two portions of the earth, Europe and America for instance, sufficiently extensive to give operation to general causes; let us consider the circumstances peculiar to each, and observe their effect on animal nature. America, running through the torrid as well as temperate zone, has more *heat* collectively taken, than Europe. But Europe, according to our hypothesis, is the *dryest*. They are equally adapted then to animal productions; each being endowed with one of those causes which befriend animal growth, and with one which opposes it. If it be thought unequal to compare Europe with America, which is so much larger, I answer, not more so than to compare America with the whole world. Besides, the purpose of the comparison is to try an hypothesis, which makes the size

* viii. 134.

of animals depend on the *heat* and *moisture* of climate. If therefore, we take a region so extensive as to comprehend a sensible distinction of climate, and so extensive too as that local accidents, or the intercourse of animals on its borders, may not materially affect the size of those in its interior parts, we shall comply with those conditions which the hypothesis may reasonably demand. The objection would be the weaker in the present case, because any intercourse of animals which may take place on the confines of Europe and Asia, is to the advantage of the former, Asia producing certainly larger animals than Europe. Let us then take a comparative view of the quadrupeds of Europe and America, presenting them to the eye in three different tables, in one of which shall be enumerated those found in both countries; in a second, those found in one only; in a third, those which have been domesticated in both. To facilitate the comparison, let those of each table be arranged in gradation according to their sizes, from the greatest to the smallest, so far as their sizes can be conjectured. The weights of the large animals shall be expressed in the English avoirdupoise and its decimals; those of the smaller, in the same ounce and its decimals. Those which are marked thus *, are actual weights of particular subjects, deemed among the largest of their species. Those marked thus †, are furnished by judicious persons, well acquainted with the species, and saying, from conjecture only, what the largest individual they had seen would probably have weighed. The other weights are taken from Messrs. Buffon and D'Aubenton, and are of such subjects as came casually to their hands for dissection. This circumstance must be remembered where their weights and mine stand opposed; the latter being stated not to produce a conclusion in favor of the American species, but to justify a suspension of opinion until we are better informed, and a suspicion, in the meantime, that there is no uniform difference n favor of either; which is all I pretend.

A comparative view of the Quadrupeds of Europe and of America.

I. ABORIGINALS OF BOTH.

	Europe. lb.	America. lb.
Mammoth		
Buffalo. Bison		*1800
White Bear. Ours blanc		
Carribou. Renne		
Bear. Ours	153.7	*410
Elk. Elan. Original palmated		
Red deer. - Cerf	288.8	*273
Fallow Deer. Daim	167.8	
Wolf. Loup	69.8	
Roe. Chevreuil	56.7	
Glutton. Glouton. Carcajou		
Wild cat. Chat sauvage		†30
Lynx. Loup cervier	25.	
Beaver. Castor	18.5	*45
Badger. Blaireau	13.6	
Red fox. Renard	13.5	
Gray fox. Isatis		
Otter. Loutre	8.9	†12
Monax. Marmotte	6.5	
Vison. Fouine	2.8	
Hedgehog. Herisson	2.2	
Marten. Marte	1.9	†6
	oz.	
Water rat. Rat d'eau	7.5	
Weasel. Belette	2.2	oz.
Flying squirrel. Polatouche	2.2	†4
Shrew moseu Musaraigne	1.	

II. ABORIGINALS OF ONE ONLY.

EUROPE.	lb.	AMERICA.	lb.
Sanglier. Wild boar	280.	Tapir	534.
Mouflon. Wild sheep	56.	Elk, round horned.	†450.
Bouquetin. Wild goat . . .		Puma	
Lievre. Hare	7.6	Jaguar	218.
Lapin. Rabbit	3.4	Cabiai	109.
Putois. Polecat	3.3	Tamanoir	109.
Genette	3.1	Tammandua	65.4
Desman. Muskrat	oz.	Cougar of North-America . .	75.
Ecureuil. Squirrel . . .	12.	Cougar of South-America . .	59.4
Hermine. Ermin	8.2	Ocelot	
Rat. Rat	7.5	Pecari	46.3
Loirs	3.1	Jaguaret	43.6
Lerot. Dormouse	1.8	Alco	
Taupe. Mole	1.2	Lama	
Hampster	.6	Paco	
Zisel . . . . , . .		Paca	32.7

II. TABLE CONTINUED.

EUROPE.	lb.	AMERICA.	lb.
Leming		Serval	
Pouris. Mouse	.6	Sloth. Unau	27.25
		Saricovienne	
		Kincajou	
		Tatou Kabassou . . .	21.8
		Urson. Urchin	
		Raccoon. Raton	16.5
		Coati	
		Coendou	16.3
		Sloth. Aï	13.
		Sapajou Ouarini	
		Sapajou Coaita	9.8
		Tatou Encubert	
		Tatou Apar	
		Tatou Cachica	7.
		Little Coendou	6.5
		Opossum. Sarigu . . .	
		Tapeti	
		Margay	
		Crabier	
		Agouti	4.2
		Sapajou Saï	3.5
		Tatou Cirquinçon . . .	
		Tatou Tatouate	8.3
		Mouffette Squash . . .	
		Mouffette Chinche . . .	
		Mouffette Conepate . . .	
		Scunk	
		Mouffette. Zorilla . . .	
		Whabus. Hare. Rabbit . .	
		Aperea	
		Akouchi	
		Ondatra. Muskrat . . .	
		Pilori	
		Great gray squirrel . .	†2.7
		Fox squirrel of Virginia . .	†2.625
		Surikate	2.
		Mink	†2.
		Sapajou. Sajou	1.8
		Indian pig. Cochon d'Inde . .	1.6
		Sapajou Saïmiri	1.5
		Phalanger	
		Coqualain	
		Lesser gray squirrel . .	†1.5
		Black squirrel	†1.5
		Red squirrel	10.oz.
		Sagoin Saki	
		Sagoin Pinche	
		Sagoin Tamarin	oz.
		Sagoin Ouistiti	4.4
		Sagoin Marakine . . .	
		Sagoin Mico	
		Cayopollin	
		Fourmillier	
		Marmose	
		Sarigue of Cayenne . . .	
		Tucan	
		Red mole	oz.
		Ground squirrel	4.

III. DOMESTICATED IN BOTH.

	Europe. lb.	America. lb.
Cow	765.	*2500
Horse		*1366
Ass		
Hog		*1200
Sheep		*125
Goat		*80
Dog	67.6	
Cat	7.	

I have not inserted in the first table the Phoca,* nor leather-winged bat, because the one living half the year in the water, and the other being a winged animal, the individuals of each species may visit both continents.

Of the animals in the first table, Monsieur de Buffon himself informs us, [XXVII. 130, XXX. 213,] that the beaver, the otter, and shrew mouse, though of the same species, are large. in America than in Europe. This should therefore have corrected the generality of his expressions, XVIII. 145, and else where, that the animals common to the two countries, are considerably less in America than in Europe, " et cela sans aucune exception." He tells us too, [Quadrup. VIII. 334, edit. Paris 1777,] that on examining a bear from America, he remarked no difference, " dans *la forme* de cet ours d'Amerique comparé a celui d'Europe," but adds from Bartram's journal, that an American bear weighed four hundred pounds, English, equal to three hundred and sixty-seven pounds French ; whereas we find the European bear examined by Mons. D'Aubenton, [XVII. 82,] weighed but one hundred and forty-one pounds French. That the palmated elk is larger in America than in Europe, we are informed by Kalm,† a naturalist, who visited the former by public appointment, for the express purpose of examining the subjects of natural

* It is said that this animal is seldom seen above thirty miles from shore, or beyond the 56th degree of latitude. The interjacent islands between Asia and America admit his passing from one continent to the other without exceeding these bounds. And in fact, travellers tell us that these islands are places of principal resort for them, and especially in the season of bringing forth their young.

† I. 233, Lon. 1772.

history. In this fact Pennant concurs with him. [Barrington's Miscellanies.] The same Kalm tells us* that the black moose, or renne of America, is as high as a tall horse ; and Catesby,† that it is about the bigness of a middle-sized ox. The same account of their size has been given me by many who have seen them. But Monsieur D'Aubenton says‡ that the renne of Europe is about the size of a red deer. The weasel is larger in America than in Europe, as may be seen by comparing its dimensions as reported by Monsieur D'Aubenton§ and Kalm. The latter tells us,‖ that the lynx, badger, red fox, and flying squirrel, are the *same* in America as in Europe ; by which expression I understand, they are the same in all material circumstances, in size as well as others ; for if they were smaller, they would differ from the European. Our gray fox is, by Catesby's account,¶ little different in size and shape from the European fox. I presume he means the red fox of Europe, as does Kalm, where he says,** that in size "they do not quite come up to our foxes." For proceeding next to the red fox of America, he says, "they are entirely the same with the European sort ;" which shows he had in view one European sort only, which was the red. So that the result of their testimony is, that the American gray fox is somewhat less than the European red ; which is equally true of the gray fox of Europe, as may be seen by comparing the measures of the Count de Buffon and Monsieur D'Aubenton.†† The white bear of America is as large as that of Europe. The bones of the mammoth which has been found in America, are as large as those found in the old world. It may be asked, why I insert the mammoth, as if it still existed ? I ask in return, why I should omit it, as if it did not exist ? Such is the economy of nature, that no instance can be produced, of her having permitted any one race of her animals to become extinct ; of her having formed any link in her great work so weak as to be broken. To add to this, the traditionary testimony of the Indians, that this animal still exists in the northern and western parts of America, would

* Ib. 233.   † I. xxvii.   ‡ XXIV. 162.   § XV. 42.
‖ I. 359. I. 48, 221, 251. II. 52.   ¶ II. 78.   ** I. 220.
†† XXVII. 63. XIV. 119. Harris, II. 387. Buffon, Quad. IX. 1.

be adding the light of a taper to that of the meridian sun. Those parts still remain in their aboriginal state, unexplored and undisturbed by us, or by others for us. He may as well exist there now, as he did formerly where we find his bones. If he be a carnivorous animal, as some anatomists have conjectured, and the Indians affirm, his early retirement may be accounted for from the general destruction of the wild game by the Indians, which commences in the first instant of their connection with us, for the purpose of purchasing match-coats, hatchets, and firelocks, with their skins. There remain then the buffalo, red deer, fallow deer, wolf, roe, glutton, wild cat, monax, bison, hedgehog, marten, and water-rat, of the comparative sizes of which we have not sufficient testimony. It does not appear that Messieurs de Buffon and D'Aubenton have measured, weighed, or seen those of America. It is said of some of them, by some travellers, that they are smaller than the European. But who were these travellers? Have they not been men of a very different description from those who have laid open to us the other three quarters of the world? Was natural history the object of their travels? Did they measure or weigh the animals they speak of? or did they not judge of them by sight, or perhaps even from report only? Were they acquainted with the animals of their own country, with which they undertake to compare them? Have they not been so ignorant as often to mistake the species? A true answer to these questions would probably lighten their authority, so as to render it insufficient for the foundation of an hypothesis. How unripe we yet are, for an accurate comparison of the animals of the two countries, will appear from the work of Monsieur de Buffon. The ideas we should have formed of the sizes of some animals, from the information he had received at his first publications concerning them, are very different from what his subsequent communications give us. And indeed his candor in this can never be too much praised. One sentence of his book must do him immortal honor. " J'aime autant une personne qui me releve d'une erreur, qu'une autre qui m'apprend une verité, parce qu'en effet une erreur corrigée est une verité."*

* Quad. IX. 158.

He seems to have thought the cabiai he first examined wanted little of its full growth. "Il n'etoit pas encore tout-a-fait adulte."* Yet he weighed but forty-six and a half pounds, and he found afterwards,† that these animals, when full grown, weigh one hundred pounds. He had supposed, from the examination of a jaguar,‡ said to be two years old, which weighed but sixteen pounds twelve ounces, that when he should have acquired his full growth, he would not be larger than a middle-sized dog. But a subsequent account§ raises his weight to two hundred pounds. Further information will, doubtless, produce further corrections. The wonder is, not that there is yet something in this great work to correct, but that there is so little. The result of this view then is, that of twenty-six quadrupeds common to both countries, seven are said to be larger in America, seven of equal size, and twelve not sufficiently examined. So that the first table impeaches the first member of the assertion, that of the animals common to both countries, the American are smallest, "et cela sans aucune exception." It shows it is not just, in all the latitude in which its author has advanced it, and probably not to such a degree as to found a distinction between the two countries.

Proceeding to the second table, which arranges the animals found in one of the two countries only, Monsieur de Buffon observes, that the tapir, the elephant of America, is but of the size of a small cow. To preserve our comparison, I will add, that the wild boar, the elephant of Europe, is little more than half that size. I have made an elk with round or cylindrical horns an animal of America, and peculiar to it; because I have seen many of them myself, and more of their horns; and because I can say, from the best information, that, in Virginia, this kind of elk has abounded much, and still exists in smaller numbers; and I could never learn that the palmated kind had been seen here at all. I suppose this confined to the more northern latitudes.‖ I have made our hare or rabbit peculiar, believing it

---

* XXV. 184.   † Quad. IX. 132.   ‡ XIX. 2.   § Quad. IX. 41.
‖ The descriptions of Theodat, Denys and La Honton, cited by Monsieur de Buffon, under the article Elan, authorize the supposition, that the flat-horned elk

to be different from both the European animals of those de-
nominations, and calling it therefore by its Algonquin name,
Whabus, to keep it distinct from these. Kalm is of the same
opinion.* I have enumerated the squirrels according to our own
knowledge, derived from daily sight of them, because I am not
able to reconcile with that the European appellations and descriptions. I have heard of other species, but they have never
come within my own notice. These, I think, are the only in-

is found in the northern parts of America. It has not however extended to our
latitudes. On the other hand, I could never learn that the round-horned elk
has been seen further north than the Hudson's river. This agrees with the
former elk in its general character, being, like that, when compared with a deer,
very much larger, its ears longer, broader, and thicker in proportion, its hair
much longer, neck and tail shorter, having a dewlap before the breast (caruncula
gutturalis Linnæi) a white spot often, if not always, of a foot diameter, on the
hinder part of the buttocks round the tail; its gait a trot, and attended with a
rattling of the hoofs ; but distinguished from that decisively by its horns, which
are not palmated, but round and pointed. This is the animal described by
Catesby as the Cervus major Americanus, the stag of America, le Cerf de l'Amerique. But it differs from the Cervus as totally as does the palmated elk from
the dama. And in fact it seems to stand in the same relation to the palmated elk,
as the red deer does to the fallow. It has abounded in Virginia, has been seen,
within my knowledge, on the eastern side of the Blue Ridge since the year 1765,
is now common beyond those mountains, has been often brought to us and tamed,
and its horns are in the hands of many. I should designate it as the "Alces
Americanus cornibus teretibus." It were to be wished, that naturalists, who are
acquainted with the renne and elk of Europe, and who may hereafter visit the
northern parts of America, would examine well the animals called there by the
names of gray and black moose, caribou, original and elk. Monsieur de Buffon
has done what could be done from the materials in his hands, toward clearing up
the confusion introduced by the loose application of these names among the animals they are meant to designate. He reduces the whole to the renne and flat-
horned elk. From all the information I have been able to collect, I strongly suspect they will be found to cover three, if not four distinct species of animals. I
have seen skins of a moose, and of the caribou: they differ more from each other,
and from that of the round-horned elk, than I ever saw two skins differ which
belonged to different individuals of any wild species. These differences are in
the color, length, and coarseness of the hair, and in the size, texture, and marks
of the skin. Perhaps it will be found that there is, 1, the moose, black and gray,
the former being said to be the male, and the latter the female ; 2, the caribou or
renne ; 3, the flat-horned elk, or original ; 4, the round-horned elk. Should this
last, though possessing so nearly the characters of the elk, be found to be the
same with the Cerf d'Ardennes or Brandhitz of Germany, still there will remain
the three species first enumerated.

* Kalm II. 340, I. 82.

stances in which I have departed from the authority of Monsieur
de Buffon in the construction of this table. I take him for my
ground work, because I think him the best informed of any
naturalist who has ever written. The result is, that there are
eighteen quadrupeds peculiar to Europe; more than four times
as many, to wit, seventy four, peculiar to America; that the*
first of these seventy-four weighs more than the whole column
of Europeans; and consequently this second table disproves the
second member of the assertion, that the animals peculiar to the
new world are on a smaller scale, so far as that assertion relied
on European animals for support; and it is in full opposition to
the theory which makes the animal volume to depend on the
circumstances of *heat* and *moisture*.

The third table comprehends those quadrupeds only which
are domestic in both countries. That some of these, in some
parts of America, have become less than their original stock, is
doubtless true; and the reason is very obvious. In a thinly-
peopled country, the spontaneous productions of the forests, and
waste fields, are sufficient to support indifferently the domestic
animals of the farmer, with a very little aid from him, in the severest and scarcest season. He therefore finds it more convenient to receive them from the hand of nature in that indifferent state, than to keep up their size by a care and nourishment
which would cost him much labor. If, on this low fare, these
animals dwindle, it is no more than they do in those parts of
Europe where the poverty of the soil, or the poverty of the owner,
reduces them to the same scanty subsistence. It is the uniform
effect of one and the same cause, whether acting on this or that
side of the globe. It would be erring, therefore, against this rule

---

* The Tapir is the largest of the animals peculiar to America. I collect his
weight thus: Monsieur de Buffon says, XXIII. 274, that he is of the size of a Zebu,
or a small cow. He gives us the measures of a Zebu, ib. 4, as taken by himself,
viz. five feet seven inches from the muzzle to the root of the tail, and five feet
one inch circumference behind the fore-legs. A bull, measuring in the same way
six feet nine inches and five feet two inches, weighed six hundred pounds, VIII.
153. The Zebu then, and of course the Tapir, would weigh about five hundred
pounds. But one individual of every species of European peculiars would probably weigh less than four hundred pounds. These are French measures and
weights.

of philosophy, which teaches us to ascribe like effects to like causes, should we impute this diminution of size in America to any imbecility or want of uniformity in the operations of nature. It may be affirmed with truth, that, in those countries, and with those individuals in America, where necessity or curiosity has produced equal attention, as in Europe, to the nourishment of animals, the horses, cattle, sheep, and hogs, of the one continent are as large as those of the other. There are particular instances, well attested, where individuals of this country have imported good breeders from England, and have improved their size by care in the course of some years. To make a fair comparison between the two countries, it will not answer to bring together animals of what might be deemed the middle or ordinary size of their species; because an error in judging of that middle or ordinary size, would vary the result of the comparison. Thus Mons. D'Aubenton* considers a horse of 4 feet five inches high and 400lb. weight French, equal to 4 feet 8.6 inches and 436lb. English, as a middle-sized horse. Such a one is deemed a small horse in America. The extremes must therefore be resorted to. The same anatomist† dissected a horse of 5 feet 9 inches height, French measure, equal to 6 feet 1.7 English. This is near 6 inches higher than any horse I have seen; and could it be supposed that I had seen the largest horses in America, the conclusion would be, that ours have diminished, or that we have bred from a smaller stock. In Connecticut and Rhode Island, where the climate is favorable to the production of grass, bullocks have been slaughtered which weighed 2,500, 2,200, and 2,100 lbs. nett; and those of 1,800 lbs. have been frequent. I have seen a hog‡ weigh 1,050 lbs. after the blood, bowels, and hair had been taken from him. Before he was killed, an attempt was made to weigh him with a pair of steel yards, graduated to 1,200 lbs., but he weighed more. Yet this hog was probably not within fifty generations of the European stock. I am well informed of another which weighed 1,100 lbs. gross. Asses have been still more neglected than any other domestic animal in America. They are neither fed or housed in the most rigorous season of

* VII. 432.   † VII. 474.   ‡ In Williamsburg, April, 1769.

the year. Yet they are larger than those measured by Mons. D'Aubenton,* of 3 feet 7¼ inches, 3 feet 4 inches, and 3 feet 2½ inches, the latter weighing only 215.8 lbs. These sizes, I suppose, have been produced by the same negligence in Europe, which has produced a like diminution here. Where care has been taken of them on that side of the water, they have been raised to a size bordering on that of the horse ; not by the *heat* and *dryness* of the climate, but by good food and shelter. Goats have been also much neglected in America. Yet they are very prolific here, bearing twice or three times a year, and from one to five kids at a birth. Mons. de Buffon has been sensible of a difference in this circumstance in favor of America.† But what are their greatest weights, I cannot say. A large sheep here weighs 100 lbs. I observe Mons. D'Aubenton calls a ram of 62 lbs. one of the middle size.‡ But to say what are the extremes of growth in these and the other domestic animals of America, would require information of which no one individual is possessed. The weights actually known and stated in the third table preceding will suffice to show, that we may conclude on probable grounds, that, with equal food and care, the climate of America will preserve the races of domestic animals as large as the European stock from which they are derived ; and, consequently, that the third member of Mons. de Buffon's assertion that the domestic animals are subject to degeneration from the climate of America, is as probably wrong as the first and second were certainly so.

That the last part of it is erroneous, which affirms that the species of American quadrupeds are comparatively few, is evident from the tables taken together. By these it appears that there are an hundred species aboriginal in America. Mons. de Buffon supposes about double that number existing on the whole earth.§ Of these Europe, Asia, and Africa, furnish suppose one hundred and twenty-six ; that is, the twenty-six common to Europe and America, and about one hundred which are not in America at all. The American species, then, are to those of the rest of the earth, as one hundred to one hundred and twenty-six, or four to

* VIII. 48, 55, 66.   † XVIII. 96.   ‡ IX. 41.   § XXX. 219.

five. But the residue of the earth being double the extent of America, the exact proportion would have been but as four to eight.

Hitherto I have considered this hypothesis as applied to brute animals only, and not in its extension to the man of America, whether aboriginal or transplanted. It is the opinion of Mons. de Buffon that the former furnishes no exception to it.*

" Quoique le sauvage du nouveau monde soit à peu près de même stature que l'homme de notre monde, cela ne suffit pas pour qu'il puisse faire une exception au fait général du rapetissement de la nature vivante dans tout ce continent; le sauvage est foible et petit par les organes de la génération; il n'a ni poil, ni barbe, and nulle ardeur pour sa femelle. Quoique plus léger que l'Européen, parce qu'il a plus d'habitude à courir, il est cependant beaucoup moins fort de corps; il est aussi bien moins sensible, et cependant plus craintif et plus lâche; il n'a nulle vivacité, nulle activité dans l'ame; celle du corps est moins un exercise, un mouvement volontaire qu'une nécessité d'action causée par le besoin; ôtez lui la faim et la soif, vous détruirez en même tems le principe actif de tous ses mouvemens; il demeurera stupidement en repos sur ses jambes ou couché pendant des jours entiers. Il ne faut pas aller chercher plus loin à cause de la vie dispersée des sauvages et de leur éloignement pour la société· la plus précieuse étincelle du feu de la nature leur a été refusée; ils manquent d'ardeur pour leur femelle, et par consequent d'amour pour leur semblables; ne connoissant pas l'attachment le plus vif, le plus tendre de tous, leurs autres sentimens de ce genre, sont froids et languissans; ils aiment foiblement leurs pères et leurs enfans; la société la plus intime de toutes, celle de la même famille, n'a donc chez eux que de foibles liens; la société d'une famille à l'autre n'en a point de tout; dès lors nulle réunion, nulle république, nulle état social. La physique de l'amour fait chez eux le moral des mœurs; leur cœur est glacé, leur societé et leur empire dur. Ils ne regardent leurs femmes que comme des servantes de peine ou des bêtes de somme qu'ils chargent, sans ménagement, du fardeau de leur chasse, et qu'ils forcent, sans pitié, sans reconnoissance, à des ouvrages qui souvent sont au dessus de leurs forces; ils n'ont que peu d'enfans; ils en ont peu de soin; tout se ressent de leur premier defaut; ils sont indifférents parce qu'ils sont peu puissants, et cette indifference pour le sexe est la tache originelle qui flétrit la nature, qui l'empeche de s'épanouir, et qui detruisant les germes de la vie, coupe en même temps la racine de société. L'homme ne fait donc point d'exception ici. La nature en lui refusant les puissances de l'amour l'a plus maltraité et plus rapetissé qu'aucun des animaux."

An afflicting picture, indeed, which for the honor of human nature, I am glad to believe has no original. Of the Indian of South America I know nothing; for I would not honor with the appellation of knowledge, what I derive from the fables pub-

* XVIII. 146.

lished of them.   These I believe to be just as true as the fable
of Æsop.   This belief is founded on what I have seen of man,
white, red, and black, and what has been written of him by
authors, enlightened themselves, and writing among an enlightened people.   The Indian of North America being more within
our reach, I can speak of him somewhat from my own knowledge, but more from the information of others better acquainted
with him, and on whose truth and judgment I can rely.   From
these sources I am able to say, in contradiction to this representation, that he is neither more defective in ardor, nor more impotent with his female, than the white reduced to the same diet
and exercise ; that he is brave, when an enterprise depends on
bravery ; education with him making the point of honor consist
in the destruction of an enemy by stratagem, and in the preservation of his own person free from injury ; or, perhaps, this is nature, while it is education which teaches us to* honor force more
than finesse ; that he will defend himself against a host of enemies, always choosing to be killed, rather than to surrender,†

* Sol Rodomonte sprezza di venire
    Se non, dove la via meno è ficura.—ARISTO, 14, 117.

    † In so judicious an author as Don Ulloa, and one to whom we are indebted for
the most precise information we have of South America, I did not expect to find
such assertions as the following : "Los Indios vencidos son los mas cobardes y
pusilanimes que se peuden vér : Se hacen inocentes, le humillan hasta el desprecio,
disculpan su inconsiderado arrojo, y con las suplicas y los ruegos dán seguras
pruebas de su pusilanimidad. ó lo que resieren las historias de la Conquista,
sobre sus grandes acciones, es en un sendito figurado, ó el caracter de estas gentes
no es ahora segun era entonces ; pero lo que no tiene duda es, que las Naciones
de la parte Septentrional subsisten en la misma libertad que siempre han tenido,
sin haber sido sojuzgados por algon Principe extrano, y que viven segun su régi-
men y costumbres de toda la vida, sin que haya habido motivo para que muden
de caracter ; y en estos se vé lo mismo, que sucede en los Peru, y de toda la
América Meridional, reducidos, y que nunca lo han estado." Noticias Americanas,
Entretenimiento xviii. §. 1.   Don Ulloa here admits, that the authors who have
described the Indians of South America, before they were enslaved, had represented them as a brave people, and therefore seems to have suspected that the
cowardice which he had observed in those of the present race might be the effect
of subjugation.   But, supposing the Indians of North America to be cowards
also, he concludes the ancestors of those of South America to have been so too,
and, therefore, that those authors have given fictions for truth.   He was probably
not acquainted himself with the Indians of North America, and had formed his
opinion from hear-say.   Great numbers of French, of English, and of Americans,

though it be to the whites, who he knows will treat him well; that in other situations, also, he meets death with more deliberation, and endures tortures with a firmness unknown almost to religious enthusiasm with us; that he is affectionate to his children, careful of them, and indulgent in the extreme; that his affections comprehend his other connections, weakening, as with us, from circle to circle, as they recede from the centre; that his friendships are strong and faithful to the uttermost* extremity; that his sensibility is keen, even the warriors weeping most bitterly on the loss of their children, though in general they endeavor to appear superior to human events; that his vivacity and activity of mind is equal to ours in the same situation; hence his eagerness for hunting, and for games of chance. The women are submitted to unjust drudgery. This I believe is the case with every barbarous people. With such, force is law. The stronger sex imposes on the weaker. It is civilization alone which replaces women in the enjoyment of their natural equality. That first teaches us to subdue the selfish passions, and to re-

are perfectly acquainted with these people. Had he had an opportunity of inquiring of any of these, they would have told him, that there never was an instance known of an Indian begging his life when in the power of his enemies; on the contrary, that he courts death by every possible insult and provocation. His reasoning, then, would have been reversed thus: "Since the present Indian of North America is brave, and authors tell us that the ancestors of those of South America were brave also, it must follow that the cowardice of their descendants is the effect of subjugation and ill treatment." For he observes, ib. §. 27, that "los obrages los aniquillan por la inhumanidad con que se les trata."

* A remarkable instance of this appeared in the case of the late Colonel Byrd, who was sent to the Cherokee nation to transact some business with them. It happened that some of our disorderly people had just killed one or two of that nation. It was therefore proposed in the council of the Cherokees that Colonel Byrd should be put to death, in revenge for the loss of their countrymen. Among them was a chief named Silòuee, who, on some former occasion, had contracted an acquaintance and friendship with Colonel Byrd. He came to him every night in his tent, and told him not to be afraid, they should not kill him. After many days' deliberation, however, the determination was, contrary to Silòuee's expectation, that Byrd should be put to death, and some warriors were despatched as executioners. Silòuee attended them, and when they entered the tent, he threw himself between them and Byrd, and said to the warriors, "This man is my friend; before you get at him, you must kill me." On which they returned, and the council respected the principle so much as to recede from their determination.

spect those rights in others which we value in ourselves. Were we in equal barbarism, our females would be equal drudges. The man with them is less strong than with us, but their women stronger than ours; and both for the same obvious reason; because our man and their woman is habituated to labor, and formed by it. With both races the sex which is indulged with ease is the least athletic. An Indian man is small in the hand and wrist, for the same reason for which a sailor is large and strong in the arms and shoulders, and a porter in the legs and thighs. They raise fewer children than we do. The causes of this are to be found, not in a difference of nature, but of circumstance. The women very frequently attending the men in their parties of war and of hunting, child-bearing becomes extremely inconvenient to them. It is said, therefore, that they have learned the practice of procuring abortion by the use of some vegetable; and that it even extends to prevent conception for a considerable time after. During these parties they are exposed to numerous hazards, to excessive exertions, to the greatest extremities of hunger. Even at their homes the nation depends for food, through a certain part of every year, on the gleanings of the forest; that is, they experience a famine once in every year. With all animals, if the female be badly fed, or not fed at all, her young perish; and if both male and female be reduced to like want, generation becomes less active, less productive. To the obstacles, then, of want and hazard, which nature has opposed to the multiplication of wild animals, for the purpose of restraining their numbers within certain bounds, those of labor and of voluntary abortion are added with the Indian. No wonder, then, if they multiply less than we do. Where food is regularly supplied, a single farm will show more of cattle, than a whole country of forests can of buffaloes. The same Indian women, when married to white traders, who feed them and their children plentifully and regularly, who exempt them from excessive drudgery, who keep them stationary and unexposed to accident, produce and raise as many children as the white women. Instances are known, under these circumstances, of their rearing a dozen children. An inhuman practice once prevailed in this country, of making slaves of the Indians. It is a fact well known with us, that the Indian women so enslaved produced and raised as numerous families as either the whites or blacks among whom they lived. It has been said that Indians have less hair than the whites, except on the head. But this is a fact of which fair proof can scarcely be had. With them it is disgraceful to be hairy on the body. They say it likens them to hogs. They therefore pluck the hair as fast as it appears. But the traders who marry their women, and prevail on them to discontinue this practice, say, that nature is the same with them as with the whites. Nor, if the fact be true, is the consequence necessary which has been drawn from it. Negroes have notoriously less hair than the whites; yet they are more ardent. But if cold and moisture be the agents of nature for diminishing the races of animals, how comes she all at once to suspend their operation as to the physical man of the new world, whom the Count acknowledges to be "à peu près de même stature que l'homme de notre monde," and to let loose their influence on his moral faculties? How has this "combination of the elements and other physical causes, so contrary to the enlargement of animal nature in this new world, these obstacles to the development and formation of great germs,"* been arrested and suspended, so as to permit the human body to acquire its just dimensions, and by what inconceivable process has their action been directed on his mind alone? To judge of the truth of this, to form a just estimate of their genius and mental powers, more facts are wanting, and great allowance to be made for those circumstances of their situation which call for a display of particular talents only. This done, we shall probably find that they are formed in mind as well as in body, on the same module with the* "Homo sapiens Europæus." The principles of their society forbidding all compulsion, they are to be led to duty and to enterprise by personal influence and persuasion. Hence eloquence in council, bravery and address in war, become the foundations of all consequence with them. To these acquirements all their faculties are directed. Of their bravery and ad-

* XVIII. 146.   * Linn. Syst. Definition of a Man.

dress in war we have multiplied proofs, because we have been the subjects on which they were exercised. Of their eminence in oratory we have fewer examples, because it is displayed chiefly in their own councils. Some, however, we have, of very superior lustre. I may challenge the whole orations of Demosthenes and Cicero, and of any more eminent orator, if Europe has furnished more eminent, to produce a single passage, superior to the speech of Logan, a Mingo chief, to Lord Dunmore, then governor of this State. And as a testimony of their talents in this line, I beg leave to introduce it, first stating the incidents necessary for understanding it.

In the spring of the year 1774, a robbery was committed by some Indians on certain land-adventurers on the river Ohio. The whites in that quarter, according to their custom, undertook to punish this outrage in a summary way. Captain Michael Cresap, and a certain Daniel Greathouse, leading on these parties, surprised, at different times, travelling and hunting parties of the Indians, having their women and children with them, and murdered many. Among these were unfortunately the family of Logan, a chief celebrated in peace and war, and long distinguished as the friend of the whites. This unworthy return provoked his vengeance. He accordingly signalized himself in the war which ensued. In the autumn of the same year a decisive battle was fought at the mouth of the Great Kanhaway, between the collected forces of the Shawanese, Mingoes and Delawares, and a detachment of the Virginia militia. The Indians were defeated and sued for peace. Logan, however, disdained to be seen among the suppliants. But lest the sincerity of a treaty should be disturbed, from which so distinguished a chief absented himself, he sent, by a messenger, the following speech, to be delivered to Lord Dunmore.

"I appeal to any white man to say, if ever he entered Logan's cabin hungry, and he gave him not meat ; if ever he came cold and naked, and he clothed him not. During the course of the last long and bloody war Logan remained idle in his cabin, an advocate for peace. Such was my love for the whites, that my countrymen pointed as they passed, and said, "Logan is the friend of white men." I had even thought to have lived with you, but for the injuries of one man. Colonel Cresap, the last spring, in cold blood, and unprovoked, murdered all the relations of Logan, not even sparing my women and children. There runs not a drop of my blood in the veins of any living creature. This called on me for revenge. I have sought it: I have killed many: I have fully glutted my vengeance: for my country I rejoice at the beams of peace. But do not harbor a thought that mine is the joy of fear. Logan never felt fear. He will not turn on his heel to save his life. Who is there to mourn for Logan?—Not one."*

Before we condemn the Indians of this continent as wanting genius, we must consider that letters have not yet been introduced among them. Were we to compare them in their present state

---

* PHILADELPHIA, December 31, 1797.

DEAR SIR,—Mr. Tazewell has communicated to me the inquiries you have been so kind as to make, relative to a passage in the "Notes on Virginia," which has lately excited some newspaper publications. I feel, with great sensibility, the interest you take in this business, and with pleasure, go into explanations with one whose objects I know to be truth and justice alone. Had Mr. Martin thought proper to suggest to me, that doubts might be entertained of the transaction respecting Logan, as stated in the "Notes on Virginia," and to inquire on what grounds that statement was founded, I should have felt myself obliged by the inquiry; have informed him candidly of the grounds, and cordially have co-operated in every means of investigating the fact, and correcting whatsoever in it should be found to have been erroneous. But he chose to step at once into the newspapers, and in his publications there and the letters he wrote to me, adopted a style which forbade the respect of an answer. Sensible, however, that no act of his could absolve me from the justice due to others, as soon as I found that the story of Logan could be doubted, I determined to inquire into it as accurately as the testimony remaining, after a lapse of twenty odd years, would permit, and that the result should be made known, either in the first new edition which should be printed of the "Notes on Virginia," or by publishing an appendix. I thought that so far as that work had contributed to impeach the memory of Cresap, by handing on an erroneous charge, it was proper it should be made the vehicle of retribution. Not that I was at all the author of the injury; I had only concurred, with thousands and thousands of others, in believing a transaction on authority which merited respect. For the story of Logan is only repeated in the "Notes on Virginia," precisely as it had been current for more than a dozen years before they were published. When Lord Dunmore returned from the expedition against the Indians, in 1774, he and his officers brought the speech of Logan, and related the circumstances of it. These were so affecting, and the

with the Europeans, north of the Alps, when the Roman arms and arts first crossed those mountains, the comparison would be unequal, because, at that time, those parts of Europe were swarming with numbers; because numbers produce emulation, and multiply the chances of improvement, and one improvement begets another. Yet I may safely ask, how many good poets, how

speech itself so fine a morsel of eloquence, that it became the theme of every conversation, in Williamsburg particularly, and generally, indeed, wheresoever any of the officers resided or resorted. I learned it in Williamsburg, I believe at Lord Dunmore's; and I find in my pocket-book of that year (1774) an entry of the narrative, as taken from the mouth of some person, whose name, however, is not noted, nor recollected, precisely in the words stated in the "Notes on Virginia." The speech was published in the Virginia Gazette of that time, (I have it myself in the volume of gazettes of that year,) and though it was the translation made by the common interpreter, and in a style by no means elegant, yet it was so admired, that it flew through all the public papers of the continent, and through the magazines and other periodical publications of Great Britain; and those who were boys at that day will now attest, that the speech of Logan used to be given them as a school exercise for repetition. It was not till about thirteen or fourteen years after the newspaper publications, that the "Notes on Virginia" were published in America. Combating, in these, the contumelious theory of certain European writers, whose celebrity gave currency and weight to their opinions, that our country from the combined effects of soil and climate, degenerated animal nature, in the general, and particularly the moral faculties of man, I considered the speech of Logan as an apt proof of the contrary, and used it as such; and I copied, verbatim, the narrative I had taken down in 1774, and the speech as it had been given us in a better translation by Lord Dunmore. I knew nothing of the Cresaps, and could not possibly have a motive to do them an injury with design. I repeated what thousands had done before, on as good authority as we have for most of the facts we learn through life, and such as, to this moment, I have seen no reason to doubt. That any body questioned it, was never suspected by me, till I saw the letter of Mr. Martin in the Baltimore paper. I endeavored then to recollect who among my contemporaries, of the same circle of society, and consequently of the same recollections, might still be alive; three and twenty years of death and dispersion had left very few. I remembered, however, that General Gibson was still living, and knew that he had been the translator of the speech. I wrote to him immediately. He, in answer, declares to me, that he was the very person sent by Lord Dunmore to the Indian town; that, after he had delivered his message there, Logan took him out to a neighboring wood; sat down with him, and rehearsing, with tears, the catastrophe of his family, gave him that speech for Lord Dunmore; that he carried it to Lord Dunmore; translated it for him; has turned to it in the Encyclopedia, as taken from the "Notes on Virginia," and finds that it was his translation I had used, with only two or three verbal variations of no importance. These, I suppose, had arisen in the course of successive copies. I cite General Gibson's letter by memory, not hav-

many able mathematicians, how many great inventors in arts or sciences, had Europe, north of the Alps, then produced? And it was sixteen centuries after this before a Newton could be formed. I do not mean to deny that there are varieties in the race of man, distinguished by their powers both of body and mind. I believe there are, as I see to be the case in the races

ing it with me; but I am sure I cite it substantially right. It establishes unquestionably, that the speech of Logan is genuine; and that being established, it is Logan himself who is author of all the important facts. "Colonel Cresap," says he, "in cold blood and unprovoked, murdered all the relations of Logan, not sparing even my women and children; there runs not a drop of my blood in the veins of any living creature." The person and the fact, in all its material circumstances, are here given by Logan himself. General Gibson, indeed, says, that the title was mistaken; that Cresap was a Captain, and not a Colonel. This was Logan's mistake. He also observes, that it was on another water of the Ohio, and not on the Kanhaway, that his family was killed. This is an error which has crept into the traditionary account; but surely of little moment in the moral view of the subject. The material question is, was Logan's family murdered, and by whom? That it was murdered has not, I believe, been denied; that it was by one of the Cresaps, Logan affirms. This is a question which concerns the memories of Logan and Cresap; to the issue of which I am as indifferent as if I had never heard the name of either. I have begun and shall continue to inquire into the evidence additional to Logan's, on which the fact was founded. Little, indeed, can now be heard of, and that little dispersed and distant. If it shall appear on inquiry, that Logan has been wrong in charging Cresap with the murder of his family, I will do justice to the memory of Cresap, as far as I have contributed to the injury, by believing and repeating what others had believed and repeated before me. If, on the other hand, I find that Logan was right in his charge, I will vindicate, as far as my suffrage may go, the truth of a Chief, whose talents and misfortunes have attached to him the respect and commiseration of the world.

I have gone, my dear Sir, into this lengthy detail to satisfy a mind, in the candor and rectitude of which I have the highest confidence. So far as you may incline to use the communication for rectifying the judgments of those who are willing to see things truly as they are, you are free to use it. But I pray that no confidence which you may repose in any one, may induce you to let it go out of your hands, so as to get into a newspaper: against a contest in that field I am entirely decided. I feel extraordinary gratification, indeed, in addressing this letter to you, with whom shades of difference in political sentiment have not prevented the interchange of good opinion, nor cut off the friendly offices of society and good correspondence. This political tolerance is the more valued by me, who consider social harmony as the first of human felicities, and the happiest moments, those which are given to the effusions of the heart. Accept them sincerely, I pray you, from one who has the honor to be, with sentiments of high respect and attachment, dear Sir, your most obedient, and most humble servant.

of other animals. I only mean to suggest a doubt, whether the bulk and faculties of animals depend on the side of the Atlantic on which their food happens to grow, or which furnishes the elements of which they are compounded? Whether nature has enlisted herself as a Cis or Trans-Atlantic partisan? I am induced to suspect there has been more eloquence than sound reasoning displayed in support of this theory; that it is one of those cases where the judgment has been seduced by a glowing pen; and whilst I render every tribute of honor and esteem to the celebrated zoologist, who has added, and is still adding, so many precious things to the treasures of science, I must doubt whether in this instance he has not cherished error also, by lending her for a moment his vivid imagination and bewitching language. (4)

So far the Count de Buffon has carried this new theory of the tendency of nature to belittle her productions on this side the Atlantic. Its application to the race of whites transplanted from Europe, remained for the Abbé Raynal. "On doit etre etonné (he says) que l'Amerique n'ait pas encore produit un bon poëte, un habile mathematicien, un homme de genie dans un seul art, ou seule science." Hist. Philos. p. 92, ed. Maestricht, 1774. "America has not yet produced one good poet." When we shall have existed as a people as long as the Greeks did before they produced a Homer, the Romans a Virgil, the French a Racine and Voltaire, the English a Shakespeare and Milton, should this reproach be still true, we will inquire from what unfriendly causes it has proceeded, that the other countries of Europe and quarters of the earth shall not have inscribed any name in the roll of poets.* But neither has America produced "one able mathematician, one man of genius in a single art or a single science." In war we have produced a Washington, whose memory will be adored while liberty shall have votaries, whose

* Has the world as yet produced more than two poets, acknowledged to be such by all nations? An Englishman only reads Milton with delight, an Italian, Tasso, a Frenchman the Henriade; a Portuguese, Camoens; but Homer and Virgil have been the rapture of every age and nation; they are read with enthusiasm in their originals by those who can read the originals, and in translations by those who cannot.

name shall triumph over time, and will in future ages assume its just station among the most celebrated worthies of the world, when that wretched philosophy shall be forgotten which would have arranged him among the degeneracies of nature. In physics we have produced a Franklin, than whom no one of the present age has made more important discoveries, nor has enriched philosophy with more, or more ingenious solutions of the phenomena of nature. We have supposed Mr. Rittenhouse second to no astronomer living; that in genius he must be the first, because he is self-taught. As an artist he has exhibited as great a proof of mechanical genius as the world has ever produced. He has not indeed made a world; but he has by imitation approached nearer its Maker than any man who has lived from the creation to this day.* As in philosophy and war, so in government, in oratory, in painting, in the plastic art, we might show that America, though but a child of yesterday, has already given hopeful proofs of genius, as well as of the nobler kinds, which arouse the best feelings of man, which call him into action, which substantiate his freedom, and conduct him to happiness, as of the subordinate, which serve to amuse him only. We therefore suppose, that this reproach is as unjust as it is unkind: and that, of the geniuses which adorn the present age, America contributes its full share. For comparing it with those countries where genius is most cultivated, where are the most excellent models for art, and scaffoldings for the attainment of science, as France and England for instance, we calculate thus: The United States contains three millions of inhabitants; France twenty millions; and the British islands ten. We produce a Washington, a Franklin, a Rittenhouse. France then should have half a dozen in each of these lines, and Great Britain half that number, equally eminent. It may be true that France has; we are but just becoming acquainted with her, and our acquaintance so far gives us high ideas of the genius of her inhabitants. It

There are various ways of keeping truth out of sight. Mr. Rittenhouse's model of the planetary system has the plagiary application of an Orrery; and the quadrant invented by Godfrey, an American also, and with the aid of which the European nations traverse the globe, is called Hadley's quadrant.

would be injuring too many of them to name particularly a Voltaire, a Buffon, the constellation of Encyclopedists, the Abbe Raynal himself, &c. &c. We, therefore, have reason to believe she can produce her full quota of genius. The present war having so long cut off all communication with Great Britain, we are not able to make a fair estimate of the state of science in that country. The spirit in which she wages war, is the only sample before our eyes, and that does not seem the legitimate offspring either of science or of civilization. The sun of her glory is fast descending to the horizon. Her philosophy has crossed the channel, her freedom the Atlantic, and herself seems passing to that awful dissolution whose issue is not given human foresight to scan.*

Having given a sketch of our minerals, vegetables, and quadrupeds, and being led by a proud theory to make a comparison of the latter with those of Europe, and to extend it to the man of America, both aboriginal and emigrant, I will proceed to the remaining articles comprehended under the present query.

Between ninety and a hundred of our birds have been described by Catesby. His drawings are better as to form and attitude than coloring, which is generally too high. They are the following:

* In a later edition of the Abbé Raynal's work, he has withdrawn his censure from that part of the new world inhabited by the Federo-Americans; but has left it still on the other parts. North America has always been more accessible to strangers than South. If he was mistaken then as to the former, he may be so as to the latter. The glimmerings which reach us from South America enable us to see that its inhabitants are held under the accumulated pressure of slavery, superstition and ignorance. Whenever they shall be able to rise under this weight, and to show themselves to the rest of the world, they will probably show they are like the rest of the world. We have not yet sufficient evidence that there are more lakes and fogs in South America than in other parts of the earth. As little do we know what would be their operation on the mind of man. That country has been visited by Spaniards and Portuguese chiefly, and almost exclusively. These, going from a country of the old world remarkably dry in its soil and climate, fancied there were more lakes and fogs in South America than in Europe. An inhabitant of Ireland, Sweden, or Finland would have formed the contrary opinion. Had South America then been discovered and settled by a people from a fenny country, it would probably have been represented as much drier than the old world. A patient pursuit of facts, and cautious combination and comparison of them, is the drudgery to which man is subjected by his Maker, if he wishes to attain sure knowledge.

BIRDS OF VIRGINIA.

Linnæan Designation.	Catesby's Designation.		Popular Names.	Buffon oiseaux.
Lanius tyrannus	Muscicapa coronâ rubrâ	1.55	Tyrant. Field martin	8.398
Vultur aura	Buteo specie Gallo-pavonis	1. 6	Turkey buzzard	1.246
Falco leucocephalus	Aquila capite albo	1. 1	Bald eagle	1.138
Falco sparverius	Accipiter minor	1. 5	Little hawk. Sparrow hawk	
Falco columbarius	Accipiter palumbarius	1. 3	Pigeon hawk	1.338
Falco furcatus	Accipiter caudâ furcatâ	1. 4	Forked tail hawk	1.286.312
	Accipiter piscatorius	1. 2	Fishing hawk	1.199
Strix asio	Noctua aurita minor	1. 7	Little owl	1.141
Psittacus Carolinensis	Psittacus Caroliniensis	1.11	Parrot of Carolina. Parroquet	11.383
Corvus cristatus	Pica glandaria, cærulea, cristata	1.15	Blue jay	5.164
Oriolus Baltimore	Icterus ex aureo nigroque varius	1.48	Baltimore bird	5.318
Oriolus spurius	Icterus minor	1.49	Bastard Baltimore	5.321
Gracula quiscula	Monedula purpurea	1.12	Purple jackdaw. Crow blackbird	5.134
Cuculus Americanus	Cuculus Caroliniensis	1. 9	Carolina cuckow	12.62
Picus principalis	Picus maximus rostro albo	1.16	White bill woodpecker	13.69
Picus pileatus	Picus niger maximus, capite rubro	1.17	Larger red-crested woodpecker	13.72
Picus erythrocephalus	Picus capite toto rubro	1.20	Red-headed woodpecker	13.83
Picus ouratus	Picus major alis aureis	1.18	Gold winged woodpecker. Yucker	13.59
Picus Carolinus	Picus ventre rubro	1.19	Red-bellied woodpecker	13.105
Picus pubescens	Picus varius minimus	1.21	Smallest spotted woodpecker	13.113
Picus villosus	Picus medius quasi-villosus	1.19	Hairy woodpecker. Spec. woodpecker	13.111
Picus varius	Picus varius minor ventre luteo	1.21	Yellow-bellied woodpecker	13.115
Sitta Europæa	{ Sitta capite nigro	1.22	Nuthatch	10.213
	{ Sitta capite fusco	1.22	Small Nuthatch	10.214
Alcedo alcyon	Ispida	1.69	Kingfisher	13.310
Certhia pinus	Parus Americanus lutescens	1.61	Pine-Creeper	9.433
Trochilus colubris	Mellivora avis Caroliniensis	1.65	Humming bird	11.16
Anas Canadensis	Anser Canadensis	1.92	Wild goose	17.122
Anas bucephala	Anas minor purpureo capite	1.95	Buffel's-head duck	17.356
Anas rustica. b.	Anas minor ex albo & fusco vario	1.98	Little brown duck	17.413
Anas discors. b.	Querquedula Americana variegata	1.10	White face teal	17.403

Linnaean Designation.	Catesby's Designation.	Popular Names.	Buffon oiseaux.
Anas discors, ♂............	Querquedula Americana fusca....	1.99 Blue wing teal........	17.405
Anas sponsa................	Anas Americanus cristatus elegans.	1.97 Summer duck.........	17.351
	Anas Americanus lato rostro.....	1.96 Blue wing shoveler.....	17.275
Mergus cucullatus.........	Anas cristata...............	1.94 Round crested duck......	15.437
Columbus podiceps.........	Prodicipes minor rostro vario.....	1.91 Pied bill dopchick......	15.383
Ardea Herodias.............	Ardea cristata maxima Americana..	3.10 Largest crested heron.....	14.113
Ardea violacea.............	Ardea stellaris cristata Americana.	1.79 Crested bittern........	14.184
Ardea caerulea.............	Ardea caerulea..............	1.76 Blue heron. Crane......	14.131
Ardea virescens	Ardea stellaris minima........	1.80 Small bittern.........	14.142
Ardea aequinoctialis.......	Ardea alba minor Caroliniensis...	1.77 Little white heron......	14.186
	Ardea stellaris Americana.....	1.78 Brown bittern. Indian hen.....	14.175
Tantalus loculator.........	Pelicanus Americanus.........	1.81 Wood pelican.........	13.403
Tantalus alber.............	Numenius albus..............	1.82 White curlew.........	15.62
Tantalus fuscus............	Numenius fuscus.	1.83 Brown curlew........	15.64
Charadrius vociferus.......	Pluvialis vociferus..........	1.71 Chattering plover. Kildee......	15.151
Haematopus ostralegus....	Haematopus...............	1.85 Oyster-catcher........	15.185
Rallus Virginianus........	Gallinula Americana.........	1.70 Soree. Ral-bird.......	15.286
Meleagris Gallopavo.......	Gallopava Sylvestris.........	xliv. Wild Turkey.........	3.187.229
Tetrao Virginianus........	Perdix Sylvestris Virginiana.....	3.12 American partridge. American quail.	4.237
	Urgallus minor, or kind of Lagopus.	3. 1 Pheasant. Mountain partridge..	3.409
Columba passerina.........	Turtur miuimus guttatus.......	1.26 Ground dove.........	4.404
Columba migratorio........	Palumbus migratorius.........	1.23 Pigeon of passage. Wild pigeon..	4.351
Columba Caroliniensis.....	Turtur Caroliniensis.........	1.24 Turtle. Turtle dove......	4.401
Alauda alpestris	Alauda gutture flavo.........	1.32 Lark. Sky lark........	9.79
Alauda magna.	Alauda magna.............	1.33 Field lark. Large lark......	6,59
	Sturnus niger allis superné rubentibus..........	1.13 Red wing. Starling. Marsh blackbird.....	5.293
Tardus migratorius.........	Turdus pilaris migratorius......	1.29 Fieldfare of Carolina. Robin redbreast....	{ 5.426 / 9.257
Tardus rufus..............	Turdus rufus...............	1.28 Fox colored thrush. Thrush.....	5.449
Tardus polyglottos.........	Turdus minor cinereo albus non maculatus........	1.27 Mocking bird........	5.451

		No. & English name	
Ampelis garrulus. b.	Turdus minimus.	1.31 Little thrush	5.400
Loxia Cardinalis.	Garrulus Caroliniensis	1.46 Chatterer	6.162
Loxia Caerulea.	Coccothranstes rubra.	1.38 Red bird. Virginia nightingale.	6.185
Emberiza hyemalis.	Coccothranstes caerulea	1.39 Blue gross beak.	8.125
Emberiza Oryzivora.	Passer nivalis.	1.36 Snow bird.	8.47
Emberiza Ciris.	Hortulanus Caroliniensis	1.14 Rice bird.	8.49
Tanagra cyanea.	Fringilla tricolor.	1.44 Painted finch.	7.247
	Linaria caerulea.	1.45 Blue linnet.	7.122
	Passerculus	1.35 Little sparrow	7.120
	Passer fuscus.	1.34 Cowpen bird.	7.196
Fringilla erythrophthalma.	Passer niger oculis rubris.	1.34 Towhe bird.	7.201
Fringilla tristis.	Carduelis Americanus.	1.43 American goldfinch. Lettuce bird.	7.297
	Fringilla purpurea.	1.41 Purple finch.	8.129
Muscicapa crinita.	Muscicapa cristata ventre luteo.	1.52 Crested flycatcher.	8.379
Muscicapa rubra.	Muscicapa rubra.	1.56 Summer red bird.	8.410
Muscicapa ruticilla.	Rubicilla Americana.	1.67 Red start.	{ 8.349 / 9.259
Muscicapa Caroliniensis.	Muscicapa vertice nigro.	1.66 Cat bird.	8.372
	Muscicapa nigrescens.	1.53 Black cap flycatcher.	8.341
	Muscicapa fusca.	1.54 Little brown flycatcher.	8.344
	Muscicapa oculis rubris.	1.54 Red-eyed flycatcher.	8.337
Motacilla Sialis.	Rubicula Americana cerulea.	1.47 Blue bird.	9.308
Motacilla regulus.	Regulus cristatus.	3.13 Wren.	10.58
Motacilla trochilus. b.	Oenanthe Americana pectore luteo.	1.50 Yellow breasted chat.	6.96
Parus bicolor.	Parus cristatus.	1.57 Crested titmouse.	10.181
Parus Americanus.	Parus fringillaris.	1.64 Finch creeper.	9.442
	Parus uropygeo luteo.	1.58 Yellow rump.	10.184
Parus Virginianus.	Parus cucullo nigro.	1.60 Hooded titmouse.	10.183
	Parus Americanus gutture luteo.	1.62 Yellow throated creeper.	
	Parus Caroliniensis.	1.63 Yellow titmouse.	9.431
Hirundo Pelasgia.	Hirundo cauda aculeata Americana.	3. 8 American swallow.	12.478
Hirundo purpurea.	Hirundo purpurea.	1.51 Purple marten. House marten.	12.445
Caprimulgus Europaeus. a.	Caprimulgus.	1. 8 Goatsucker. Great bat.	12.243
Caprimulgus Europaeus. b.	Caprimulgus minor Americanus.	3.16 Whip poor Will.	12.246

Besides these, we have,

The Royston crow.   Corvus cornix.
  Crane.   Ardea Canadensis.
  House swallow.   Hirundo rustica.
  Ground swallow.   Hirundo riparia.
  Greatest gray eagle.
  Smaller turkey buzzard, with a
    feathered head.
  Greatest owl, or night hawk.
  Wet hawk, which feeds flying.
  Raven.
  Water Pelican of the Mississippi,
    whose pouch holds a peck.
  Swan.
  Loon.
  Cormorant.
  Duck and mallard.
  Widgeon.
  Sheldrach, or Canvas back.

The Black head.
  Ballcoot.
  Sprigtail.
  Didapper, or dopchick
  Spoon-billed duck.
  Water-witch.
  Water-pheasant.
  Mow-bird.
  Blue Peter.
  Water Wagtail.
  Yellow-legged Snipe.
  Squatting Snipe.
  Small Plover.
  Whistling Plover.
  Woodcock.
  Red bird, with black head, wings
    and tail.

And doubtless many others which have not yet been described and classed.

To this catalogue of our indigenous animals, I will add a short account of an anomaly of nature, taking place sometimes in the race of negroes brought from Africa, who, though black themselves, have, in rare instances, white children, called Albinos. I have known four of these myself, and have faithful accounts of three others. The circumstances in which all the individuals agree are these. They are of a pallid cadaverous white, untinged with red, without any colored spots or seams; their hair of the same kind of white, short, coarse, and curled as is that of the negro; all of them well formed, strong, healthy, perfect in their senses, except that of sight, and born of parents who had no mixture of white blood. Three of these Albinos were sisters, having two other full sisters, who were black. The youngest of the three was killed by lightning, at twelve years of age. The eldest died at about 27 years of age, in child-bed, with her second child. The middle one is now alive, in health, and has issue, as the eldest had, by a black man, which issue was black. They are uncommonly shrewd, quick in their apprehensions and in reply. Their eyes are in a perpetual tremulous vibration, very weak, and much affected by the sun; but they see much better in the night than we do. They are of the property of Colonel Skipwith, of Cumberland. The fourth is a negro woman, whose parents came from Guinea, and had three other children, who were of their own color. She is freckled, her eye-sight so weak that she is obliged to wear a bonnet in the summer; but it is better in the night than day. She had an Albino child by a black man. It died at the age of a few weeks. These were the property of Col. Carter, of Albemarle. A sixth instance is a women the property of a Mr. Butler, near Petersburg. She is stout and robust, has issue a daughter, jet black, by a black man. I am not informed as to her eye-sight. The seventh instance is of a male belonging to a Mr. Lee of Cumberland. His eyes are tremulous and weak. He is tall of stature, and now advanced in years. He is the only male of the Albinos which have come within my information. Whatever be the cause of the disease in the skin, or in its coloring matter, which produces this change, it seems more incident to the female than male sex. To these I may add the mention of a negro man within my own knowledge, born black, and of black parents; on whose chin, when a boy, a white spot appeared. This continued to increase till he became a man, by which time it had extended over his chin, lips, one cheek, the under jaw, and neck on that side. It is of the Albino white, without any mixture of red, and has for several years been stationary. He is robust and healthy, and the change of color was not accompanied with any sensible disease, either general or topical.

Of our fish and insects there has been nothing like a full description or collection. More of them are described in Catesby than in any other work. Many also are to be found in Sir Hans Sloane's Jamaica, as being common to that and this country. The honey-bee is not a native of our continent. Marcgrave, indeed, mentions a species of honey-bee in Brazil. But this has no sting, and is therefore different from the one we have, which resembles perfectly that of Europe. The Indians concur with us in the tradition that it was brought from Europe; but when, and by whom, we know not. The bees have generally extended themselves into the country, a little in advance of the white settlers. The Indians, therefore, call them the white man's fly, and consider their approach as indicating the approach of the settlements of the whites. A question here occurs, How far northwardly have these insects been found? That they are unknown in Lapland, I infer from Scheffer's information, that the Laplanders eat the pine bark, prepared in a certain way, instead of those things sweetened with sugar. "Hoc comedunt pro rebus saccharo conditis." Scheff. Lapp. c. 18. Certainly if they had honey, it would be a better substitute for sugar than any preparation of the pine bark. Kalm tells us* the honey-bee cannot live through the winter in Canada. They furnish then an additional fact first observed by the Count de Buffon, and which has thrown such a blaze of light on the field of natural history, that no animals are found in both continents, but those which are able to bear the cold of those regions where they probably join.

QUERY VII.

A notice of all that can increase the progress of Human Knowledge?

Under the latitude of this query, I will presume it not improper nor unacceptable to furnish some data for estimating the climate of Virginia. Journals of observations on the quantity of rain, and degree of heat, being lengthy, confused, and too minute to produce general and distinct ideas, I have taken five years' observations, to wit, from 1772 to 1777, made in Williamsburg and its neighborhood, have reduced them to an average for every month in the year, and stated those averages in the following table, adding an analytical view of the winds during the same period.

The rains of every month, (as of January, for instance,) through the whole period of years, were added separately, and an average drawn from them. The coolest and warmest point of the same day in each year of the period, were added separately, and an average of the greatest cold and greatest heat of

* I. 126.

that day was formed. From the averages of every day in the month, a general average was formed. The point from which the wind blew, was observed two or three times in every day. These observations, in the month of January, for instance, through the whole period, amounted to three hundred and thirty-seven. At seventy-three of these, the wind was from the north; forty-seven from the north-east, &c. So that it will be easy to see in what proportion each wind usually prevails in each month; or, taking the whole year, the total of observations through the whole period having been three thousand six hundred and ninety-eight, it will be observed that six hundred and eleven of them were from the north, five hundred and fifty-eight from the north-east, &c.

	Fall of rain. etc., in inches.	Least and greatest daily heat, by Fahrenheit's thermometer.	WINDS.								
			N.	N.E.	E.	S.E.	S.	S.W.	W.	N.W.	Total.
Jan. ...	3.192	38½ to 44	73	47	32	10	11	78	40	46	337
Feb. ...	2.049	41 .. 47½	61	52	24	11	4	63	30	31	276
March..	3.95	48 .. 54½	49	44	38	28	14	83	29	33	318
April ..	3.68	56 .. 62½	35	44	54	19	9	58	18	20	257
May ...	2.871	63 .. 70½	27	36	62	23	7	74	32	20	281
June...	3.751	71½ .. 78½	22	34	43	24	13	81	25	25	267
July ...	4.497	77 .. 83½	41	44	75	15	7	95	32	19	328
August.	9.153	76½ .. 81	43	52	40	30	9	103	27	30	334
Sept ...	4.761	69¼ .. 74½	70	60	51	18	10	81	18	37	345
Oct. ...	3.633	61¼ .. 66½	52	77	64	15	6	56	23	34	327
Nov ...	2.617	47¼ .. 53½	74	21	20	14	9	63	35	58	294
Dec....	2.877	43 .. 48¼	64	37	18	16	10	91	42	56	334
Total.	47.038	8 A.M. to 4 PM.	611	548	521	223	109	926	351	409	3,698

Though by this table it appears we have on an average forty-seven inches of rain annually, which is considerably more than usually falls in Europe, yet from the information I have collected, I suppose we have a much greater proportion of sunshine here than there. Perhaps it will be found, there are twice as many cloudy days in the middle parts of Europe, as in the United States of America. I mention the middle parts of Europe, because my information does not extend to its northern or southern parts.

In an extensive country, it will of course be expected that the climate is not the same in all its parts. It is remarkable, that proceeding on the same parallel of latitude westwardly, the

climate becomes colder in like manner as when you proceed
northwardly. This continues to be the case till you attain the
summit of the Alleghany, which is the highest land between the
ocean and the Mississippi. From thence, descending in the
same latitude to the Mississippi, the change reverses; and, if we
may believe travellers, it becomes warmer there than it is in the
same latitude on the sea-side. Their testimony is strengthened
by the vegetables and animals which subsist and multiply there
naturally, and do not on the sea-coast. Thus Catalpas grow
spontaneously on the Mississippi, as far as the latitude of 37°,
and reeds as far as 38°. Parroquets even winter on the Scioto,
in the 39th degree of latitude. In the summer of 1779, when
the thermometer was at 90° at Monticello, and 96° at Williamsburg, it was 110° at Kaskaskia. Perhaps the mountain,
which overhangs this village on the north side, may, by its reflection, have contributed somewhat to produce this heat. The
difference of temperature of the air at the sea-coast, or on the
Chesapeake bay, and at the Alleghany, has not been ascertained;
but contemporary observations, made at Williamsburg, or in its
neighborhood, and at Monticello, which is on the most eastern
ridge of the mountains, called the South-West, where they are
intersected by the Rivanna, have furnished a ratio by which that
difference may in some degree be conjectured. These observations make the difference between Williamsburg and the nearest mountains, at the position before mentioned, to be on an
average $6\frac{1}{3}°$ of Fahrenheit's thermometer. Some allowance,
however, is to be made for the difference of latitude between
these two places, the latter being 38° 8′ 17″, which is 52′ 22″
north of the former. By contemporary observations of between
five and six weeks, the averaged and almost unvaried difference
of the height of mercury in the barometer, at those two places,
was .784 of an inch, the atmosphere at Monticello being so
much the lightest, that is to say, about one-thirty-seventh of its
whole weight. It should be observed, however, that the hill of
Monticello is of five hundred feet perpendicular height above the
river which washes its base. This position being nearly central
between our northern and southern boundaries, and between the

bay and Alleghany, may be considered as furnishing the best average of the temperature of our climate. Williamsburg is much too near the south-eastern corner to give a fair idea of our general temperature.

But a more remarkable difference is in the winds which prevail in the different parts of the country. The following table exhibits a comparative view of the winds prevailing at Williamsburg, and at Monticello. It is formed by reducing nine months' observations at Monticello to four principal points, to wit, the north-east, south-east, south-west, and north-west; these points being perpendicular to, or parallel with our coast, mountains, and rivers; and by reducing in like manner, an equal number of observations, to wit, four hundred and twenty-one from the preceding table of winds at Williamsburg, taking them proportionably from every point:

	N.E.	S.E.	S.W.	N.W.	Total.
Williamsburg	127	61	132	101	421
Monticello	32	91	126	172	421

By this it may be seen that the south-west wind prevails equally at both places; that the north-east is, next to this, the principal wind towards the sea-coast, and the north-west is the predominent wind at the mountains. The difference between these two winds to sensation, and in fact, is very great. The north-east is loaded with vapor, insomuch, that the salt-makers have found that their crystals would not shoot while that blows; it brings a distressing chill, and is heavy and oppressive to the spirits. The north-west is dry, cooling, elastic, and animating. The eastern and south-eastern breezes come on generally in the afternoon. They have advanced into the country very sensibly within the memory of people now living. They formerly did not penetrate far above Williamsburg. They are now frequent at Richmond, and every now and then reach the mountains. They deposit most of their moisture, however, before they get that far. As the lands become more cleared, it is probable they will extend still further westward.

Going out into the open air, in the temperate, and warm

months of the year, we often meet with bodies of warm air, which passing by us in two or three seconds, do not afford time to the most sensible thermometer to seize their temperature. Judging from my feelings only, I think they approach the ordi nary heat of the human body. Some of them, perhaps, go a little beyond it. They are of about twenty to thirty feet diam eter horizontally. Of their height we have no experience, but probably they are globular volumes wafted or rolled along with the wind. But whence taken, where found, or how generated ? They are not to be ascribed to volcanos, because we have none. They do not happen in the winter when the farmers kindle large fires in clearing up their grounds. They are not confined to the spring season, when we have fires which traverse whole counties, consuming the leaves which have fallen from the trees. And they are too frequent and general to be ascribed to accidental fires. I am persuaded their cause must be sought for in the at mosphere itself, to aid us in which I know but of these constant circumstances: a dry air ; a temperature as warm, at least, as that of the spring or autumn ; and a moderate current of wind. They are most frequent about sun-set ; rare in the middle parts of the day ; and I do not recollect having ever met with them in the morning.

The variation in the weight of our atmosphere, as indicated by the barometer, is not equal to two inches of mercury. Dur ing twelve months' observation at Williamsburg, the extremes 29 and 30.86 inches, the difference being 1.86 of an inch ; and in nine months, during which the height of the mercury was noted at Monticello, the extremes were 28.48 and 29.69 inches, the variation being 1.21 of an inch. A gentleman, who has ob served his barometer many years, assures me it has never varied two inches. Contemporary observations made at Monticello and Williamsburg, proved the variations in the weight of air to be simultaneous and corresponding in these two places.

Our changes from heat to cold, and cold to heat, are very sud den and great. The mercury in Fahrenheit's thermometer has been known to descend from 92° to 47° in thirteen hours.

It was taken for granted, that the preceding table of average heat will not give a false idea on this subject, as it proposes to state only the ordinary heat and cold of each month, and not those which are extraordinary. At Williamsburg, in August 1766, the mercury in Fahrenheit's thermometer was at 98°, corresponding with 29⅓ of Reaumur. At the same place in January 1780, it was 6°, corresponding with 11½ below zero of Reaumur. I believe* these may be considered to be nearly the extremes of heat and cold in that part of the country. The latter may most certainly, as that time York river, at Yorktown, was frozen over, so that people walked across it; a circumstance which proves it to have been colder than the winter of 1740, 1741, usually called the cold winter, when York river did not freeze over at that place. In the same season of 1780, Chesapeake bay was solid, from its head to the mouth of Potomac. At Annapolis, where it is 5¼ miles over between the nearest points of land, the ice was from five to seven inches thick quite across, so that loaded carriages went over on it. Those, our extremes of heat and cold, of 6° and 98°, were indeed very distressing to us, and were thought to put the extent of the human constitution to considerable trial. Yet a Siberian would have considered them as scarcely a sensible variation. At Jenniseitz in that country, in latitude 58° 27', we are told that the cold in 1735 sunk the mercury by Fahrenheit's scale to 126° below nothing; and the inhabitants of the same country use stove rooms two or three times a week, in which they stay two hours at a time, the atmosphere of which raises the mercury to 135° above nothing. Late experiments show that the human body will exist in rooms heated to 140° of Reaumur, equal to 347° of Fahrenheit's, and 135° above boiling water. The hottest point of the twenty-four hours is about four o'clock, P. M., and the dawn of day the coldest.

The access of frost in autumn, and its recess the spring, do not seem to depend merely on the degree of cold; much less on

---

* At Paris, in 1753, the mercury in Reaumur's thermometer was at 30½ above zero, and in 1776, it was at 16 below zero. The extremities of heat and cold therefore at Paris, are greater than at Williamsburg, which is in the hottest part of Virginia.

the air's being at the freezing point. White frosts are frequent when the thermometer is at 47°, have killed young plants of Indian corn at 48°, and have been known at 54°. Black frost, and even ice, have been produced at 38½°, which is 6½ degrees above the freezing point. That other circumstances must be combined with this cold to produce frost, is evident from this also, on the higher parts of mountains, where it is absolutely colder than in the plains on which they stand, frosts do not appear so early by a considerable space of time in autumn, and go off sooner in the spring, than in the plains. I have known frosts so severe as to kill the hickory trees round about Monticello, and yet not injure the tender fruit blossoms then in bloom on the top and higher parts of the mountain ; and in the course of forty years, during which it had been settled, there have been but two instances of a general loss of fruit on it ; while in the circumjacent country, the fruit has escaped but twice in the last seven years. The plants of tobacco, which grow from the roots of those which have been cut off in the summer, are frequently green here at Christmas. This privilege against the frost is undoubtedly combined with the want of dew on the mountains. That the dew is very rare on their higher parts, I may say with certainty, from twelve years' observations, having scarcely ever, during that time, seen an unequivocal proof of its existence on them at all during summer. Severe frosts in the depth of winter prove that the region of dews extends higher in that season than the tops of the mountains; but certainly, in the summer season, the vapors, by the time they attain that height, are so attenuated as not to subside and form a dew when the sun retires.

The weavil has not yet ascended the high mountains.

A more satisfactory estimate of our climate to some, may perhaps be formed, by noting the plants which grow here, subject, however, to be killed by our severest colds. These are the fig, pomegranate, artichoke, and European walnut. In mild winters, lettuce and endive require no shelter ; but, generally, they need a slight covering. I do not know that the want of long moss, reed, myrtle, swamp laurel, holly, and cypress, in the upper country proceeds from a greater degree of cold, nor that they were ever killed with any degree of cold, nor that they were ever killed with any degree of cold in the lower country. The aloe lived in Williamsburg, in the open air, through the severe winter of 1779, 1780.

A change in our climate, however, is taking place very sensibly. Both heats and colds are become much more moderate within the memory even of the middle-aged. Snows are less frequent and less deep. They do not often lie, below the mountains, more than one, two, or three days, and very rarely a week. They are remembered to have been formerly frequent, deep, and of long continuance. The elderly inform me, the earth used to be covered with snow about three months in every year. The rivers, which then seldom failed to freeze over in the course of the winter, scarcely ever do so now. This change has produced an unfortunate fluctuation between heat and cold, in the spring of the year, which is very fatal to fruits. From the year 1741 to 1769, an interval of twenty-eight years, there was no instance of fruit killed by the frost in the neighborhood of Monticello. An intense cold, produced by constant snows, kept the buds locked up till the sun could obtain, in the spring of the year, so fixed an ascendency as to dissolve those snows, and protect the buds, during their development, from every danger of returning cold. The accumulated snows of the winter remaining to be dissolved all together in the spring, produced those overflowings of our rivers, so frequent then, and so rare now.

Having had occasion to mention the particular situation of Monticello for other purposes, I will just take notice that its elevation affords an opportunity of seeing a phenomenon which is rare at land, though frequent at sea. The seamen call it *looming*. Philosophy is as yet in the rear of the seamen, for so far from having accounted for it, she has not given it a name. Its principal effect is to make distant objects appear larger, in opposition to the general law of vision, by which they are diminished. I knew an instance, at Yorktown, from whence the water prospect eastwardly is without termination, wherein a canoe with three men, at a great distance was taken for a ship with its three masts. I am little acquainted with the phenom-

enon as it shows itself at sea; but at Monticello it is familiar.
There is a solitary mountain about forty miles off in the South,
whose natural shape, as presented to view there, is a regular
cone; but by the effect of looming, it sometimes subsides almost
totally in the horizon; sometimes it rises more acute and more
elevated; sometimes it is hemispherical; and sometimes its sides
are perpendicular, its top flat, and as broad as its base.   In short,
it assumes at times the most whimsical shapes, and all these perhaps successively in the same morning.   The blue ridge of
mountains comes into view, in the north-east, at about one hundred miles distance, and approaching in a direct line, passes by
within twenty miles, and goes off to the south-west.   This phenomenon begins to show itself on these mountains, at about
fifty miles distance, and continues beyond that as far as they are
seen.   I remark no particular state, either in the weight, moisture, or heat of the atmosphere, necessary to produce this.   The
only constant circumstances are its appearance in the morning
only, and on objects at least forty or fifty miles distant.   In this
latter circumstance, if not in both, it differs from the looming on
the water.   Refraction will not account for the metamorphosis.
That only changes the proportions of length and breadth, base
and altitude, preserving the general outlines.   Thus it may
make a circle appear elliptical, raise or depress a cone, but by
none of its laws, as yet developed, will it make a circle appear a
square, or a cone a sphere.

QUERY VIII.

The number of its inhabitants?

The following table shows the number of persons imported
for the establishment of our colony in its infant state, and the
census of inhabitants at different periods, extracted from our historians and public records, as particularly as I have had opportunities and leisure to examine them.   Successive lines in the

Years.	Settlers Imported.	Census of Inhabitants	Census of Tythes.
1607	100	....	....
..	 120	 40	....
1608	....	 130	....
..	70	....	....
1609	....	 490	....
..	16	....	....
..	....	 60	....
1610	150	....	....
..	....	 200	....
1611	3 ship loads. 300	....	....
..			
1612	80	....	....
1617	....	 400	....
1618	200	....	....
..	40	....	....
..	....	 600	....
1619	1,216	....	....
1621	1,300	....	....
1622	....	3,800	....
..	....	2,500	....
1628	....	3,000	....
1632	....	....	2,000
1644	....	....	4,822
1645	....	....	5,000
1652	....	....	7,000
1654	....	....	7,209
1700	....	....	22,000
1748	....	....	82,100
1759	....	....	105,000
1772	....	....	153,000
1782	....	567,614	....

same year show successive periods of time in that year. I have stated the census in two different columns, the whole inhabitants having been sometimes numbered, and sometimes the *tythes* only. This term, with us, includes the free males above sixteen years of age, and slaves above that age of both sexes. A further examination of our records would render this history of our population much more satisfactory and perfect, by furnishing a greater number of intermediate terms. These, however, which are here stated will enable us to calculate, with a considerable degree of precision, the rate at which we have increased. During the infancy of the colony, while numbers were small, wars, importations, and other accidental circumstances render the progression fluctuating and irregular. By the year 1654, however, it becomes tolerably uniform, importations having in a great measure ceased from the dissolution of the company, and the inhabitants become too numerous to be sensibly affected by Indian wars. Beginning at that period, therefore, we find that from thence to the year 1772, our tythes had increased from 7,209 to 153,000. The whole term being of one hundred and eighteen

years, yields a duplication once in every twenty-seven and a
quarter years. The intermediate enumerations taken in 1700,
1748, and 1759, furnish proofs of the uniformity of this progression. Should this rate of increase continue, we shall have
between six and seven millions of inhabitants within ninety-
five years. If we suppose our country to be bounded, at some
future day, by the meridian of the mouth of the Great Kanhaway, (within which it has been before conjectured, are 64,-
461 square miles) there will then be one hundred inhabitants for
every square mile, which is nearly the state of population in the
British Islands.

Here I will beg leave to propose a doubt. The present desire
of America is to produce rapid population by as great importations of foreigners as possible. But is this founded in good
policy? 'The advantage proposed is the multiplication of numbers. Now let us suppose (for example only) that, in this state,
we could double our numbers in one year by the importation of
foreigners; and this is a greater accession than the most san-
guine advocate for emigration has a right to expect. Then I
say, beginning with a double stock, we shall attain any given
degree of population only twenty-seven years, and three months
sooner than if we proceed on our single stock. If we propose
four millions and a half as a competent population for this State,
we should be fifty-four and a half years attaining it, could we at
once double our numbers; and eighty-one and three quarter
years, if we rely on natural propagation, as may be seen by the
following tablet:

	Procceding on our present stock.	Proceeding on a double stock.
1781	567,614	1,135,228
1808¼	1,135,228	2,270,456
1835¼	2,270,456	4,540,912
1862¾	4,540,912	

In the first column are stated periods of twenty-seven and a
quarter years; in the second are our numbers at each period, as
they will be if we proceed on our actual stock; and in the third
are what they would be, at the same periods, were we to set out

rom the double of our present stock. I have taken the term of our million and a half of inhabitants for example's sake only. Yet I am persuaded it is a greater number than the country spoken of, considering how much inarable land it contains, can clothe and feed without a material change in the quality of their diet. But are there no inconveniences to be thrown into the scale against the advantage expected from a multiplication of numbers by the importation of foreigners? It is for the happiness of those united in society to harmonize as much as possible in matters which they must of necessity transact together. Civil government being the sole object of forming societies, its administration must be conducted by common consent. Every species of government has its specific principles. Ours perhaps are more peculiar than those of any other in the universe. It is a composition of the freest principles of the English constitution, with others derived from natural right and natural reason. To these nothing can be more opposed than the maxims of absolute monarchies. Yet from such we are to expect the greatest number of emigrants. They will bring with them the principles of the governments they leave, imbibed in their early youth; or, if able to throw them off, it will be in exchange for an unbounded licentiousness, passing, as is usual, from one extreme to another. It would be a miracle were they to stop precisely at the point of temperate liberty. These principles, with their language, they will transmit to their children. In proportion to their numbers, they will share with us the legislation. They will infuse into it their spirit, warp and bias its directions, and render it a heterogenious, incoherent, distracted mass. I may appeal to experience, during the present contest, for a verification of these conjectures. But, if they be not certain in event, are they not possible, are they not probable? Is it not safer to wait with patience twenty-seven years and three months longer, for the attainment of any degree of population desired or expected? May not our government be more homogeneous, more peaceable, more durable? Suppose twenty millions of republican Americans thrown all of a sudden into France, what would be the condition of that kingdom? If it would be more turbulent, less happy, less strong, we may believe that the addition of half a million of foreigners to our present numbers would produce a similar effect here. If they come of themselves they are entitled to all the rights of citizenship; but I doubt the expediency of inviting them by extraordinary encouragements. I mean not that these doubts should be extended to the importation of useful artificers. The policy of that measure depends on very different considerations. Spare no expense in obtaining them. They will after a while go to the plough and the hoe; but, in the mean time, they will teach us something we do not know. It is not so in agriculture. The indifferent state of that among us does not proceed from a want of knowledge merely; it is from our having such quantities of land to waste as we please. In Europe the object is to make the most of their land, labor being abundant; here it is to make the most of our labor, land being abundant.

It will be proper to explain how the numbers for the year 1782 have been obtained; as it was not from a perfect census of the inhabitants. It will at the same time develope the proportion between the free inhabitants and slaves. The following return of taxable articles for that year was given in.

53,289 free males above twenty-one years of age.

211,698 slaves of all ages and sexes.

23,766 not distinguished in the returns, but said to be tytheable slaves.

195,439 horses.

609,734 cattle.

5,126 wheels of riding-carriages.

191 taverns.

There were no returns from the eight counties of Lincoln, Jefferson, Fayette, Monongahelia, Yohogania, Ohio, Northampton, and York. To find the number of slaves which should have been returned instead of the 23,766 tytheables, we must mention that some observations on a former census had given reason to believe that the numbers above and below sixteen years of age were equal. The double of this number, therefore, to wit, 47,532 must be added to 211,698, which will give us 259,230 slaves of all ages and sexes. To find the number of free inhabitants we must repeat the observation that those above and below sixteen are nearly equal.   But as the number 53,289 omits the males below sixteen and twenty-one we must supply them from conjecture.   On a former experiment it had appeared that about one-third of our militia, that is, of the males between sixteen and fifty, were unmarried.   Knowing how early marriage takes place here, we shall not be far wrong in supposing that the unmarried part of our militia are those between sixteen and twenty-one.   If there be young men who do not marry till after twenty-one, there are many who marry before that age. But as men above fifty were not included in the militia, we will suppose the unmarried, or those between sixteen and twenty-one, to be one-fourth of the whole number above sixteen, then we have the following calculation :

53,289 free males above twenty-one years of age.

17,763 free males between sixteen and twenty-one.

17,052 free males under sixteen.

142,104 free males of all ages.

284,208 free inhabitants of all ages.

259,230 slaves of all ages.

543,438 inhabitants, exclusive of the eight counties from which were no returns.   In these eight counties in the years 1779 and 1780, were 3,161 militia.   Say then,

3,161 free males above the age of sixteen.

3,161 free males under sixteen.

6,322 free females.

12,644 free inhabitants in these eight counties.   To find the number of slaves, say, as 284,208 to 259,230, so is 12,644 to 11,532.   Adding the third of these numbers to the first, and the fourth to the second, we have,

296,852 free inhabitants.

270,762 slaves.

567,614 inhabitants of every age, sex and condition.   But 296,852, the number of free inhabitants, are to 270,762, the number of slaves, nearly as 11 to 10.   Under the mild treatment our slaves experience, and their wholesome, though coarse food, this blot in our country increases as fast, or faster than the whites. During the regal government we had at one time obtained a law which imposed such a duty on the importation of slaves as amounted nearly to a prohibition, when one inconsiderate assembly, placed under a peculiarity of circumstance repealed the law. This repeal met a joyful sanction from the then reigning sovereign, and no devices, no expedients, which could ever be attempted by subsequent assemblies, and they seldom met without attempting them, could succeed in getting the royal assent to a renewal of the duty. In the very first session held under the republican government, the assembly passed a law for the perpetual prohibition of the importation of slaves. This will in some measure stop the increase of this great political and moral evil, while the minds of our citizens may be ripening for a complete emancipation of human nature.

QUERY IX.

The number and condition of the Militia and Regular Troops, and their Pay?

The following is a state of the militia, taken from returns of 1780 and 1781, except in those counties marked with an asterisk, the returns from which are somewhat older.

Every able-bodied freeman, between the ages of sixteen and fifty, is enrolled in the militia. Those of every county are formed into companies, and these again into one or more battalions, according to the numbers in the county. They are commanded by colonels, and other subordinate officers, as in the regular service. In every county is a county-lieutenant, who commands the whole militia of his county, but ranks only as a colonel in the field. We have no general officers always existing. These are appointed occasionally, when an invasion or insurrection happens, and their commission determines with the occasion. The governor is head of the military, as well as civil power. The law requires every militia-man to provide himself

Situation.	Counties.	Militia.	Situation.	Counties.	Militia.
Westward of the Alleghaney. 4,458.	Lincoln	600	On the Tide Waters, and in that Parallel. 19,012.	Between James River and Carolina. 6,959.	Greensville	500
	Jefferson	300			Dinwiddie	*750
	Fayette	156			Chesterfield	665
	Ohio	..			Prince George	328
	Monongalia	*1,000			Surrey	380
	Washington	*829			Sussex	*700
	Montgomery	1,071			Southampton	874
	Greenbriar	502			Isle of White	*600
Between the Alleghany and Blue Ridge. 7,613.	Hampshire	930			Nansemond	*644
	Berkeley	*1,100			Norfolk	*880
	Frederick	1,143			Prince Anne	*594
	Shenando	*925		Between James & York rivers. 3,009.	Henrico	619
	Rockingham	875			Hanover	706
	Augusta	1,375			New Kent	*418
	Rockbridge	*625			Charles City	286
	Boutetourt	*700			James City	235
Between the Blue Ridge and Tide Waters. 18,828.	Loudoun	1,746			Williamsburgh	129
	Faquier	1,078			York	*244
	Culpepper	1,513			Warwick	*100
	Spotsylvania	480			Elizabeth City	182
	Orange	*600		Bet. York & Rappahannock. 3,269.	Caroline	805
	Louisa	603			King William	436
	Goochland	*550			King and Queen	500
	Fluvanna	*296			Essex	468
	Albemarle	873			Middlesex	*210
	Amherst	896			Gloucester	850
	Buckingham	*625		Betw'n Rappahannock and Powtomac. 4,137.	Fairfax	652
	Bedford	1,300			Prince William	614
	Henry	1,004			Stafford	*500
	Pittsylvania	*725			King George	483
	Halifax	*1,139			Richmond	412
	Charlotte	612			Westmoreland	544
	Prince Edward	589			Northumberland	630
	Cumberland	408			Lancaster	332
	Powhatan	330		East'n shore. 1,638.	Accomac	*1,208
	Amelia	*1,125			Northampton	*430
	Lunenburg	677				
	Mecklenburg	1,100		Whole Militia of the State		49,971
	Brunswick	559				

with the arms usual in the regular service. But this injunction
was always indifferently complied with, and the arms they had,
have been so frequently called for to arm the regulars, that in
the lower parts of the country they are entirely disarmed. In
the middle country a fourth or fifth part of them may have such
firelocks as they had provided to destroy the noxious animals
which infest their farms; and on the western side of the Blue
ridge they are generally armed with rifles. The pay of our
militia, as well as of our regulars, is that of the continental regulars. The condition of our regulars, of whom we have none
but continentals, and part of a battalion of state troops, is so constantly on the change, that a state of it at this day would not be
its state a month hence. It is much the same with the condition of the other continental troops, which is well enough
known.

QUERY X.

The Marine?

Before the present invasion of this State by the British, under the command of General Phillips, we had three vessels of sixteen guns, one of fourteen, five small gallies, and two or three armed boats. They were generally so badly manned as seldom to be in a condition for service. Since the perfect possession of our rivers assumed by the enemy, I believe we are left with a single armed boat only.

QUERY XI.

A description of the Indians established in that State?

When the first effectual settlement of our colony was made, which was in 1607, the country from the sea-coast to the mountains, and from the Potomac to the most southern waters of James' river, was occupied by upwards of forty different tribes of Indians. Of these the *Powhatans*, the *Mannahoacs*, and *Monacans*, were the most powerful. Those between the seacoast and falls of the rivers, were in amity with one another, and attached to the *Powhatans* as their link of union. Those between the falls of the rivers and the mountains, were divided into two confederacies; the tribes inhabiting the head waters of Potomac and Rappahannock, being attached to the *Mannahoacs*; and those on the upper parts of James' river to the *Monacans*. But the *Monacans* and their friends were in amity with the *Mannahoacs* and their friends, and waged joint and perpetual war against the *Powhatans*. We are told that the *Powhatans*, *Mannahoacs*, and *Monacans*, spoke languages so radically different, that interpreters were necessary when they transacted business. Hence we may conjecture, that this was not the case between all the tribes, and, probably, that each spoke the language of the nation

WEST.

MANNAHOACS.

Region	Tribes	Country	Cf. Towns	War's 1669
Between Patowmac and Rappahannoc.	Whonkenties. Terminaties. Oniponies. Tauxitanians. Hassinungaes.	Fauquier. Culpepper. Orange. Fauquier. Culpepper.		
Bet. Rappahannoc & York.	Stegarakies. Shackakonies. Manahoacs.	Orange. Spotsylvania. Stafford. Spotsylvania.		
Between York and James. (MONACANS.)	Monasiccapan-oes.	James river, above the falls. Louisa. Fluvanna.	Fork of James river.	30
Between James & Carolina.	Monacans.	Bedford. Buckingham. Cumberland. Powhatan.		
	Monahassanoes. Massinnacacs. Mohemenchoes.			
Eastern shore.				

NORTH.

POWHATANS.

Tribes	Country	Chief Towns	Warriors 1607.	Warriors 1669.	
Tauxenents.	Fairfax.	About Gen. Washing- [ton's.	40		
Patowomekes.	Stafford.	Pawtomac cr.	200		
Cuttatawomans.	King George.	About Lamb creek.	20	60	
	King George.				
Pissasecs.	King George. Richmond.	Above Leeds Town.	100	..	
Onaumanients.	Westmoreland.	Nomony river.	100		
Rappahannocs.	Richmond co.	Rappahannoc creek.	100	30	By the name of Mat-chotics, U. Match-odic, Nanzaticon, Nanzatico, Appo-matox, Matox.
Moraughtacunds.	Lancaster. Richmond.	Moratico river.	80	40	
Secacaonies.	Northumberland.	Coan river.	30		
Wighcocomicoes.	Northumberland.	Wicocomico river.	130	70	By the name of Totus-keys.
Cuttatawomans.	Lancaster.	Corotoman.	30		
Nantaughtacunds.	Essex. Caroline.	Port Tobacco creek.	150	60	
Mattapoments.	Mattapony river.		30	20	
Pamunkies.	King William.	Romuncock.	300	50	
Werowocomicos.	Gloucester.	....	30		
Payankatonks.	Plankatank river.	About Rosewell, [Dy.	300		
	Pamunkey river.	Turk's Ferry, Grimes	55		
Youghtanunds.			60		
Chickahominies.	Chickahominy r.	....	250	60	
Powhatans.	Powhatan.	Orapaks.	40	40	
Arrowhatocs.	Henrico.	Powhatan. Mayo's.	30	10	
Weanocs.	Henrico.	Arrohatocs.	30		
Paspaheghes.	Charles city.	Weynoke.	100	15	
	Charles city.	Sandy-Point.	40		
	James city.		40	15	
Chiskiacs.	York.	Chiskiac.	45		
Kecoughtans.	Elizabeth city.	Rosow's.	20	50	
Appamattocs.	Chesterfield.	Bermuda Hundred.	60		
Quiocohanocs.	Surry.	About Upp. Chipoak.	60		
Warrasqueaks.	Isle of Wight.	Warrasquenoc.	25	15	
Nansamonds.	Nansamond.	A't mouth W. branch	200	3 Pohles	
Chesapeaks.	Princess Anne. Accom.	About Lynhaven riv.	100	45	Nottoways, Meherrica, Tuteloes.
Accohanocs.	Northampton.	Accohanoc river.	40		
Accomacks.	Northampton.	About Cherton's.	80	50	1699.

SOUTH.

EAST.

to which it was attached; which we know to have been the case in many particular instances. Very possibly there may have been anciently three different stocks, each of which multiplying in a long course of time, had separated into so many little societies. This practice results from the circumstance of their having never submitted themselves to any laws, any coercive power, any shadow of government. Their only controls are their manners, and that moral sense of right and wrong, which, like the sense of tasting and feeling in every man, makes a part of his nature. An offence against these is punished by contempt, by exclusion from society, or, where the case is serious, as that of murder, by the individuals whom it concerns. Imperfect as this species of coercion may seem, crimes are very rare among them; insomuch that were it made a question, whether no law, as among the savage Americans, or too much law, as among the civilized Europeans, submits man to the greatest evil, one who has seen both conditions of existence would pronounce it to be the last; and that the sheep are happier of themselves, than under care of the wolves. It will be said, that great societies cannot exist without government. The savages, therefore, break them into small ones.

The territories of the *Powhatan* confederacy, south of the Potomac, comprehended about eight thousand square miles, thirty tribes, and two thousand four hundred warriors. Captain Smith tells us, that within sixty miles of Jamestown were five thousand people, of whom one thousand five hundred were warriors. From this we find the proportion of their warriors to their whole inhabitants, was as three to ten. The *Powhatan* confederacy, then, would consist of about eight thousand inhabitants, which was one for every square mile; being about the twentieth part of our present population in the same territory, and the hundredth of that of the British islands.

Besides these were the *Nottoways*, living on Nottoway river, the *Meherrins* and *Tuteloes* on Meherrin river, who were connected with the Indians of Carolina, probably with the Chowanocs.

The preceding table contains a state of these several tribes, according to their confederacies and geographical situation, with their numbers when we first became acquainted with them, where these numbers are known. The numbers of some of them are again stated as they were in the year 1669, when an attempt was made by assembly to enumerate them. Probably the enumeration is imperfect, and in some measure conjectural, and that a farther search into the records would furnish many more particulars. What would be the melancholy sequel of their history, may, however, be argued from the census of 1669; by which we discover that the tribes therein enumerated were, in the space of sixty-two years, reduced to about one-third of their former numbers. Spirituous liquors, the small-pox, war, and an abridgement of territory to a people who lived principally on the spontaneous productions of nature, had committed terrible havoc among them, which generation, under the obstacles opposed to it among them, was not likely to make good. That the lands of this country were taken from them by conquest, is not so general a truth as is supposed. I find in our historians and records, repeated proofs of purchase, which cover a considerable part of the lower country; and many more would doubtless be found on further search. The upper country, we know, has been acquired altogether acquired by purchases made in the most unexceptionable form.

Westward of all these tribes, beyond the mountains, and extending to the great lakes, were the *Maffawomees*, a most powerful confederacy, who harrassed unremittingly the *Powhatans* and *Manahoacs*. These were probably the ancestors of tribes known at present by the name of the *Six Nations*.

Very little can now be discovered of the subsequent history of these tribes severally. The *Chickahominies* removed about the year 1661, to Mattapony river. Their chief, with one from each of the Pamunkies and Mattaponies, attended the treaty of Albany in 1685. This seems to have been the last chapter in their history. They retained, however, their separate name so late as 1705, and were at length blended with the Pamunkies and Mattaponies, and exist at present only under their names. There remain of the *Mattaponies* three or four men only, and have more negro than Indian blood in them. They have lost their language, have reduced themselves, by voluntary sales, to about fifty acres of land, which lie on the river of their own name, and have from time to time, been joining the Pamunkies, from whom they are distant but ten miles. The *Pamunkies* are reduced to about ten or twelve men, tolerably pure from mixture with other colors. The older ones among them preserve their language in a small degree, which are the last vestiges on earth, as far as we know, of the Powhatan language. They have about three hundred acres of very fertile land, on Pamunkey river, so encompassed by water that a gate shuts in the whole. Of the *Nottoways*, not a male is left. A few women constitute the remains of that tribe. They are seated on Nottoway river, in Southampton country, on very fertile lands. At a very early period, certain lands were marked out and appropriated to these tribes, and were kept from encroachment by the authority of the laws. They have usually had trustees appointed, whose duty was to watch over their interests, and guard them from insult and injury.

The *Monacans* and their friends, better known latterly by the name of *Tuscaroras*, were probably connected with the Massawomecs, or Five Nations. For though we are* told their languages were so different that the intervention of interpreters was necessary between them, yet do we also† learn that the Erigas, a nation formerly inhabiting on the Ohio, were of the same original stock with the Five Nations, and that they partook also of the Tuscarora language. Their dialects might, by long separation, have become so unlike as to be unintelligible to one another. We know that in 1712, the Five Nations received the Tuscaroras into their confederacy, and made them the Sixth Nation. They received the Meherrins and Tuteloes also into their protection; and it is most probable, that the remains of many other of the tribes, of whom we find no particular account, retired westwardly in like manner, and were incorporated with one or the other of the western tribes. (5).

I know of no such thing existing as an Indian monument; for

* Smith.   † Evans.

I would not honor with that name arrow points, stone hatchets, stone pipes, and half-shapen images. Of labor on the large scale, I think there is no remain as respectable as would be a common ditch for the draining of lands; unless indeed it would be the barrows, of which many are to be found all over this country. These are of different sizes, some of them constructed of earth, and some of loose stones. That they were repositories of the dead, has been obvious to all; but on what particular occasion constructed, was a matter of doubt. Some have thought they covered the bones of those who have fallen in battles fought on the spot of interment. Some ascribed them to the custom, said to prevail among the Indians, of collecting, at certain periods, the bones of all their dead, wheresoever deposited at the time of death. Others again supposed them the general sepulchres for towns, conjectured to have been on or near these grounds; and this opinion was supported by the quality of the lands in which they are found, (those constructed of earth being generally in the softest and most fertile meadow-grounds on river sides,) and by a tradition, said to be handed down from the aboriginal Indians, that, when they settled in a town, the first person who died was placed erect, and earth put about him, so as to cover and support him; that when another died, a narrow passage was dug to the first, the second reclined against him, and the cover of earth replaced, and so on. There being one of these in my neighborhood, I wished to satisfy myself whether any, and which of these opinions were just. For this purpose I determined to open and examine it thoroughly. It was situated on the low grounds of the Rivanna, about two miles above its principal fork, and opposite to some hills, on which had been an Indian town. It was of a spheroidical form, of about forty feet diameter at the base, and had been of about twelve feet altitude, though now reduced by the plough to seven and a half, having been under cultivation about a dozen years. Before this it was covered with trees of twelve inches diameter, and round the base was an excavation of five feet depth and width, from whence the earth had been taken of which the hillock was formed. I first dug superficially in several parts of it, and came to collections of human bones, at different depths, from six inches to three feet below the surface. These were lying in the utmost confusion, some vertical, some oblique, some horizontal, and directed to every point of the compass, entangled and held together in clusters by the earth. Bones of the most distant parts were found together, as, for instance, the small bones of the foot in the hollow of a scull; many sculls would sometimes be in contact, lying on the face, on the side, on the back, top or bottom, so as, on the whole, to give the idea of bones emptied promiscuously from a bag or a basket, and covered over with earth, without any attention to their order. The bones of which the greatest numbers remained, were sculls, jaw-bones, teeth, the bones of the arms, thighs, legs, feet and hands. A few ribs remained, some vertebræ of the neck and spine, without their processes, and one instance only of the* bone which serves as a base to the vertebral column. The sculls were so tender, that they generally fell to pieces on being touched. The other bones were stronger. There were some teeth which were judged to be smaller than those of an adult; a scull, which on a slight view, appeared to be that of an infant, but it fell to pieces on being taken out, so as to prevent satisfactory examination; a rib, and a fragment of the under-jaw of a person about half grown; another rib of an infant; and a part of the jaw of a child, which had not cut its teeth. This last furnishing the most decisive proof of the burial of children here, I was particular in my attention to it. It was part of the right half of the under-jaw. The processes, by which it was attenuated to the temporal bones, were entire, and the bone itself firm to where it had been broken off, which, as nearly as I could judge, was about the place of the eye-tooth. Its upper edge, wherein would have been the sockets of the teeth, was perfectly smooth. Measuring it with that of an adult, by placing their hinder processes together, its broken end extended to the penultimate grinder of the adult. This bone was white, all the others of a sand color. The bones of infants being soft, they probably decay sooner, which might be the cause so few were found here. I proceeded then to make a perpendicular cut through the

* The os sacrum.

body of the barrow, that I might examine its internal structure. This passed about three feet from its centre, was opened to the former surface of the earth, and was wide enough for a man to walk through and examine its sides.   At the bottom, that is, on the level of the circumjacent plain, I found bones; above these a few stones, brought from a cliff a quarter of a mile off, and from the river one-eighth of a mile off; then a large interval of earth, then a stratum of bones, and so on.   At one end of the section were four strata of bones plainly distinguishable; at the other, three; the strata in one part not ranging with those in another.   The bones nearest the surface were least decayed. 'No holes were discovered in any of them, as if made with bullets, arrows, or other weapons.   I conjectured that in this barrow might have been a thousand skeletons.   Every one will readily seize the circumstances above related, which militate against the opinion, that it covered the bones only of persons fallen in battle; and against the tradition also, which would make it the common sepulchre of a town, in which the bodies were placed upright, and touching each other.   Appearances certainly indicate that it has derived both origin and growth from the accustomary collection of bones, and deposition of them together; that the first collection had been deposited on the common surface of the earth, a few stones put over it, and then a covering of earth, that the second had been laid on this, had covered more or less of it in proportion to the number of bones, and was then also covered with earth; and so on.   The following are the particular circumstances which give it this aspect.   1. The number of bones.   2. Their confused position.   3. Their being in different strata.   4. The strata in one part having no correspondence with those in another.   5. The different states of decan in these strata, which seem to indicate a difference in the time of inhumation.   6. The existence of infant bones among them.

But on whatever occasion they may have been made, they are of considerable notoriety among the Indians; for a party passing, about thirty years ago, through the part of the country where this barrow is, went through the woods directly to it, without any instructions or inquiry, and having staid about it for some time, with expressions which were construed to be those of sorrow, they returned to the high road, which they had left about half a dozen miles to pay this visit, and pursued their journey. There is another barrow much resembling this, in the low grounds of the south branch of Shenandoah, where it is crossed by the road leading from the Rockfish gap to Staunton. Both of these have, within these dozen years, been cleared of their trees and put under cultivation, are much reduced in their height, and spread in width, by the plough, and will probably disappear in time. There is another on a hill in the Blue Ridge of mountains, a few miles north of Wood's gap, which is made up of small stones thrown together. This has been opened and found to contain human bones, as the others do. There are also many others in other parts of the country.

Great question has arisen from whence came those aboriginals of America? Discoveries, long ago made, were sufficient to show that the passage from Europe to America was always practicable, even to the imperfect navigation of ancient times. In going from Norway to Iceland, from Iceland to Greenland, from Greenland to Labrador, the first traject is the widest; and this having been practised from the earliest times of which we have any account of that part of the earth, it is not difficult to suppose that the subsequent trajects may have been sometimes passed. Again, the late discoveries of Captain Cook, coasting from Kamschatka to California, have proved that if the two continents of Asia and America be separated at all, it is only by a narrow strait. So that from this side also, inhabitants may have passed into America; and the resemblance between the Indians of America and the eastern inhabitants of Asia, would induce us to conjecture, that the former are the descendants of the latter, or the latter of the former; excepting indeed the Esquimaux, who, from the same circumstance of resemblance, and from identity of language must be derived from the Greenlanders, and these probably from some of the northern parts of the old continent. A knowledge of their several languages would be the most certain evidence of their derivation which could be produced. In fact, it is the best proof of the affinity of nations which ever can be referred to. How many ages have elapsed since the English, the Dutch, the Germans, the Swiss, the Norwegians, Danes and Swedes have separated from their common stock? Yet how many more must elapse before the proofs of their common origin, which exist in their several languages, will disappear? It is to be lamented then, very much to be lamented, that we have suffered so many of the Indian tribes already to extinguish, without our having previously collected and deposited in the records of literature, the general rudiments at least of the languages they spoke. Were vocabularies formed of all the languages spoken in North and South America, preserving their appellations of the most common objects in nature, of those which must be present to every nation barbarous or civilized, with the inflections of their nouns and verbs, their principles of regimen and concord, and these deposited in all the public libraries, it would furnish opportunities to those skilled in the languages of the old world to compare them with these, now, or at any future time, and hence to construct the best evidence of the derivation of this part of the human race.

But imperfect as is our knowledge of the tongues spoken in America, it suffices to discover the following remarkable fact: Arranging them under the radical ones to which they may be palpably traced, and doing the same by those of the red men of Asia, there will be found probably twenty in America, for one in Asia, of those radical languages, so called because if they were ever the same they have lost all resemblance to one another. A separation into dialects may be the work of a few ages only, but for two dialects to recede from one another till they have lost all vestiges of their common origin, must require an immense course of time; perhaps not less than many people give to the age of the earth. A greater number of those radical changes of language having taken place among the red men of America, proves them of greater antiquity than those of Asia.

I will now proceed to state the nations and numbers of the Aborigines which still exist in a respectable and independent form. And as their undefined boundaries would render it difficult to specify those only which may be within any certain limits, and it may not be unacceptable to present a more general view of them, I will reduce within the form of a catalogue all those within, and circumjacent to, the United States, whose names and numbers have come to my notice. These are taken from four different lists, the first of which was given in the year 1759 to General Stanwix by George Croghan, deputy agent for Indian affairs under Sir William Johnson; the second was drawn up by a French trader of considerable note, resident among the Indians many years, and annexed to Colonel Bouquet's printed account of his expedition in 1764. The third was made out by Captain Hutchins, who visited most of the tribes, by order, for the purpose of learning their numbers, in 1768; and the fourth by John Dodge, an Indian trader, in 1779, except the numbers marked *, which are from other information.

INDIAN TRIBES.

TRIBES.	Croghan, 1759.	Bouquet, 1764.	Hutchins, 1768.	Where they reside.
Oswegatchies			100	At Swagatchy, on the river St. Laurence.
Connasedagoes			300	Near Montreal.
Cohunnewugoes		900		Near Trois Rivieres.
Orondocs			100	Near Trois Rivieres.
Abenakies		350	150	Near Trois Rivieres.
Little Alkonkins			100	River St. Laurence.
Michmacs		700		River St. Laurence.
Amelistes		550		River St. Laurence.
Chalas		130		Towards the heads of the Ottawas river
Nipissins		400		Towards the heads of the Ottawas river.
Algonquins		300		Riviere aux Tetes boules, on the east side of Lake Superior.
Round Heads		2,500		Lakes Huron and Superior.
Messasagues		2,000		Lake Christianaux,
Christianaux—Kris		3,000		Lake Assinaboes,
Assinaboos		1,500		
Blancs, or Barbus		1,500		
Sioux of the Meadows		2,500		On the heads of the Mississippi and westward of that river.
Sioux of the Woods		1,800		
Sioux	10,000		10,000	
Ajoues		1,100		North of the Padoucas,
Panis—White		2,000		South of the Missouri.
Panis—Freckled		1,769		South of the Missouri.
Padoucas		500		South of the Missouri.
Grandes-Eaux		1,000		
Canses		1,000		South of the Missouri.
Osges	400	600		South of the Missouri.
Missouris		3,000		On the river Missouri.
Arkansas		2,000		On the river Arkansas,
Caouitas		700		East of the Allibamous.

Northward and Westward of the United States.

TRIBES.	Croghan, 1759.	Bouquet, 1764.	Hutchins, 1768.	Dodge, 1779.	Where they reside.
Mohocks	...	...	160	100	Mohocks river.
Oneidas	...	...	300 }	400	East side of Oneida Lake and head branches of Susquehanna.
Tuscaroras	...	...	200 }	230	Between the Oneidas and Onondagoes.
Onondagoes	...	1,550	260	220	Near Onondago Lake.
Cayugas	...	...	200		On the Cayuga Lake, near the north branch of Susquehanna.
Senecas	...	...	1,000	650	On the waters of Susquehanna, of Ontario, and the heads of the Ohio.
Aughquagahs	...	...	150	...	East branch of Susquehanna, and on Aughquagah.
Nanticoes	...	...	100	...	Utsanango, Chagbnet, and Owegy, on the east branch of Susquehanna.
Mohiccons	...	...	100	...	In the same parts.
Conoies	...	...	100	...	In the same parts.
Saponies	...	...	30	...	At Diahago and other villages up the north branch of Susquehanna.
Munsies	...	...	150	*150	At Diahago and other villages up the north branch of Susquehanna.
Delawares, or Linnelinopies	600	600	150 }	*500	At Diahago and other villages up the north branch of Susquehanna.
Delawares, or Linnelinopies	500	400	600 }	*500	Between Ohio and Lake Erie and the branches of Beaver creek, Cayahoga and Muskingum.
Shawanees	...	300 }	300	300	Sioto and the branches of Muskingum.
Mingoes	...		...	60	On a branch of Sioto.
Mohiccons	...		...	*60	
Cohunnewagos	...	300 }	300		Near Sandusky.
Wyandots	300 }		250	180	Near Fort St. Joseph's and Detroit.
Wyandots	300 }		250		Miami river near Fort Miami.
Twightwees	...	350	...		Miami river, about Fort St. Joseph.
Miamis	200	400	300	300	On the banks of the Wabash, near Fort Ouiatonon.
Outanons	300	250	300	*400	On the banks of the Wabash, near Fort Ouiatonon.
Piankishas	...	...	200	...	On the banks of the Wabash, near Fort Ouiatonon.
Shakirs	...	...	300	...	Near Kaskaskia.
Kaskaskias	...	...	300	...	Near Cahokia.
Illinois	400	600	300	...	Query, if not the same with the Mitchigamis?
Piorias	...	800	...	...	On the Illinois river, called Pianrias, but supposed to mean Piorias.
Poutedtamies	...	350	300	450	Near Fort St. Joseph's and Fort-Detroit.

Within the limits of the United States.

Ottawas	...	...	550	*300	Near Fort St. Joseph's and Fort Detroit.
Chippawas	...	...	200	...	On Saguinam bay of Lake Huron.
Ottawas	...	...	400	...	On Saguinam bay of Lake Huron.
Chippawas	...	...	250	...	Near Michillimackinac.
Ottawas	2,000	...	400	...	Near Michillimackinac.
Chippawas	...	5,900	...	5,450	Near Fort St. Mary's on Lake Superior. Several other villages along the banks of Lake Superior. Numbers unknown.
Chippawas	...	...	...	...	Near Puans bay on Lake Michigan.
Shakies	200	400	550	...	Near Puans bay on Lake Michigan.
Myuonimies	...	...	...	...	Near Puans bay on Lake Michigan.
Ouisconsings	...	550	...	...	Ouisconsing river.
Kickapous	600	300	...	...	
Otogamies—Foxes	...	500	...	250	On Lake Michigan, and between that and the Mississippi.
Mascoutens	...	...	4,000	...	
Miscóthins	...	...	...	...	
Outimacs	200	250	...	250	
Musquakies	...	...	...	500	On the eastern heads of the Mississippi, and the islands of Lake Superior.
Sioux. Eastern.	...	...	Galphin, 1878.	...	
Cherokees	1,500	2,500	3,000	...	Western parts of North Carolina.
Chickasaws	...	750	500	...	Western parts of Georgia.
Catawbas	...	150	...	...	On the Catawba river in South Carolina.
Chacktaws	2,000	4,500	6,000	...	Western parts of Georgia.
Upper Creeks	...	1,180	...	...	
Lower Creeks	...	150	3,000	...	Western parts of Georgia.
Natchez	...	600	...	...	
Allibamous	...	...	...	...	Alabama river, in the western parts of Georgia.

Within the limits of the United States.

The following tribes are also mentioned :

Croghan's Catal.	Lezar	400	From the mouth of Ohio to the mouth of Wabash.
	Webings	200	On the Mississippi below the Shakies.
	Ousasoys } Grand Tuc }	4,000	On White Creek, a branch of the Mississippi.
	Linways	1,000	On the Mississippi.

Bouquet's.	Les Puans	700	Near Puans Bay.
	Folle Avoine	350	Near Puans Bay.
	Ouanakina	300	
	Chiakanessou	350	Conjectured to be tribes of the Creeks.
	Machecous	800	
	Souikilas	200	

Dodge's.	Minneamis	2,000	North-west of Lake Michigan, to the heads of Mississippi, and up to Lake Superior.
	Piankishas, } Mascoutins, } Vermillions, }	800	On and near the Wabash toward the Illinois.

But apprehending these might be different appellations for some of the tribes already enumerated, I have not inserted them in the table, but state them separately as worthy of further inquiry. The variations observable in numbering the same tribe may sometimes be ascribed to imperfect information, and sometimes to a greater or less comprehension of settlements under the same name. (7)

QUERY XII.

A notice of the counties, cities, townships, and villages ?

The counties have been enumerated under Query IX. They are seventy-four in number, of very unequal size and population. Of these thirty-five are on the tide waters, or in that parallel; twenty-three are in the midlands, between the tide waters and Blue Ridge of mountains; eight between the Blue Ridge and Alleghany; and eight westward of the Alleghany.

The State, by another division, is formed into parishes, many of which are commensurate with the counties; but sometimes a county comprehends more than one parish, and sometimes a parish more than one county. This division had relation to the religion of the State, a portion of the Anglican church, with a fixed salary, having been heretofore established in each parish. The care of the poor was another object of the parochial division.

We have no townships. Our country being much intersected with navigable waters, and trade brought generally to our doors, instead of our being obliged to go in quest of it, has probably been one of the causes why we have no towns of any consequence. Williamsburg, which, till the year 1780, was the seat of our government, never contained above 1,800 inhabitants ; and Norfolk, the most populous town we ever had, contained but 6,000. Our towns, but more properly our villages and hamlets, are as follows :

On *James River* and its waters, Norfolk, Portsmouth, Hampton, Suffolk, Smithfield, Williamsburg, Petersburg, Richmond, the seat of our government, Manchester, Charlottesville, New London.

On *York River* and its waters, York, Newcastle, Hanover.

On *Rappahannock*, Urbanna, Port-Royal, Fredericksburg, Falmouth.

On *Potomac* and its waters, Dumfries, Colchester, Alexandria, Winchester, Staunton.

On *Ohio*, Louisville.

There are other places at which, like some of the foregoing, the *laws* have said there shall be towns ; but *nature* has said there shall not, and they remain unworthy of enumeration. *Norfolk* will probably be the emporium for all the trade of the Chesapeake bay and its waters ; and a canal of eight or ten miles will bring to it all that of Albermale sound and its waters. Secondary to this place, are the towns at the head of the tide waters, to wit, Petersburg on Appomattox ; Richmond on James river ; Newcastle on York river ; Alexandria on Potomac, and Baltimore on Patapsco. From these the distribution will be to subordinate situations in the country. Accidental circumstances, however, may control the indications of nature, and in no instance do they do it more frequently than in the rise and fall of towns.

QUERY XIII.

The constitution of the State and its several charters ?

Queen Elizabeth by her letters patent, bearing date March 25, 1584, licensed Sir Walter Raleigh to search for remote heathen lands, not inhabited by Christian people, and granted to him in fee simple, all the soil within two hundred leagues of the places where his people should, within six years, make their dwellings or abidings ; reserving only to herself and her successors, their allegiance and one-fifth part of all the gold and silver ore they should obtain. Sir Walter immediately sent out two ships, which visited Wococon island in North Carolina, and the next year despatched seven with one hundred and seven men, who settled in Roanoke island, about latitude 35° 50′. Here Okisko, king of the Weopomeiocs, in a full council of his people is said to have acknowledged himself the homager of the Queen of England, and, after her, of Sir Walter Raleigh. A supply of fifty men were sent in 1586, and one hundred and fifty in 1587. With these last Sir Walter sent a governor, appointed him twelve assistants, gave them a charter of incorporation, and instructed them to settle on Chesapeake bay. They landed, however, at Hatorask. In 1588, when a fleet was ready to sail with a new supply of colonists and necessaries, they were detained by the Queen to assist against the Spanish armada. Sir Walter having now expended £40,000 in these enterprises, obstructed occasionally by the crown without a shilling of aid from it, was under a necessity of engaging others to adventure their money. He, therefore, by deed bearing date the 7th of March, 1589, by the name of Sir Walter Raleigh, Chief Governor of Assamàcomòc, (probably Acomàc,) alias Wingadacoia, alias Virginia, granted to Thomas Smith and others, in consideration of their adventuring certain sums of money, liberty to trade to this new country free from all customs and taxes for seven years, excepting the fifth part of the gold and silver ore to be obtained ; and stipulated with them and the other assistants, then in Virginia, that he would confirm the deed of incorporation which he had given in 1587, with all the prerogatives, jurisdictions, royalties and privileges granted to him by the Queen. Sir Walter, at different times, sent five other adventurers hither, the last of which was in 1602; for in 1603 he was attainted and put into close imprisonment, which put an end to his cares over his infant colony. What was the particular fate of the colonists he had before sent and seated, has never been known; whether they were murdered, or incorporated with the savages.

Some gentlemen and merchants, supposing that by the attainder of Sir Walter Raleigh the grant to him was forfeited, not inquiring over carefully whether the sentence of an English court could affect lands not within the jurisdiction of that court, petitioned king James for a new grant of Virginia to them. He accordingly executed a grant to Sir Thomas Gates and others, bearing date the 9th of March, 1607, under which, in the same year, a settlement was effected at Jamestown, and ever after maintained. Of this grant, however, no particular notice need be taken, as it was superceded by letters patent of the same king, of May 23, 1609, to the Earl of Salisbury and others, incorporating them by the name of "The Treasurer and company of Adventurers and Planters of the City of London for the first colony in Virginia," granting to them and their successors all the lands in Virginia from Point Comfort along the sea-coast, to the northward two hundred miles, and from the same point along the sea-coast to the southward two hundred miles, and all the space from this precinct on the sea-coast up into the land, west and north-west, from sea to sea, and the islands within one hundred miles of it, with all the communities, jurisdictions, royalties, privileges, franchises, and pre-eminencies, within the same, and thereto and thereabouts, by sea and land, appertaining in as ample manner as had before been granted to any adventurer; to be held of the king and his successors, in common soccage, yielding one-fifth part of the gold and silver ore to be therein found, for all manner of services; establishing a counsel in England for the direction of the enterprise, the members of which were to be chosen and displaced by the voice of the majority of the company and adventurers, and were to have the nomination and revocation of governors, officers, and ministers, which by them should be thought needful for the colony, the power of establishing laws and forms of government and magistracy, obligatory not only within the colony, but also on the seas in going and coming to and from it; authorizing them to carry thither any persons who should consent to go, freeing them forever from all taxes and impositions on any goods or merchandise on importations into the colony, or exportation out of it, except the five per cent. due for custom on all goods imported into the British dominions, according to the ancient trade of merchants; which five per cent. only being paid they might, within thirteen months, re-export the same goods into foreign parts, without any custom, tax, or other duty, to the king or any of his officers, or deputies; with powers of waging war against those who should annoy them; giving to the inhabitants of the colony all the rights of natural subjects, as if born and abiding in England; and declaring that these letters should be construed, in all doubtful parts, in such manner as should be most for the benefit of the grantees.

Afterwards on the 12th of March, 1612, by other letters patent, the king added to his former grants, all islands in any part of the ocean between the 30th and 41st degrees of latitude, and within three hundred leagues of any of the parts before granted to the treasurer and company, not being possessed or inhabited by any other Christian prince or state, nor within the limits of the northern colony.

In pursuance of the authorities given to the company by these charters, and more especially of that part in the charter of 1609, which authorized them to establish a form of government, they on the 24th of July, 1621, by charter under their common seal, declared that from thenceforward there should be two supreme councils in Virginia, the one to be called the council of state, to be placed and displaced by the treasurer, council in England, and company from time to time, whose office was to be that of assisting and advising the governor; the other to be called the general assembly, to be convened by the governor once yearly or oftener, which was to consist of the council of state, and two burgesses out of every town, hundred, or plantation, to be respectively chosen by the inhabitants. In this all matters were to be decided by the greater part of the votes present; reserving to the governor a negative voice; and they were to have power to treat, consult, and conclude all emergent occasions concerning the public weal, and to make laws for the behoof and government of the colony, imitating and following the laws and policy of England as nearly as might be; providing that these laws should have no force till ratified in a general court of the company in England, and returned under their common seal; and declaring that, after the government of the colony should be well framed and settled, no orders of the council in England should bind the colony unless ratified in the said general assembly. The king and company quarrelled, and by a mixture of law and force, the latter were ousted of all their rights without retribution, after having expended one hundred thousand pounds in establishing the colony, without the smallest aid from government. King James suspended their powers by proclamation of July 15, 1624, and Charles I. took the government into his own hands. Both sides had their partisans in the colony, but, in truth, the people of the colony in general thought themselves little concerned in the dispute. There being three parties interested in these several charters, what passed between the first and second, it was thought could not affect the third. If the king seized on the powers of the company, they only passed into other hands, without increase or diminution, while the rights of the people remained as they were. But they did not remain so long. The northern parts of their country were granted away to the lords Baltimore and Fairfax; the first of these obtaining also the rights of separate jurisdiction and government. And in 1650 the parliament, considering itself as standing in the place of their deposed king, and as having succeeded to all his powers, without as well as within the realm, began to assume a right over the colonies, passing an act for inhibiting their trade with foreign nations. This succession to the exercise of kingly authority gave the first color for parliamentary interference with the colonies, and produced that fatal precedent which they continued to follow, after they had retired, in other respects, within their proper functions. When this colony, therefore, which still maintained its opposition to Cromwell and the parliament, was induced in 1651 to lay down their arms, they previously secured their most essential rights by a solemn convention, which, having never seen in print, I will here insert literally from the records.

"ARTICLES agreed on and concluded at James Cittie in Virginia for the surrendering and settling of that plantation under the obedience and government of the commonwealth of England by the commissioners of the Councill of State by authoritie of the parliamt of England, and by the Grand assembly of the Governour, Councill, and Burgesses of that countrey.

"First it is agreed and consted that the plantation of Virginia, and all the inhabitants thereof, shall be and remain in due obedience and subjection to the Commonwealth of England, according to the laws there established, and that this submission and subscription bee acknowledged a voluntary act not forced nor constrained by a conquest upon the countrey, and that they shall have and enjoy such freedoms and priviledges as belong to the free borne people of England, and that the former government by the Commissions and Instructions be void and null.

"2ly. That the Grand assembly as formerly shall convene and transact the affairs of Virginia, wherein nothing is to be acted or done contrairie to the government of the Commonwealth of England and the lawes there established.

"3ly. That there shall be a full and totall remission and indempnitie of all acts. words, or writeings done or spoken against the parliament of England in relation to the same.

"4ly. That Virginia shall have and enjoy the antient bounds and lymitts granted by the charters of the former kings, and that we shall seek a new charter from the parliament to that purpose against any that have intrencht upon the rights thereof.

"5ly. That all the pattents of land granted under the colony seal by any of the precedent governours shall be and remaine in their full force and strength.

"6ly. That the priviledge of haveing ffiftie acres of land for every person transported in that collonie shall continue as formerly granted.

"7ly. That the people of Virginia have free trade as the people of England do enjoy to all places and with all nations according to the lawes of that commonwealth, and that Virginia shall enjoy all priviledges equall with any English plantations in America.

"8ly. That Virginia shall be free from all taxes, customs and impositions whatsoever, and none to be imposed on them without consent of the Grand assembly; and soe that neither fforts nor castle bee erected or garrisons maintained without their consent.

"9ly. That noe charge shall be required from this country in respect of this present ffleet.

"10ly. That for the future settlement of the countrey in their due obedience, the engagement shall be tendred to all the inhabitants according to act of parliament made to that purpose, that all persons who shall refuse to subscribe the said engagement, shall have a yeare's time if they please to remove themselves and their estates out of Virginia, and in the meantime during the said yeare to have equall justice as formerly.

"11ly. That the use of the booke of common prayer shall be permitted for one yeare ensueinge with referrence to the consent of the major part of the parishes, provided that those which relate to kingshipp or that government be not used publiquely, and the continuance of ministers in their places, they not misdemeaning themselves, and the payment of their accustomed dues and agreements made with them respectively shall be left as they now stand dureing this ensueing yeare.

"12ly. That no man's cattell shall be questioned as the companies, unless such as have been entrusted with them or have disposed of them without order.

"13ly. That all ammunition, powder and armes, other than for private use, shall be delivered up, securitie being given to make satisfaction for it.

"14ly. That all goods allreadie brought hither by the Dutch or others which are now on shoar shall be free from surprizall.

"15ly. That the quittrents granted unto us by the late kinge for seaven yeares bee confirmed.

"16ly. That the commissioners for the parliament subscribeing these articles engage themselves and the honour of parliament for the full performance thereof; and that the present governour, and the councill, and the burgesses do likewise subscribe and engage the whole collony on their parts.

RICHARD BENNETT.—Seale.
WILLIAM CLAIBORNE.—Seale.
EDMOND CURTIS.—Seale.

"Theise articles were signed and sealed by the Commissioners of the Councill of state for the Commonwealth of England the twelveth day of March 1651."

Then follow the articles stipulated by the governor and council, which relate merely to their own persons and property, and then the ensuing instrument :

"An act of indempnitie made att the surrender of the countrey.

"Whereas, by the authoritie of the parliament wee the commissioners appointed by the councill of state authorized thereto, having brought a ffleet and force before James cittie in Virginia to reduce that collonie under the obedience of the commonwealth of England, and finding force raised by the Governour and countrey to make opposition against the said ffleet, whereby assured danger appearinge of the ruine and destruction of the plantation, for prevention whereof the burgesses of all the severall plantations being called to advise and assist therein, uppon long and serious debate, and in sad contemplation of the great miseries and certain destruction which were soe neerely hovering over the whole countrey; Wee the said Commissioners have thought fitt and condescending and granted to signe and confirme under our hands, seales and by our oath, Articles bearinge date with theise presents, and do further declare that by the authoritie of the parliament and commonwealth of England derived unto us their commissioners, that according to the articles in generall wee have granted an act of indempnitie and oblivion to all the inhabitants of this collonie from all words, actions, or writings that have been spoken acted or writt against the parliament or commonwealth of Englana or any other person from the beginning of the world to this daye. And this we have done that all the inhabitants of the collonie may live quietly and securely under the commonwealth of England. And we do promise that the parliament and commonwealth of England shall confirm and make good all those transactions of ours. Witness our hands and seales this 12th of March 1651.

RICHARD BENNETT.—Seale.
WILLIAM CLAIBORNE.—Seale.
EDMOND CURTIS.—Seale.

The colony supposed, that, by this solemn convention, entered into with arms in their hands, they had secured the ancient limits* of their country, its free trade,† its exemption from taxation‡ but by their own assembly, and exclusion of military force§ from among them. Yet in every of these points was this convention violated by subsequent kings and parliaments, and other infractions of their constitution, equally dangerous committed. Their general assembly, which was composed of the council of state and burgesses, sitting together and deciding by plurality of voices, was split into two houses, by which the council obtained a separate negative on their laws. Appeals from their supreme court, which had been fixed by law in their general assembly, were arbitrarily revoked to England, to be there heard before the king and council. Instead of four hundred miles on the seacoast, they were reduced, in the space of thirty years, to about one hundred miles. Their trade with foreigners was totally suppressed, and when carried to Great Britain, was there loaded with imposts. It is unnecessary, however, to glean up the several instances of injury, as scattered through American and British history, and the more especially as, by passing on to the accession of the present king, we shall find specimens of them all, aggravated, multiplied and crowded within a small compass of time, so as to evince a fixed design of considering our rights natural, conventional and chartered as mere nullities. The following is an epitome of the first sixteen years of his reign : The colonies were taxed internally and externally ; their essential interests sacrificed to individuals in Great Britain ; their

* Art. 4.   † Art. 7.   ‡ Art. 8.   § Art. 8.

legislatures suspended ; charters annulled ; trials by juries taken away ; their persons subjected to transportation across the Atlantic, and to trial before foreign judicatories ; their supplications for redress thought beneath answer ; themselves published as cowards, in the councils of their mother country and courts of Europe ; armed troops sent among them to enforce submission to these violences; and actual hostilities commenced against them. No alternative was presented but resistance, or unconditional submission. Between these could be no hesitation. They closed in the appeal to arms. They declared themselves independent states. They confederated together into one great republic ; thus securing to every State the benefit of an union of their whole force. In each State separately a new form of government was established. Of ours particularly the following are the outlines : The executive powers are lodged in the hands of a governor, chosen annually, and incapable of acting more then three years in seven. He is assisted by a council of eight members. The judiciary powers are divided among several courts, as will be hereafter explained. Legislation is exercised by two houses of assembly, the one called the house of Delegates, composed of two members from each county, chosen annually by the citizens, possessing an estate for life in one hundred acres of uninhabited land, or twenty-five acres with a house on it, or in a house or lot in some town : the other called the Senate, consisting of twenty-four members, chosen quadrenially by the same electors, who for this purpose are distributed into twenty-four districts. The concurrence of both houses is necesary to the passage of a law. They have the appointment of the governor and council, the judges of the superior courts, auditors, attorney-general, treasurer, register of the land office, and delegates to Congress. As the dismemberment of the State had never had its confirmation, but, on the contrary, had always been the subject of protestation and complaint, that it might never be in our own power to raise scruples on that subject, or to disturb the harmony of our new confederacy, the grants to Maryland, Pennsylvania, and the two Carolinas, were ratified.

This constitution was formed when we were new and unexperienced in the science of government. It was the first, too, which was formed in the whole United States. No wonder then that time and trial have discovered very capital defects in it.

1. The majority of the men in the State, who pay and fight for its support, are unrepresented in the legislature, the roll of freeholders entitled to vote not including generally the half of those on the roll of the militia, or of the tax-gatherers.

2. Among those who share the representation, the shares are very unequal. Thus the county of Warwick, with only one hundred fighting men, has an equal representation with the county of Loudon, which has one thousand seven hundred and forty-six. So that every man in Warwick has as much influence in the government as seventeen men in Loudon. But lest it should be thought that an equal interspersion of small among large counties, through the whole State, may prevent any danger of injury to particular parts of it, we will divide it into districts, and show the proportions of land, of fighting men, and of representation in each :

	Square miles.	Fighting men.	Delegates.	Senators.
Between the sea-coast and falls of the rivers	*11,205	19,012	71	12
Between the falls of the rivers and and Blue Ridge of mountains	18,759	18,828	46	8
Between the Blue Ridge and the Alleghany	11,911	7,673	16	2
Between the Alleghany and Ohio	†79,650	4,458	16	2
Total	121,525	49,971	149	24

An inspection of this table will supply the place of commentaries on it. It will appear at once that nineteen thousand men, living below the falls of the rivers, possess half the senate, and want four members only of possessing a majority of the house of delegates; a want more than supplied by the vicinity of their situation to the seat of government, and of course the greater degree of convenience and punctuality with which their members may and will attend in the legislature. These nineteen thousand,

* Of these 542 are on the eastern shore.

† Of these, 22,616 are eastward of the meridian of the north of the Great Kanhaway.

therefore, living in one part of the country, give law to upwards
of thirty thousand living in another, and appoint all their chief
officers, executive and judiciary.   From the difference of their
situation and circumstances, their interests will often be very different.

3. The senate is, by its constitution, too homogenous with the
house of delegates.   Being chosen by the same electors, at the
same time, and out of the same subjects, the choice falls of course
on men of the same description.   The purpose of establishing
different houses of legislation is to introduce the influence of different interests or different principles.   Thus in Great Britain it
is said their constitution relies on the house of commons for honesty, and the lords for wisdom ; which would be a rational reliance, if honesty were to be bought with money, and if wisdom
were hereditary.   In some of the American States, the delegates
and senators are so chosen, as that the first represent the persons,
and the second the property of the State.   But with us, wealth
and wisdom have equal chance for admission into both houses.
We do not, therefore, derive from the separation of our legislature into two houses, those benefits which a proper complication
of principles are capable of producing, and those which alone can
compensate the evils which may be produced by their dissensions.

4. All the powers of government, legislative, executive, and
judiciary, result to the legislative body.   The concentrating
these in the same hands is precisely the definition of despotic
government.   It will be no alleviation that these powers will be
exercised by a plurality of hands, and not by a single one.   One
hundred and seventy-three despots would surely be as oppressive
as one.   Let those who doubt it turn their eyes on the republic
of Venice.   As little will it avail us that they are chosen by ourselves.   An *elective despotism* was not the government we fought
for, but one which should not only be founded on free principles,
but in which the powers of government should be so divided and
balanced among several bodies of magistracy, as that no one
could transcend their legal limits, without being effectually
checked and restrained by the others.   For this reason that con-

vention which passed the ordinance of government, laid its foundation on this basis, that the legislative, executive, and judiciary departments should be separate and distinct, so that no person should exercise the powers of more than one of them at the same time. But no barrier was provided between these several powers. The judiciary and executive members were left dependent on the legislative, for their subsistence in office, and some of them for their continuance in it. If, therefore, the legislature assumes executive and judiciary powers, no opposition is likely to be made ; nor, if made, can it be effectual ; because in that case they may put their proceedings into the form of an act of assembly, which will render them obligatory on the other branches. They have, accordingly, in many instances, decided rights which should have been left to judiciary controversy ; and the direction of the executive, during the whole time of their session, is becoming habitual and familiar. And this is done with no ill intention. The views of the present members are perfectly upright. When they are led out of their regular province, it is by art in others, and inadvertence in themselves. And this will probably be the case for some time to come. But it will not be a very long time. Mankind soon learn to make interested uses of every right and power which they possess, or may assume. The public money and public liberty, intended to have been deposited with three branches of magistracy, but found inadvertently to be in the hands of one only, will soon be discovered to be sources of wealth and dominion to those who hold them ; distinguished, too, by this tempting circumstance, that they are the instrument, as well as the object of acquisition. With money we will get men, said Cæsar, and with men we will get money. Nor should our assembly be deluded by the integrity of their own purposes, and conclude that these unlimited powers will never be abused, because themselves are not disposed to abuse them. They should look forward to a time, and that not a distant one, when a corruption in this, as in the country from which we derive our origin, will have seized the heads of government, and be spread by them through the body of the people ; when they will purchase the voices of the people, and make them pay the price. Human nature is the same on every side of the Atlantic, and will be alike influenced by the same causes. The time to guard against corruption and tyranny, is before they shall have gotten hold of us. It is better to keep the wolf out of the fold, than to trust to drawing his teeth and talons after he shall have entered. To render these considerations the more cogent, we must observe in addition :

5. That the ordinary legislature may alter the constitution itself. On the discontinuance of assemblies, it became necessary to substitute in their place some other body, competent to the ordinary business of government, and to the calling forth the powers of the State for the maintenance of our opposition to Great Britain. Conventions were therefore introduced, consisting of two delegates from each county, meeting together and forming one house, on the plan of the former house of burgesses, to whose places they succeeded. These were at first chosen anew for every particular session. But in March 1775, they recommended to the people to choose a convention, which should continue in office a year. This was done, accordingly, in April 1775, and in the July following that convention passed an ordinance for the election of delegates in the month of April annually. It is well known, that in July 1775, a separation from Great Britain and establishment of republican government, had never yet entered into any person's mind. A convention, therefore, chosen under that ordinance, cannot be said to have been chosen for the purposes which certainly did not exist in the minds of those who passed it. Under this ordinance, at the annual election in April 1776, a convention for the year was chosen. Independence, and the establishment of a new form of government, were not even yet the objects of the people at large. One extract from the pamphlet called Common Sense had appeared in the Virginia papers in February, and copies of the pamphlet itself had got in a few hands. But the idea had not been opened to the mass of the people in April, much less can it be said that they had made up their minds in its favor. So that the electors of April 1776, no more than the legislators of July 1775, not thinking of independence and a perma-

nent republic, could not mean to vest in these delegates powers of establishing them, or any authorities other than those of the ordinary legislature. So far as a temporary organization of government was necessary to render our opposition energetic, so far their organization was valid. But they received in their creation no power but what were given to every legislature before and since. They could not, therefore, pass an act transcendent to the powers of other legislatures. If the present assembly pass an act, and declare it shall be irrevocable by subsequent assemblies, the declaration is merely void, and the act repealable, as other acts are. So far, and no farther authorized, they organized the government by the ordinance entitled a constitution or form of government. It pretends to no higher authority than the other ordinances of the same session; it does not say that it shall be perpetual; that it shall be unalterable by other legislatures; that it shall be transcendent above the powers of those who they knew would have equal power with themselves. Not only the silence of the instrument is a proof they thought it would be alterable, but their own practice also; for this very convention, meeting as a house of delegates in general assembly with the Senate in the autumn of that year, passed acts of assembly in contradiction to their ordinance of government; and every assembly from that time to this has done the same. I am safe, therefore, in the position that the constitution itself is alterable by the ordinary legislature. Though this opinion seems founded on the first elements of common sense, yet is the contrary maintained by some persons. 1. Because, say they, the conventions were vested with every power necessary to make effectual opposition to Great Britain. But to complete this argument, they must go on, and say further, that effectual opposition could not be made to Great Britain without establishing a form of government perpetual and unalterable by the legislature; which is not true. An opposition which at some time or other was to come to an end, could not need a perpetual institution to carry it on; and a government amendable as its defects should be discovered, was as likely to make effectual resistance, as one that should be unalterably wrong. Besides, the assemblies were as much vested with all powers requisite for resistance as the conventions were. If, therefore, these powers included that of modelling the form of government in the one case, they did so in the other. The assemblies then as well as the conventions may model the government; that is, they may alter the ordinance of government. 2. They urge, that if the convention had meant that this instrument should be alterable, as their other ordinances were, they would have called it an ordinance; but they have called it a *constitution,* which, ex vi termini, means " an act above the power of the ordinary legislature." I answer that *constitutio, constitutium, statutum, lex,* are convertible terms. " *Constitutio* dicitur jus quod a principe conditure." " *Constitutium,* quod ab imperatoribus rescriptum statutumve est." " *Statutum,* idem quod lex." Calvini Lexicon juridicum. *Constitution* and *statute* were originally terms of the* civil law, and from thence introduced by ecclesiastics into the English law. Thus in the statute 25 Hen. VIII. c. 19, §. 1, " *Constitutions* and *ordinances"* are used as synonymous. The term *constitution* has many other significations in physics and politics; but in jurisprudence, whenever it is applied to any act of the legislature, it invariably means a statute, law, or ordinance, which is the present case. No inference then of a different meaning can be drawn from the adoption of this title; on the contrary, we might conclude that, by their affixing to it a term synonymous with ordinance or statute. But of what consequence is their meaning, where their power is denied? If they meant to do more than they had power to do, did this give them power? It is not the name, but the authority that renders an act obligatory. Lord Coke says, " an article of the statute, 11 R. II. c. 5, that no person should attempt to revoke any ordinance then made, is repealed, for that such restrainst is against the jurisdiction and power of the parliament." 4. Inst. 42. And again, " though divers parliaments have attempted to restrain subsequent parliaments, yet could they never effect it; for the latter parliament hath ever power to abrogate, suspend, qualify, explain, or make void the former in the

* To bid, to set, was the ancient legislative word of the English. Ll. Hlothari and Eadrici. Ll. Inæ. Ll. Eadwerdi. Ll. Aathelstani.

whole or in any part thereof, notwithstanding any words of restraint, prohibition, or penalty, in the former; for it is a maxim
in the laws of the parliament, quod leges posteriores priores con-
trarias abrogant." 4. Inst. 43. To get rid of the magic supposed to be in the word *constitution*, let us translate it into its
definition as given by those who think it above the power of the
law; and let us suppose the convention, instead of saying, "We
the ordinary legislature, establish a *constitution*," had said, "We
the ordinary legislature, establish an act *above the power of the
ordinary legislature*." Does not this expose the absurdity of
the attempt? 3. But, say they, the people have acquiesced, and
this has given it an authority superior to the laws. It is true
that the people did not rebel against it; and was that a time for
the people to rise in rebellion? Should a prudent acquiescence,
at a critical time, be construed into a confirmation of every illegal thing done during that period? Besides, why should they
rebel? At an annual election they had chosen delegates for the
year, to exercise the ordinary powers of legislation, and to manage the great contest in which they were engaged. These delegates thought the contest would be best managed by an organized
government. They therefore, among others, passed an ordinance
of government. They did not presume to call it perpetual and
unalterable. They well knew they had no power to make it
so; that our choice of them had been for no such purpose, and
at a time when we could have no such purpose in contemplation.
Had an unalterable form of government been meditated, perhaps
we should have chosen a different set of people. There was no
cause then for the people to rise in rebellion. But to what dangerous lengths will this argument lead? Did the acquiescence
of the colonies under the various acts of power exercised by
Great Britain in our infant State, confirm these acts, and so far
invest them with the authority of the people as to render them
unalterable, and our present resistance wrong? On every un-
authoritative exercise of power by the legislature must the people rise in rebellion, or their silence be construed into a surrender of that power to them? If so, how many rebellions should
we have had already? One certainly for every session of as-

sembly. The other States in the union have been of opinion that to render a form of government unalterable by ordinary acts of assembly, the people must delegate persons with special powers. They have accordingly chosen special conventions to form and fix their governments. The individuals then who maintain the contrary opinion in this country, should have the modesty to suppose it possible that they may be wrong, and the rest of America right. But if there be only a possibility of their being wrong, if only a plausible doubt remains of the validity of the ordinance of government, is it not better to remove that doubt by placing it on a bottom which none will dispute? If they be right we shall only have the unnecessary trouble of meeting once in convention. If they be wrong, they expose us to the hazard of having no fundamental rights at all. True it is, this is no time for deliberating on forms of government. While an enemy is within our bowels, the first object is to expel him. But when this shall be done, when peace shall be established, and leisure given us for intrenching within good forms, the rights for which we have bled, let no man be found indolent enough to decline a little more trouble for placing them beyond the reach of question. If anything more be requisite to produce a conviction of the expediency of calling a convention at a proper season to fix our form of government, let it be the reflection:

6. That the assembly exercises a power of determining the quorum of their own body which may legislate for us. After the establishment of the new form they adhered to the *Lex majoris partis*, founded in* common law as well as common right. It is the† natural law of every assembly of men, whose numbers are not fixed by any other law. They continued for some time to require the presence of a majority of their whole number, to pass an act. But the British parliament fixes its own quorum; our former assemblies fixed their own quorum; and one precedent in favor of power is stronger than an hundred against it. The house of delegates, therefore, have‡ lately voted that, during the present dangerous invasion, forty members shall be a house

* Bro. abr. Corporations, 31, 34. Hakewell, 93.
† Puff. Off. hom. l. 2, c. 6, §. 12.   ‡ June 4, 1781.

to proceed to business. They have been moved to this by the fear of not being able to collect a house. But this danger could not authorize them to call that a house which was none ; and if they may fix it at one number, they may at another, till it loses its fundamental character of being a representative body. As this vote expires with the present invasion, it is probable the former rule will be permitted to revive ; because at present no ill is meant. The power, however, of fixing their own quorum has been avowed, and a precedent set. From forty it may be reduced to four, and from four to one ; from a house to a committee, from a committee to a chairman or speaker, and thus an oligarchy or monarchy be substituted under forms supposed to be regular. " Omnia mala exempla ex bonis orta sunt ; sed ubi imperium ad ignaros aut minus bonos pervenit, novum illud exemplum ab dignis et idoneis adindignos et non idoneos fertur." When, therefore, it is considered, that there is no legal obstacle to the assumption by the assembly of all the powers legislative, executive, and judiciary, and that these may come to the hands of the smallest rag of delegation, surely the people will say, and their representatives, while yet they have honest representatives, will advise them to say, that they will not acknowledge as laws any acts not considered and assented to by the major part of their delegates.

In enumerating the defects of the constitution, it would be wrong to count among them what is only the error of particular persons. In December 1776, our circumstances being much distressed, it was proposed in the house of delegates to create a *dictator*, invested with every power legislative, executive, and judiciary, civil and military, of life and of death, over our persons and over our properties ; and in June 1781, again under calamity, the same proposition was repeated, and wanted a few votes only of being passed. One who entered into this contest from a pure love of liberty, and a sense of injured rights, who determined to make every sacrifice, and to meet every danger, for the re-establishment of those rights on a firm basis, who did not mean to expend his blood and substance for the wretched purpose of changing this matter for that, but to place the powers of

governing him in a plurality of hands of his own choice, so that
the corrupt will of no one man might in future oppress him,
must stand confounded and dismayed when he is told, that a
considerable portion of that plurality had mediated the surrender
of them into a single hand, and, in lieu of a limited monarchy,
to deliver him over to a despotic one ! How must we find his
efforts and sacrifices abused and baffled, if he may still, by a
single vote, be laid prostrate at the feet of one man ! In God's
name, from whence have they derived this power ? Is it from
our ancient laws ? None such can be produced. Is it from any
principle in our new constitution expressed or implied ? Every
lineament expressed or implied, is in full opposition to it. Its
fundamental principle is, that the State shall be governed as a
commonwealth. It provides a republican organization, pro-
scribes under the name of *prerogative* the exercise of all powers
undefined by the laws ; places on this basis the whole system of
our laws ; and by consolidating them together, chooses that they
should be left to stand or fall together, never providing for any
circumstances, nor admitting that such could arise, wherein
either should be suspended ; no, not for a moment. Our ancient
laws expressly declare, that those who are but delegates themselves shall not delegate to others powers which require judgment and integrity in their exercise. Or was this proposition
moved on a supposed right in the movers, of abandoning their
posts in a moment of distress ? The same laws forbid the aban-
donment of that post, even on ordinary occasions ; and much
nore a transfer of their powers into other hands and other forms,
without consulting the people. They never admit the idea that
these, like sheep or cattle, may be given from hand to hand without an appeal to their own will. Was it from the necessity of
the case ? Necessities which dissolve a government, do not convey its authority to an oligarchy or a monarchy. They throw
back, into the hands of the people, the powers they had delegated, and leave them as individuals to shift for themselves. A
leader may offer, but not impose himself, nor be imposed on them.
Much less can their necks be submitted to his sword, their breath
to be held at his will or caprice. The necessity which should

operate these tremendous effects should at least be palpable and irresistible. Yet in both instances, where it was feared, or pretended with us, it was belied by the event. It was belied, too, by the preceding experience of our sister States, several of whom had grappled through greater difficulties without abandoning their forms of government. When the proposition was first made, Massachusetts had found even the government of committees sufficient to carry them through an invasion. But we at the time of that proposition, were under no invasion. When the second was made, there had been added to this example those of Rhode Island, New York, New Jersey, and Pennsylvania, in all of which the republican form had been found equal to the task of carrying them through the severest trials. In this State alone did there exist so little virtue, that fear was to be fixed in the hearts of the people, and to become the motive of their exertions, and principle of their government? The very thought alone was treason against the people ; was treason against mankind in general ; as rivetting forever the chains which bow down their necks, by giving to their oppressors a proof, which they would have trumpeted through the universe, of the imbecility of republican government, in times of pressing danger, to shield them from harm. Those who assume the right of giving away the reins of government in any case, must be sure that the herd, whom they hand on to the rods and hatchet of the dictator, will lay their necks on the block when he shall nod to them. But if our assemblies supposed such a recognition in the people, I hope they mistook their character. I am of opinion, that the government, instead of being braced and invigorated for greater exertions under their difficulties, would have been thrown back upon the bungling machinery of county committees for administration, till a convention could have been called, and its wheels again set into regular motion. What a cruel moment was this for creating such an embarrassment, for putting to the proof the attachment of our countrymen to republican government ! Those who meant well, of the advocates of this measure, (and most of them meant well, for I know them personally, had been their fellow-laborer in the common cause, and had often proved the purity of their principles,) had been seduced in their judgment by the example of an ancient republic, whose constitution and circumstances were fundamentally different. They had sought this precedent in the history of Rome, where alone it was to be found, and where at length, too, it had proved fatal. They had taken it from a republic rent by the most bitter factions and tumults, where the government was of a heavy-handed unfeeling aristocracy, over a people ferocious, and rendered desperate by poverty and wretchedness; tumults which could not be allayed under the most trying circumstances, but by the omnipotent hand of a single despot. Their constitution, therefore, allowed a temporary tyrant to be erected, under the name of a dictator; and that temporary tyrant, after a few examples, became perpetual. They misapplied this precedent to a people mild in their dispositions, patient under their trial, united for the public liberty, and affectionate to their leaders. But if from the constitution of the Roman government there resulted to their senate a power of submitting all their rights to the will of one man, does it follow that the assembly of Virginia have the same authority? What clause in our constitution has substituted that of Rome, by way of residuary provision, for all cases not otherwise provided for? Or if they may step *ad libitum* into any other form of government for precedents to rule us by, for what oppression may not a precedent be found in this world of the *ballum omnium in omnia* ? Searching for the foundations of this proposition, I can find none which may pretend a color of right or reason, but the defect before developed, that there being no barrier between the legislative, executive, and judiciary departments, the legislature may seize the whole; that having seized it, and possessing a right to fix their own quorum, they may reduce that quorum to one, whom they may call a chairman, speaker, dictator, or by any other name they please. Our situation is indeed perilous, and I hope my countrymen will be sensible of it, and will apply, at a proper season, the proper remedy; which is a convention to fix the constitution, to amend its defects, to bind up the several branches of government by certain laws, which, when they transgress, their acts shall become nullities; to render unnecessary an appeal to the people, or in other words a rebellion, on every in-fraction of their rights, on the peril that their acquiescence shall be construed into an intention to surrender those rights.

QUERY XIV.

The administration of justice and the description of the laws?

The State is divided into counties. In every county are ap-pointed magistrates, called justices of the peace, usually from eight to thirty or forty in number, in proportion to the size of the county, of the most discreet and honest inhabitants. They are nominated by their fellows, but commissioned by the gover-nor, and act without reward. These magistrates have jurisdic-tion both criminal and civil. If the question before them be a question of law only, they decide on it themselves ; but if it be of fact, or of fact and law combined, it must be referred to a jury. In the latter case, of a combination of law and fact, it is usual for the jurors to decide the fact, and to refer the law aris-ing on it to the decision of the judges. But this division of the subject lies with their discretion only. And if the question re-late to any point of public liberty, or if it be one of those in which the judges may be suspected of bias, the jury undertake to decide both law and fact. If they be mistaken, a decision against right, which is casual only, is less dangerous to the State, and less afflicting to the loser, than one which makes part of a regular and uniform system. In truth, it is better to toss up cross and pile in a cause, than to refer it to a judge whose mind is warped by any motive whatever, in that particular case. But the common sense of twelve honest men gives still a better chance of just decision, than the hazard of cross and pile. These judges execute their process by the sheriff or coroner of the county, or by constables of their own appointment. If any free person commit an offence against the commonwealth, if it be below the degree of felony, he is bound by a justice to appear before their court, to answer it on an indictment or information.

If it amount to felony, he is committed to jail; a court of these justices is called; if they on examination think him guilty, they send him to the jail of the general court, before which court he is to be tried first by a grand jury of twenty-four, of whom thirteen must concur in opinion; if they find him guilty, he is then tried by a jury of twelve men of the county where the offence was committed, and by their verdict, which must be unanimous, he is acquitted or condemned without appeal. If the criminal be a slave, the trial by the county court is final. In every case, however, except that of high treason, there resides in the governor a power of pardon. In high treason the pardon can only flow from the general assembly. In civil matters these justices have jurisdiction in all cases of whatever value, not appertaining to the department of the admiralty. This jurisdiction is twofold. If the matter in dispute be of less value than four dollars and one-sixth, a single member may try it at any time and place within his county, and may award execution on the goods of the party cast. If it be of that or greater value, it is determinable before the county court, which consists of four at the least of those justices and assembles at the court-house of the county on a certain day in every month. From their determination, if the matter be of the value of ten pounds sterling, or concern the title or bounds of lands, an appeal lies to one of the superior courts.

There are three or four superior courts, to wit, the high court of chancery, the general court, and the court of admiralty. The first and second of these receive appeals from the county courts, and also have original jurisdiction, where the subject of controversy is of the value of ten pounds sterling, or where it concerns the title or bounds of lands. The jurisdiction of the admiralty is original altogether. The high court of chancery is composed of three judges; the general court of five, and the court of admiralty of three. The two first hold their sessions at Richmond at stated times, the chancery twice in the year, and the general court twice for business civil and criminal, and twice more for criminal only. The court of admiralty sits at Williamsburg whenever a controversy arises.

There is one supreme court, called the court of appeals, composed of the judges of the three superior courts, assembling twice a year at stated times at Richmond. This court receives appeals in all civil cases from each of the superior courts, and determines them finally. But it has no original jurisdiction.

If a controversy arise between two foreigners of a nation in alliance with the United States, it is decided by the Consul for their State, or, if both parties choose it, by the ordinary courts of justice. If one of the parties only be such a foreigner, it is triable before the courts of justice of the country. But if it shall have been instituted in a county court, the foreigner may remove it into the general court, or court of chancery, who are to determine it at their first sessions, as they must also do if it be originally commenced before them. In cases of life and death, such foreigners have a right to be tried by a jury, the one-half foreigners, the other natives.

All public accounts are settled with a board of auditors, consisting of three members appointed by the general assembly, any two of whom may act. But an individual, dissatisfied with the determination of that board, may carry his case into the proper superior court.

A description of the laws.

The general assembly was constituted, as has been already shown, by letters-patent of March the 9th, 1607, in the fourth year of the reign of James the first. The laws of England seem to have been adopted by consent of the settlers, which might easily enough be done whilst they were few and living all together. Of such adoption, however, we have no other proof than their practice till the year 1661, when they were expressly adopted by an act of the assembly, except so far as "a difference of condition" rendered them inapplicable. Under this adoption, the rule, in our courts of judicature was, that the common law of England, and the general statutes previous to the fourth of James, were in force here; but that no subsequent statutes were, *unless we were named in them,* said the judges and other partisans of the crown, but *named or not named,* said those who reflected freely. It will be unnecessary to attempt a description of the laws of England, as that may be found in English publications. To those which were established here, by the adoption of the legislature, have been since added a number of acts of assembly passed during the monarchy, and ordinances of convention and acts of assembly enacted since the establishment of the republic. The following variations from the British model are perhaps worthy of being specified :

Debtors unable to pay their debts, and making faithful delivery of their whole effects, are released from confinement, and their persons forever discharged from restraint for such previous debts ; but any property they may afterwards acquire will be subject to their creditors.

The poor unable to support themselves, are maintained by an assessment on the tytheable persons in their parish. This assessment is levied and administered by twelve persons in each parish, called vestrymen, originally chosen by the housekeepers of the parish, but afterwards filling vacancies in their own body by their own choice. These are usually the most discreet farmers, so distributed through their parish, that every part of it may be under the immediate eye of some one of them. They are well acquainted with the details and economy of private life, and they find sufficient inducements to execute their charge well, in their philanthropy, in the approbation of their neighbors, and the distinction which that gives them. The poor who have neither property, friends, nor strength to labor, are boarded in the houses of good farmers, to whom a stipulated sum is annually paid. To those who are able to help themselves a little, or have friends from whom they derive some succors, inadequate however to their full maintenance, supplementary aids are given which enable them to live comfortably in their own houses, or in the nouses of their friends. Vagabonds without visible property or vocation, are placed in work houses, where they are well clothed, fed, lodged, and made to labor. Nearly the same method of providing for the poor prevails through all our States ; and from Savannah to Portsmouth you will seldom meet a beggar. In the large towns, indeed, they sometimes present themselves. These are usually foreigners, who have never obtained a settlement in any parish. I never yet saw a native American begging in the streets or highways. A subsistence is easily gained here, and if, by misfortunes, they are thrown on the charities of the world, those provided by their own country are so comfortable and so certain, that they never think of relinquishing them to become strolling beggars. Their situation too, when sick, in the family of a good farmer, where every member is emulous to do them kind offices, where they are visited by all the neighbors, who bring them the little rarities which their sickly appetites may crave, and who take by rotation the nightly watch over them, when their condition requires it, is without comparison better than in a general hospital, where the sick, the dying and the dead are crammed together in the same rooms, and often in the same beds. The disadvantages, inseparable from general hospitals, are such as can never be counterpoised by all the regularities of medicine and regimen. Nature and kind nursing save a much greater proportion in our plain way, at a smaller expense, and with less abuse. One branch only of hospital institution is wanting with us; that is, a general establishment for those laboring under difficult cases of chirurgery. The aids of this art are not equivocal. But an able chirurgeon cannot be had in every parish. Such a receptacle should therefore be provided for those patients; but no others should be admitted.

Marriages must be solemnized either on special license, granted by the first magistrate of the county, on proof of the consent of the parent or guardian of either party under age, or after solemn publication, on three several Sundays, at some place of religious worship, in the parishes where the parties reside. The act of solemnization may be by the minister of any society of Christians, who shall have been previously licensed for this purpose by the court of the county. Quakers and Menonists, however, are exempted from all these conditions, and marriage among them is to be solemnized by the society itself.

A foreigner of any nation, not in open war with us, becomes naturalized by removing to the State to reside, and taking an oath of fidelity; and thereupon acquires every right of a native citizen; and citizens may divest themselves of that character, by declaring, by solemn deed, or in open court, that they mean to expatriate themselves, and no longer to be citizens of this State.

Conveyances of land must be registered in the court of the county wherein they lie, or in the general court, or they are void, as to creditors, and subsequent purchasers.

Slaves pass by descent and dower as lands do. Where the descent is from a parent, the heir is bound to pay an equal share of their value in money to each of their brothers and sisters.

Slaves, as well as lands, were entailable during the monarchy; but, by an act of the first republican assembly, all donees in tail, present and future, were vested with the absolute dominion of the entailed subject.

Bills of exchange, being protested, carry ten per cent. interest from their date.

No person is allowed, in any other case, to take more than five per cent. per annum simple interest for the loan of moneys.

Gaming debts are made void, and moneys actually paid to discharge such debts (if they exceed forty shillings) may be recovered by the payer within three months, or by any other person afterwards.

Tobacco, flour, beef, pork, tar, pitch, and turpentine, must be inspected by persons publicly appointed, before they can be exported.

The erecting iron-works and mills is encouraged by many privileges; with necessary cautions however to prevent their dams from obstructing the navigation of the water-courses. The general assembly have on several occasions shown a great desire to encourage the opening the great falls of James and Potomac rivers. As yet, however, neither of these have been effected.

The laws have also descended to the preservation and improvement of the races of useful animals, such as horses, cattle, deer; to the extirpation of those which are noxious, as wolves, squirrels, crows, blackbirds; and to the guarding our citizens against infectious disorders, by obliging suspected vessels coming into the State, to perform quarantine, and by regulating the conduct of persons having such disorders within the State.

The mode of acquiring lands, in the earliest times of our settlement, was by petition to the general assembly. If the lands prayed for were already cleared of the Indian title, and the assembly thought the prayer reasonable, they passed the property by their vote to the petitioner. But if they had not yet been ceded by the Indians, it was necessary that the petitioner should previously purchase their right. This purchase the assembly verified, by inquiries of the Indian proprietors; and being satisfied of its reality and fairness, proceeded further to examine the reasonableness of the petition, and its consistence with policy; and according to the result, either granted or rejected the petition. The company also sometimes, though very rarely, granted lands, independently of the general assembly. As the colony increased, and individual applications for land multiplied, it was found to give too much occupation to the general assembly to inquire into and execute the grant in every special case. They therefore thought it better to establish general rules, according to which all grants should be made, and to leave to the governor the execution of them, under these rules. This they did by what have been usually called the land laws, amending them from time to time, as their defects were developed. According to these laws, when an individual wished a portion of unappropriated land, he was to locate and survey it by a public officer, appointed for that purpose; its breadth was to bear a certain proportion to its length: the grant was to be executed by the governor; and the lands were to be improved in a certain manner, within a given time. From these regulations there resulted to the State a sole and exclusive power of taking conveyances of the Indian right of soil; since, according to them an Indian conveyance alone could give no right to an individual, which the laws would acknowledge. The State, or the crown, thereafter, made general purchases of the Indians from time to time, and the governor parcelled them out by special grants, conformable to the rules before described, which it was not in his power, or in that of the crown, to dispense with. Grants, unaccompanied by their proper legal circumstances, were set aside regularly by *fiere facias*, or by bill in chancery. Since the establishment of our new government, this order of things is but little changed

An individual, wishing to appropriate to himself lands still unappropriated by any other, pays to the public treasurer a sum of money proportioned to the quantity he wants. He carries the treasurer's receipt to the auditors of public accounts, who thereupon debit the treasurer with the sum, and order the register of the land-office to give the party a warrant for his land. With this warrant from the register, he goes to the surveyor of the county where the land lies on which he has cast his eye. The surveyor lays it off for him, gives him its exact description, in the form of a certificate, which certificate he returns to the land office, where a grant is made out, and is signed by the governor. This vests in him a perfect dominion in his lands, transmissible to whom he pleases by deed or will, or by descent to his heirs, if he die intestate.

Many of the laws which were in force during the monarchy being relative merely to that form of government, or inculcating principles inconsistent with republicanism, the first assembly which met after the establishment of the commonwealth appointed a committee to revise the whole code, to reduce it into proper form and volume, and report it to the assembly. This work has been executed by three gentlemen, and reported ; but probably will not be taken up till a restoration of peace shall leave to the legislature leisure to go through such a work.

The plan of the revisal was this. The common law of England, by which is meant, that part of the English law which was anterior to the date of the oldest statutes extant, is made the basis of the work. It was thought dangerous to attempt to reduce it to a text ; it was therefore left to be collected from the usual monuments of it. Necessary alterations in that, and so much of the whole body of the British statutes, and of acts of assembly, as were thought proper to be retained, were digested into one hundred and twenty-six new acts, in which simplicity of style was aimed at, as far as was safe. The following are the most remarkable alterations proposed :

To change the rules of descent, so as that the lands of any person dying intestate shall be divisible equally among all his children, or other representatives, in equal degree.

To make slaves distributable among the next of kin, as othe. movables.

To have all public expenses, whether of the general treasury, or of a parish or county, (as for the maintenance of the poor, building bridges, court-houses, &c.,) supplied by assessment on the citizens, in proportion to their property.

To hire undertakers for keeping the public roads in repair, and indemnify individuals through whose lands new roads shall be opened.

To define with precision the rules whereby aliens should become citizens, and citizens make themselves aliens.

To establish religious freedom on the broadest bottom.

To emancipate all slaves born after the passing the act. The bill reported by the revisers does not itself contain this proposition; but an amendment containing it was prepared, to be offered to the legislature whenever the bill should be taken up, and farther directing, that they should continue with their parents to a certain age, then to be brought up, at the public expense, to tillage, arts, or sciences, according to their geniuses, till the females should be eighteen, and the males twenty-one years of age, when they should be colonized to such place as the circumstances of the time should render most proper, sending them out with arms, implements of household and of the handicraft arts, seeds, pairs of the useful domestic animals, &c., to declare them a free and independent people, and extend to them our alliance and protection, till they have acquired strength; and to send vessels at the same time to other parts of the world for an equal number of white inhabitants; to induce them to migrate hither, proper encouragements were to be proposed. It will probably be asked, Why not retain and incorporate the blacks into the State, and thus save the expense of supplying by importation of white settlers, the vacancies they will leave? Deep-rooted prejudices entertained by the whites; ten thousand recollections, by the blacks, of the injuries they have sustained; new provocations; the real distinctions which nature has made; and many other circumstances, will divide us into parties, and produce convulsions, which will probably never end but in the extermination of the one or the other race. To these objections, which are political, may be added others, which are physical and moral. The first difference which strikes us is that of color. Whether the black of the negro resides in the reticular membrane between the skin and scarf-skin, or in the scarf-skin itself; whether it proceeds from the color of the blood, the color of the bile, or from that of some other secretion, the difference is fixed in nature, and is as real as if its seat and cause were better known to us. And is this difference of no importance? Is it not the foundation of a greater or less share of beauty in the two races? Are not the fine mixtures of red and white, the expressions of every passion by greater or less suffusions of color in the one, preferable to that eternal monotony, which reigns in the countenances, that immovable veil of black which covers the emotions of the other race? Add to these, flowing hair, a more elegant symmetry of form, their own judgment in favor of the whites, declared by their preference of them, as uniformly as is the preference of the Oranootan for the black woman over those of his own species. The circumstance of superior beauty, is thought worthy attention in the propagation of our horses, dogs, and other domestic animals; why not in that of man? Besides those of color, figure, and hair, there are other physical distinctions proving a difference of race. They have less hair on the face and body. They secrete less by the kidneys, and more by the glands of the skin, which gives them a very strong and disagreeable odor. This greater degree of transpiration, renders them more tolerant of heat, and less so of cold than the whites. Perhaps, too, a difference of structure in the pulminary apparatus, which a late ingenious* experimentalist has discovered to be the principal regulator of animal heat, may have disabled them from extricating, in the act of inspiration, so much of that fluid from the outer air, or obliged them in expiration, to part with more of it. They seem to require less sleep. A black after hard labor through the day, will be induced by the slightest amusements to sit up till midnight, or later, though knowing he must be out with the first dawn of the morning. They are at least as brave,

* Crawford.

and more adventuresome. But this may perhaps proceed from a
want of forethought, which prevents their seeing a danger till it
be present. When present, they do not go through it with more
coolness or steadiness than the whites. They are more ardent
after their female; but love seems with them to be more an eager
desire, than a tender delicate mixture of sentiment and sensation.
Their griefs are transient. Those numberless afflictions, which
render it doubtful whether heaven has given life to us in mercy
or in wrath, are less felt, and sooner forgotten with them. In
general, their existence appears to participate more of sensation
than reflection. To this must be ascribed their disposition to
sleep when abstracted from their diversions, and unemployed in
labor. An animal whose body is at rest, and who does not reflect, must be disposed to sleep of course. Comparing them
by their faculties of memory, reason, and imagination, it appears
to me that in memory they are equal to the whites; in reason
much inferior, as I think one could scarcely be found capable of
tracing and comprehending the investigations of Euclid; and
that in imagination they are dull, tasteless, and anomalous. It
would be unfair to follow them to Africa for this investigation.
We will consider them here, on the same stage with the whites,
and where the facts are not apochryphal on which a judgment
is to be formed. It will be right to make great allowances for
the difference of condition, of education, of conversation, of the
sphere in which they move. Many millions of them have been
brought to, and born in America. Most of them, indeed, have
been confined to tillage, to their own homes, and their own society; yet many have been so situated, that they might have
availed themselves of the conversation of their masters; many
have been brought up to the handicraft arts, and from that circumstance have always been associated with the whites. Some
have been liberally educated, and all have lived in countries
where the arts and sciences are cultivated to a considerable degree, and all have had before their eyes samples of the best
works from abroad. The Indians, with no advantages of this
kind, will often carve figures on their pipes not destitute of design and merit. They will crayon out an animal, a plant. or a

country, so as to prove the existence of a germ in their minds which only wants cultivation. They astonish you with strokes of the most sublime oratory ; such as prove their reason and sentiment strong, their imagination glowing and elevated. But never yet could I find that a black had uttered a thought above the level of plain narration ; never saw even an elementary trait of painting or sculpture. In music they are more generally gifted than the whites with accurate ears for tune and time, and they have been found capable of imagining a small catch.* Whether they will be equal to the composition of a more extensive run of melody, or of complicated harmony, is yet to be proved. Misery is often the parent of the most affecting touches in poetry. Among the blacks is misery enough, God knows, but no poetry. Love is the peculiar œstrum of the poet. Their love is ardent, but it kindles the senses only, not the imagination. Religion, indeed, has produced a Phyllis Whately ; but it could not produce a poet. The compositions published under her name are below the dignity of criticism. The heroes of the Dunciad are to her, as Hercules to the author of that poem. Ignatius Sancho has approached nearer to merit in composition ; yet his letters do more honor to the heart than the head. They breathe the purest effusions of friendship and general philanthropy, and show how great a degree of the latter may be compounded with strong religious zeal. He is often happy in the turn of his compliments, and his style is easy and familiar, except when he affects a Shandean fabrication of words. But his imagination is wild and extravagant, escapes incessantly from every restraint of reason and taste, and, in the course of its vagaries, leaves a tract of thought as incoherent and eccentric, as is the course of a meteor through the sky. His subjects should often have led him to a process of sober reasoning ; yet we find him always substituting sentiment for demonstration. Upon the whole, though we admit him to the first place among those of his own color who have presented themselves to the

* The instrument proper to them is the Banjar, which they brought hither from Africa, and which is the original of the guitar, its chords being precisely the four lower chords of the guitar.

public judgment, yet when we compare him with the writers of the race among whom he lived and particularly with the epistolary class in which he has taken his own stand, we are compelled to enrol him at the bottom of the column. This criticism supposes the letters published under his name to be genuine, and to have received amendment from no other hand ; points which would not be of easy investigation. The improvement of the blacks in body and mind, in the first instance of their mixture with the whites, has been observed by every one, and proves that their inferiority is not the effect merely of their condition of life. We know that among the Romans, about the Augustan age especially, the condition of their slaves was much more deplorable than that of the blacks on the continent of America. The two sexes were confined in separate apartments, because to raise a child cost the master more than to buy one. Cato, for a very restricted indulgence to his slaves,in this particular*, took from them a certain price. But in this country the slaves multiply as fast as the free inhabitants. Their situation and manners place the commerce between the two sexes almost without restraint. The same Cato, on a principle of economy, always sold his sick and superannuated slaves. He gives it as a standing precept to a master visiting his farm, to sell his old oxen, old wagons, old tools, old and diseased servants, and everything else become useless. " Vendat boves vetulos, plaustrum vetus, feramenta vetera, servum senem, servum mòrbosum, et si quid aliud supersit vendat." Cato de re rusticâ, c. 2. The American slaves cannot enumerate this among the injuries and insults they receive. It was the common practice to expose in the island Æsculapius, in the Tyber, diseased slaves whose cure was like to become tedious.† The emperor Claudius, by an edict, gave freedom to such of them as should recover, and first declared that if any person chose to kill rather than to expose them, it should not be deemed homicide. The exposing them is a crime of which no instance has existed with us ; and were it to be followed by death, it would be punished capitally. We are told of a certain

* Tous doulous etaxen örismenou nomesmatos homilein tais therapainsin.— Plutarch. Cato. † Suet. Claud. 25.

Vedius Pollio, who, in the presence of Augustus, would have given a slave as food to his fish, for having broken a glass. With the Romans, the regular method of taking the evidence of their slaves was under torture. Here it has been thought better never to resort to their evidence. When a master was murdered, all his slaves, in the same house, or within hearing, were condemned to death. Here punishment falls on the guilty only, and as precise proof is required against him as against a freeman. Yet notwithstanding these and other discouraging circumstances among the Romans, their slaves were often their rarest artists. They excelled too in science, insomuch as to be usually employed as tutors to their master's children. Epictetus, Terence, and Phædrus, were slaves. But they were of the race of whites. It is not their condition then, but nature, which has produced the distinction. Whether further observation will or will not verify the conjecture, that nature has been less bountiful to them in the endowments of the head, I believe that in those of the heart she will be found to have done them justice. That disposition to theft with which they have been branded, must be ascribed to their situation, and not to any depravity of the moral sense. The man in whose favor no laws of property exist, probably feels himself less bound to respect those made in favor of others. When arguing for ourselves, we lay it down as a fundamental, that laws, to be just, must give a reciprocation of right ; that, without this, they are mere arbitrary rules of conduct, founded in force, and not in conscience ; and it is a problem which I give to the master to solve, whether the religious precepts against the violation of property were not framed for him as well as his slave ? And whether the slave may not as justifiably take a little from one who has taken all from him, as he may slay one who would slay him ? That a change in the relations in which a man is placed should change his ideas of moral right or wrong, is neither new, nor peculiar to the color of the blacks. Homer tells us it was so two thousand six hundred years ago.

'Emisu, ger t' aretes apoainutai euruopa Zeus
Haneros, eut' an min kata doulion ema elesin.
Odd. 17, 323.

> Jove fix'd it certain, that whatever day
> Makes man a slave, takes half his worth away.

But the slaves of which Homer speaks were whites. Notwithstanding these considerations which must weaken their respect for the laws of property, we find among them numerous instances of the most rigid integrity, and as many as among their better instructed masters, of benevolence, gratitude, and unshaken fidelity. The opinion that they are inferior in the faculties of reason and imagination, must be hazarded with great diffidence. To justify a general conclusion, requires many observations, even where the subject may be submitted to the anatomical knife, to optical glasses, to analysis by fire or by solvents. How much more then where it is a faculty, not a substance, we are examining; where it eludes the research of all the senses; where the conditions of its existence are various and variously combined; where the effects of those which are present or absent bid defiance to calculation; let me add too, as a circumstance of great tenderness, where our conclusion would degrade a whole race of men from the rank in the scale of beings which their Creater may perhaps have given them. To our reproach it must be said, that though for a century and a half we have had under our eyes the races of black and of red men, they have never yet been viewed by us as subjects of natural history. I advance it, therefore, as a suspicion only, that the blacks, whether originally a distinct race, or made distinct by time and circumstances, are inferior to the whites in the endowments both of body and mind. It is not against experience to suppose that different species of the same genus, or varieties of the same species, may possess different qualifications. Will not a lover of natural history then, one who views the gradations in all the races of animals with the eye of philosophy, excuse an effort to keep those in the department of man as distinct as nature has formed them? This unfortunate difference of color, and perhaps of faculty, is a powerful obstacle to the emancipation of these people. Many of their advocates, while they wish to vindicate the liberty of human nature, are anxious also to preserve its dignity and beauty. Some of these, embarrassed by the question, " What further is to be done with them ?" join themselvse in opposition with those who are actuated by sordid avarice only. Among the Romans emancipation required but one effort. The slave, when made free, might mix with, without staining the blood of his master. But with us a second is necessary, un-known to history. When freed, he is to be removed beyond the each of mixture.

The revised code further proposes to proportion crimes and punishments. This is attempted on the following scale :

ı. Crimes whose punishment extends to Life.
    1. High treason. Death by hanging.
        Forfeiture of lands and goods to the commonwealth.
    2. Petty treason. Death by hanging. Dissection.
        Forfeiture of half the lands and goods to the representatives of the party slain.
    3. Murder. 1. By poison. Death by poison.
                Forfeiture of one-half, as before.
          2. In duel. Death by hanging. Gibbeting, if the challenger.
                Forfeiture of one-half as before, unless it be the party challenged, then the forfeiture is to the commonwealth.
          3. In any other way. Death by hanging.
                Forfeiture of one-half as before.
    4. Manslaughter. The second offence is murder.
II. Crimes whose punishment goes to Limb.
    1. Rape......
    2. Sodomy ...   } Dismemberment.
    3. Maiming...
    4. Disfiguring } Retaliation, and the forfeiture of half of the lands and goods to the sufferer.

III. Crimes punishable by Labor.

1. Manslaughter, 1st offence.	Labor VII. years for the public.		Forfeiture of half, as in murder.
2. Counterfeiting money.	Labor VI. years	..	Forfeiture of lands and goods to the commonwealth.
3. Arson. 4. Asportation of vessels.	} Labor V. years	..	Reparation three-fold.
5. Robbery. 6. Burglary.	} Labor IV. years	..	Reparation double.
7. House-breaking. 8. Horse-stealing.	} Labor III. years	..	Reparation.
9. Grand larceny.	Labor II. years	..	Reparation. Pillory.
10. Petty larceny.	Labor I. year	..	Reparation. Pillory. Stripes.
11. Pretensions to witchcraft, &c.	Ducking.		
12. Excusable homicide. 13. Suicide. 14. Apostasy. Heresy.	} To be pitied, not punished.		

Pardon and privilege of clergy are proposed to be abolished ; but if the verdict be against the defendant, the court in their discretion may allow a new trial. No attainder to cause a cor-ruption of blood, or forfeiture of dower. Slaves guilty of of-fences punishable in others by labor, to be transported to Africa, or elsewhere, as the circumstances of the time admit, there to be continued in slavery. A rigorous regimen proposed for those condemned to labor.

Another object of the revisal is, to diffuse knowledge more

generally through the mass of the people. This bill proposes to lay off every county into small districts of five or six miles square, called hundreds, and in each of them to establish a school for teaching, reading, writing, and arithmetic. The tutor to be supported by the hundred, and every person in it entitled to send their children three years gratis, and as much longer as they please, paying for it. These schools to be under a visitor who is annually to choose the boy of best genius in the school, of those whose parents are too poor to give them further education, and to send him forward to one of the grammar schools, of which twenty are proposed to be erected in different parts of the country, for teaching Greek, Latin, Geography, and the higher branches of numerical arithmetic. Of the boys thus sent in one year, trial is to be made at the grammar schools one or two years, and the best genius of the whole selected, and continued six years, and the residue dismissed. By this means twenty of the best geniuses will be raked from the rubbish annually, and be instructed, at the public expense, so far as the grammar schools go. At the end of six years instruction, one half are to be discontinued (from among whom the grammar schools will probably be supplied with future masters) ; and the other half, who are to be chosen for the superiority of their parts and disposition, are to be sent and continued three years in the study of such sciences as they shall choose, at William and Mary college, the plan of which is proposed to be enlarged, as will be hereafter explained, and extended to all the useful sciences. The ultimate result of the whole scheme of education would be the teaching all the children of the State reading, writing, and common arithmetic ; turning out ten annually, of superior genius, well taught in Greek, Latin, Geography, and the higher branches of arithmetic ; turning out ten others annually, of still superior parts, who, to those branches of learning, shall have added such of the sciences as their genius shall have led them to ; the furnishing to the wealthier part of the people convenient schools at which their children may be educated at their own expense. The general objects of this law are to provide an education adapted to the years, to the capacity, and the condition of every one, and directed to their freedom and happiness. Specific details were not proper for the law. These must be the business of the vistors entrusted with its execution. The first stage of this education being the schools of the hundreds, wherein the great mass of the people will receive their instruction, the principal foundations of future order will be laid here. Instead, therefore, of putting the Bible and Testament into the hands of the children at an age when their judgments are not sufficiently matured for religious inquiries, their memories may here be stored with the most useful facts from Grecian, Roman, European and American history. The first elements of morality too may be instilled into their minds; such as, when further developed as their judgments advance in strength, may teach them how to work out their own greatest happiness, by showing them that it does not depend on the condition of life in which chance has placed them, but is always the result of a good conscience, good health, occupation, and freedom in all just pursuits. Those whom either the wealth of their parents or the adoption of the State shall destine to higher degrees of learning, will go on to the grammar schools, which constitute the next stage, there to be instructed in the languages. The learning Greek and Latin, I am told, is going into disuse in Europe. I know not what their manners and occupations may call for; but it would be very ill-judged in us to follow their example in this instance. There is a certain period of life, say from eight to fifteen or sixteen years of age, when the mind like the body is not yet firm enough for laborious and close operations. If applied to such, it falls an early victim to premature exertion; exhibiting, indeed, at first, in these young and tender subjects, the flattering appearance of their being men while they are yet children, but ending in reducing them to be children when they should be men. The memory is then most susceptible and tenacious of impressions; and the learning of languages being chiefly a work of memory, it seems precisely fitted to the powers of this period, which is long enough too for acquiring the most useful languages, ancient and modern. I do not pretend that language is science. It is only an instrument for the attainment of science. But that time is not lost which is employed in providing tools for future operation; more especially as in this case the books put into the hands of the youth for this purpose may be such as will at the same time impress their minds with useful facts and good principles. If this period be suffered to pass in idleness, the mind becomes lethargic and impotent, as would the body it inhabits if unexercised during the same time. The sympathy between body and mind during their rise, progress and decline, is too strict and obvious to endanger our being missed while we reason from the one to the other. As soon as they are of sufficient age, it is supposed they will be sent on from the grammar schools to the university, which constitutes our third and last stage, there to study those sciences which may be adapted to their views. By that part of our plan which prescribes the selection of the youths of genius from among the classes of the poor, we hope to avail the State of those talents which nature has sown as liberally among the poor as the rich, but which perish without use, if not sought for and cultivated. But of the views of this law none is more important, none more legitimate, than that of rendering the people the safe, as they are the ultimate, guardians of their own liberty. For this purpose the reading in the first stage, where *they* will receive their whole education, is proposed, as has been said, to be chiefly historical. History, by apprizing them of the past, will enable them to judge of the future; it will avail them of the experience of other times and other nations; it will qualify them as judges of the actions and designs of men; it will enable them to know ambition under every disguise it may assume; and knowing it, to defeat its views. In every government on earth is some trace of human weakness, some germ of corruption and degeneracy, which cunning will discover, and wickedness insensibly open, cultivate and improve. Every government degenerates when trusted to the rulers of the people alone. The people themselves therefore are its only safe depositories. And to render even them safe, their minds must be improved to a certain degree. This indeed is not all that is necessary, though it be essentially necessary. An amendment of our constitution must here come in aid of the public education. The influence over government must be shared among all the people.   If every individual which composes their mass participates of the ultimate authority, the government will be safe ; because the corrupting the whole mass will exceed any private resources of wealth ; and public ones cannot be provided but by levies on the people. In this case every man would have to pay his own price.   The government of Great Britain has been corrupted, because but one man in ten has a right to vote for members of parliament.   The sellers of the government, therefore, get nine-tenths of their price clear.   It has been thought that corruption is restrained by confining the right of suffrage to a few of the wealthier of the people ; but it would be more effectually restrained by an extension of that right to such numbers as would bid defiance to the means of corruption.

Lastly, it is proposed, by a bill in this revisal, to begin a public library and gallery, by laying out a certain sum annually in books, paintings, and statues.

QUERY XV.

The Colleges and Public Establishments, the Roads, Buildings, &c.

The college of William and Mary is the only public seminary of learning in this State.   It was founded in the time of king William and queen Mary, who granted to it twenty thousand acres of land, and a penny a pound duty on certain tobaccoes exported from Virginia and Maryland, which had been levied by the statute of 25 Car. II.   The assembly also gave it, by temporary laws, a duty on liquors imported, and skins and furs exported.   From these resources it received upwards of three thousand pounds *communibus annis*.   The buildings are of brick, sufficient for an indifferent accommodation of perhaps an hundred students.   By its charter it was to be under the government of twenty visitors, who were to be its legislators, and to have a president and six professors, who were incorporated. It was allowed a representative in the general assembly. Under this charter, a professorship of the Greek and Latin languages, a professorship of mathematics, one of moral philosophy, and two of divinity, were established. To these were annexed, for a sixth professorship, a considerable donation by Mr. Boyle, of England, for the instruction of the Indians, and their conversion to Christianity. This was called the professorship of Brafferton, from an estate of that name in England, purchased with the monies given. The admission of the learners of Latin and Greek filled the college with children. This rendering it disagreeable and degrading to young gentlemen already prepared for entering on the sciences, they were discouraged from resorting to it, and thus the schools for mathematics and moral philosophy, which might have been of some service, became of very little. The revenues, too, were exhausted in accommodating those who came only to acquire the rudiments of science. After the present revolution, the visitors, having no power to change those circumstances in the constitution of the college which were fixed by the charter, and being therefore confined in the number of the professorships, undertook to change the objects of the professorships. They excluded the two schools for divinity, and that for the Greek and Latin languages, and substituted others; so that at present they stand thus:

A Professorship for Law and Police;
 Anatomy and Medicine;
 Natural Philosophy and Mathematics;
 Moral Philosophy, the Law of Nature and Nations, the Fine
  Arts;
 Modern Languages;
 For the Brafferton.

And it is proposed, so soon as the legislature shall have leisure to take up this subject, to desire authority from them to increase the number of professorships, as well for the purpose of subdividing those already instituted, as of adding others for other branches of science. To the professorships usually established in the universities of Europe, it would seem proper to add one for the ancient languages and literature of the north, on account of their connection with our own language, laws, customs, and history. The purposes of the Brafferton institution would be better answered by maintaining a perpetual mission among the Indian tribes, the object of which, besides instructing them in the principles of Christianity, as the founder requires, should be to collect their traditions, laws, customs, languages, and other circumstances which might lead to a discovery of their relation with one another, or descent from other nations. When these objects are accomplished with one tribe, the missionary might pass on to another.

The roads are under the government of the county courts, subject to be controlled by the general court. They order new roads to be opened wherever they think them necessary. The inhabitants of the county are by them laid off into precincts, to each of which they allot a convenient portion of the public roads to be kept in repair. Such bridges as may be built without the assistance of artificers, they are to build. If the stream be such as to require a bridge of regular workmanship, the court employs workmen to build it, at the expense of the whole county. If it be too great for the county, application is made to the general assembly, who authorize individuals to build it, and to take a fixed toll from all passengers, or give sanction to such other proposition as to them appears reasonable.

Ferries are admitted only at such places as are particularly pointed out by law, and the rates of ferriage are fixed.

Taverns are licensed by the courts, who fix their rates from time to time.

The private buildings are very rarely constructed of stone or brick, much the greatest portion being of scantling and boards, plastered with lime. It is impossible to devise things more ugly, uncomfortable, and happily more perishable. There are two or three plans, on one of which, according to its size, most of the houses in the State are built. The poorest people build huts of logs, laid horizontally in pens, stopping the interstices with mud. These are warmer in winter, and cooler in summer, than the more expensive construction of scantling and plank. The wealthy are attentive to the raising of vegetables, but very little so to fruits. The poorer people attend to neither, living principally on milk and animal diet. This is the more inexcusable, as the climate requires indispensably a free use of vegetable food, for health as well as comfort, and is very friendly to the raising of fruits. The only public buildings worthy mention are the capitol, the palace, the college, and the hospital for lunatics, all of them in Williamsburg, heretofore the seat of our government. The capitol is a light and airy structure, with a portico in front of two orders, the lower of which, being Doric, is tolerably just in its proportions and ornaments, save only that the intercolonations are too large. The upper is Ionic, much too small for that on which it is mounted, its ornaments not proper to the order, nor proportioned within themselves. It is crowned with a pediment, which is too high for its span. Yet, on the whole, it is the most pleasing piece of architecture we have. The palace is not handsome without, but it is spacious and commodious within, is prettily situated, and with the grounds annexed to it, is capable of being made an elegant seat. The college and hospital are rude, misshapen piles, which, but that they have roofs, would be taken for brick-kilns. There are no other public buildings but churches and court-houses, in which no attempts are made at elegance. Indeed, it would not be easy to execute such an attempt, as a workman could scarcely be found capable of drawing an order. The genius of architecture seems to have shed its maledictions over this land. Buildings are often erected, by individuals, of considerable expense. To give these symmetry and taste, would not increase their cost. It would only change the arrangement of the materials, the form and combination of the members. This would often cost less than the burthen of barbarous ornaments with which these buildings are sometimes charged. But the first principles of the art are unknown, and there exists scarcely a model among us sufficiently chaste to give an idea of them. Architecture being one of the fine arts, and as such within the department of a professor of the college, according to the new arrangement, perhaps a spark may fall on some young subjects of natural taste, kindle up their genius, and produce a reformation in this elegant and useful art. But all we shall do in this way will produce no permanent improvement to our country, while the unhappy prejudice prevails that houses of brick or stone are less wholesome than those of wood. A dew is often observed on the walls of the former in rainy weather, and the most obvious solution is, that the rain has penetrated through these walls. The following facts, however, are sufficient to prove the error of this solution : 1. This dew upon the walls appears when there is no rain, if the state of the atmosphere be moist. 2. It appears upon the partition as well as the exterior walls. 3. So, also, on pavements of brick or stone. 4. It is more copious in proportion as the walls are thicker ; the reverse of which ought to be the case, if this hypothesis were just. If cold water be poured into a vessel of stone, or glass, a dew forms instantly on the outside ; but if it be poured into a vessel of wood, there is no such appearance. It is not supposed, in the first case, that the water has exuded through the glass, but that it is precipitated from the circumambient air ; as the humid particles of vapor, passing from the boiler of an alembic through its refrigerant, are precipitated from the air, in which they are suspended, on the internal surface of the refrigerant. Walls of brick and stone act as the refrigerant in this instance. They are sufficiently cold to condense and precipitate the moisture suspended in the air of the room, when it is heavily charged therewith. But walls of wood are not so. The question then is, whether the air in which this moisture is left floating, or that which is deprived of it, be most wholesome ? In both cases the remedy is easy. A little fire kindled in the room, whenever the air is damp, prevents the precipitation on the walls ; and this practice, found healthy in the warmest as well as coldest seasons, is as necessary in a wooden as in a stone or brick house. I do not mean to say, that the rain never penetrates through walls of brick. On the contrary, I have seen instances of it. But with us it is only through the northern and eastern walls of the house, after a north-easterly storm, this being the only one which continues long enough to force through the walls. This, however, happens too rarely to give a just character of unwholesomeness to such houses. In a house, the walls of which are of well-burnt brick and good mortar, I have seen the rain penetrate through but twice in a dozen or fifteen years. The inhabitants of Europe, who dwell chiefly in houses of stone or brick, are surely as healthy as those of Virginia. These houses have the advantage, too, of being warmer in winter and cooler in summer than those of wood; of being cheaper in their first construction, where lime is convenient, and infinitely more durable. The latter consideration renders it of great importance to eradicate this prejudice from the minds of our countrymen. A country whose buildings are of wood, can never increase in its improvements to any considerable degree. Their duration is highly estimated at fifty years. Every half century then our country becomes a *tabula rasa*, whereon we have to set out anew, as in the first moment of seating it. Whereas when buildings are of durable materials, every new edifice is an actual and permanent acquisition to the State, adding to its value as well as to its ornament.

QUERY XVI.

The measures taken with regard to the estates and possessions of the Rebels, commonly called Tories ?

A tory has been properly defined to be a traitor in thought but not in deed. The only description, by which the laws have endeavored to come at them, was that of non-jurors, or persons refusing to take the oath of fidelity to the State. Persons of this description were at one time subjected to double taxation, at another to treble, and lastly were allowed retribution, and placed on a level with good citizens. It may be mentioned as a proof, both of the lenity of our government, and unanimity of its inhabitants, that though this war has now raged near seven years, not a single execution for treason has taken place.

Under this query I will state the measures which have been adopted as to British property, the owners of which stand on a much fairer footing than the tories. By our laws, the same as the English as in this respect, no alien can hold lands, nor alien enemy maintain an action for money, or other movable thing. Lands acquired or held by aliens become forfeited to the State ; and, on an action by an alien enemy to recover money, or other movable property, the defendant may plead that he is an alien enemy. This extinguishes his right in the hands of the debtor or holder of his movable property. By our separation from Great Britain, British subjects became aliens, and being at war, they were alien enemies. Their lands were of course forfeited, and their debts irrecoverable. The assembly, however, passed laws at various times, for saving their property. They first sequestered their lands, slaves, and other property on their farms in the hands of commissioners, who were mostly the confidential friends or agents of the owners, and directed their clear profits to be paid into the treasury ; and they gave leave to all persons owing debts to British subjects to pay them also into the treasury. The monies so to be brought in were declared to remain the property of the British subject, and if used by the State, were to be repaid, unless an improper conduct in Great Britain should render a detention of it reasonable. Depreciation had at that time, though unacknowledged and unperceived by the whigs, begun in some small degree. Great sums of money were paid in by debtors. At a later period, the assembly, adhering to the political principles which forbid an alien to hold lands in the State, ordered all British property to be sold ; and, become sensible of the real progress of depreciation, and of the losses which would thence occur, if not guarded against, they ordered that the proceeds of the sales should be converted into their then worth in tobacco, subject to the future direction of the legislature. This act has left the question of retribution more problematical. In May, 1780, another act took away the permission to pay into the public treasury debts due to British subjects.

QUERY XVII.

The different religions received into that State?

The first settlers in this country were emigrants from England, of the English Church, just at a point of time when it was flushed with complete victory over the religious of all other persuasions. Possessed, as they became, of the powers of making, administering, and executing the laws, they showed equal intolerance in this country with their Presbyterian brethren, who had emigrated to the northern government. The poor Quakers were flying from persecution in England. They cast their eyes on these new countries as asylums of civil and religious freedom; but they found them free only for the reigning sect. Several acts of the Virginia assembly of 1659, 1662, and 1693, had made it penal in parents to refuse to have their children baptized; had prohibited the unlawful assembling of Quakers; had made it penal for any master of a vessel to bring a Quaker into the State; had ordered those already here, and such as should come thereafter, to be imprisoned till they should abjure the country; provided a milder punishment for their first and second return, but death for their third; had inhibited all persons from suffering their meetings in or near their houses, entertaining them individually, or disposing of books which supported their tenets. If no execution took place here, as did in New England, it was not owing to the moderation of the church, or spirit of the legislature, as may be inferred from the law itself; but to historical circumstances which have not been handed down to us. The Anglicans retained full possession of the country about a century. Other opinions began then to creep in, and the great care of the government to support their own church, having begotten an equal degree of indolence in its clergy, two-thirds of the people had become dissenters at the commencement of the present revolution. The laws, indeed, were still oppressive on them, but the spirit of the one party had subsided into moderation, and of the other had risen to a degree of determination which commanded respect.

The present state of our laws on the subject of religion is this. The convention of May 1776, in their declaration of rights, de-

clared it to be a truth, and a natural right, that the exercise of
religion should be free; but when they proceeded to form on
that declaration the ordinance of government, instead of taking
up every principle declared in the bill of rights, and guarding it
by legislative sanction, they passed over that which asserted our
religious rights, leaving them as they found them. The same
convention, however, when they met as a member of the general
assembly in October, 1776, repealed all *acts of Parliament* which
had rendered criminal the maintaining any opinions in matters
of religion, the forbearing to repair to church, and the exercising
any mode of worship; and suspended the laws giving salaries to
the clergy, which suspension was made perpetual in October,
1779. Statutory oppressions in religion being thus wiped away,
we remain at present under those only imposed by the common
law, or by our own acts of assembly. At the common law,
heresy was a capital offence, punishable by burning. Its definition was left to the ecclesiastical judges, before whom the conviction was, till the statute of the 1 El. c. 1 circumscribed it,
by declaring, that nothing should be deemed heresy, but what
had been so determined by authority of the canonical scriptures, or by one of the four first general councils, or by other
council, having for the grounds of their declaration the express
and plain words of the scriptures. Heresy, thus circumscribed,
being an offence against the common law, our act of assembly
of October 1777, c. 17, gives cognizance of it to the general
court, by declaring that the jurisdiction of that court shall be
general in all matters at the common law. The execution is by
the writ *De hæretico comburendo*. By our own act of assembly
of 1705, c. 30, if a person brought up in the Christian religion
denies the being of a God, or the Trinity, or asserts there are
more gods than one, or denies the Christian religion to be true,
or the scriptures to be of divine authority, he is punishable on
the first offence by incapacity to hold any office or employment
ecclesiastical, civil, or military; on the second by disability to
sue, to take any gift or legacy, to be guardian, executor, or ad-
ministrator, and by three years' imprisonment without bail. A
father's right to the custody of his own children being founded

in law on his right of guardianship, this being taken away, they may of course be severed from him, and put by the authority of a court into more orthodox hands.   This is a summary view of that religious slavery under which a people have been willing to remain, who have lavished their lives and fortunes for the establishment of their civil freedom.   *The error seems not sufficiently eradicated, that the operations of the mind, as well as the acts of the body, are subject to the coercion of the laws.   But our rulers can have no authority over such natural rights, only as we have submitted to them.   The rights of conscience we never submitted, we could not submit.   We are answerable for them to our God.   The legitimate powers of government extend to such acts only as are injurious to others.   But it does me no injury for my neighbor to say there are twenty gods, or no God. It neither picks my pocket nor breaks my leg.   If it be said, his testimony in a court of justice cannot be relied on, reject it then, and be the stigma on him.   Constraint may make him worse by making him a hypocrite, but it will never make him a truer man. It may fix him obstinately in his errors, but will not cure them. Reason and free inquiry are the only effectual agents against error.   Give a loose to them, they will support the true religion by bringing every false one to their tribunal, to the test of their investigation.   They are the natural enemies of error, and of error only.   Had not the Roman government permitted free inquiry, Christianity could never have been introduced.   Had not free inquiry been indulged at the era of the reformation, the corruptions of Christianity could not have been purged away.   If it be restrained now, the present corruptions will be protected, and new ones encouraged.   Was the government to prescribe to us our medicine and diet, our bodies would be in such keeping as our souls are now.   Thus in France the emetic was once forbidden as a medicine, and the potato as an article of food.   Government is just as infallible, too, when it fixes systems in physics. Galileo was sent to the Inquisition for affirming that the earth was a sphere ; the government had declared it to be as flat as a trencher, and Galileo was obliged to abjure his error.   This

* Furneaux passim.

error, however, at length prevailed, the earth became a globe, and Descartes declared it was whirled round its axis by a vortex. The government in which he lived was wise enough to see that this was no question of civil jurisdiction, or we should all have been involved by authority in vortices. In fact, the vortices have been exploded, and the Newtonian principle of gravitation is now more firmly established, on the basis of reason, than it would be were the government to step in, and to make it an article of necessary faith. Reason and experiment have been indulged, and error has fled before them. It is error alone which needs the support of government. Truth can stand by itself. Subject opinion to coercion : whom will you make your inquisitors ? Fallible men ; men governed by bad passions, by private as well as public reasons. And why subject it to coercion ? To produce uniformity. But is uniformity of opinion desirable ? No more than of face and stature. Introduce the bed of Procrustes then, and as there is danger that the large men may beat the small, make us all of a size, by lopping the former and stretching the latter. Difference of opinion is advantageous in religion. The several sects perform the office of a *censor morum* over such other. Is uniformity attainable ? Millions of innocent men, women, and children, since the introduction of Christianity, have been burnt, tortured, fined, imprisoned ; yet we have not advanced one inch towards uniformity. What has been the effect of coercion ? To make one half the world fools, and the other half hypocrites. To support roguery and error all over the earth. Let us reflect that it is inhabited by a thousand millions of people. That these profess probably a thousand different systems of religion. That ours is but one of that thousand. That if there be but one right, and ours that one, we should wish to see the nine hundred and ninety-nine wandering sects gathered into the fold of truth. But against such a majority we cannot effect this by force. Reason and persuasion are the only practicable instruments. To make way for these, free inquiry must be indulged ; and how can we wish others to indulge it while we refuse it ourselves. But every State, says an inquisitor, has established some religion. No two, say I, have established the same. Is this a proof of the infallibility of establishments? Our sister States of Pennsylvania and New York, however, have long subsisted without any establishment at all. The experiment was new and doubtful when they made it. It has answered beyond conception. They flourish infinitely. Religion is well supported; of various kinds, indeed, but all good enough; all sufficient to preserve peace and order; or if a sect arises, whose tenets would subvert morals, good sense has fair play, and reasons and laughs it out of doors, without suffering the State to be troubled with it. They do not hang more malefactors than we do. They are not more disturbed with religious dissensions. On the contrary, their harmony is unparalleled, and can be ascribed to nothing but their unbounded tolerance, because there is no other circumstance in which they differ from every nation on earth. They have made the happy discovery, that the way to silence religious disputes, is to take no notice of them. Let us too give this experiment fair play, and get rid, while we may, of those tyrannical laws. It is true, we are as yet secured against them by the spirit of the times. I doubt whether the people of this country would suffer an execution for heresy, or a three years' imprisonment for not comprehending the mysteries of the Trinity. But is the spirit of the people an infallible, a permanent reliance? Is it government? Is this the kind of protection we receive in return for the rights we give up? Besides, the spirit of the times may altar, will altar. Our rulers will become corrupt, our people careless. A single zealot may commence persecutor, and better men be his victims. It can never be too often repeated, that the time for fixing every essential right on a legal basis is while our rulers are honest, and ourselves united. From the conclusion of this war we shall be going down hill. It will not then be necessary to resort every moment to the people for support. They will be forgotten, therefore, and their rights disregarded. They will forget themselves, but in the sole faculty of making money, and will never think of uniting to effect a due respect for their rights. The shackles, therefore, which shall not be knocked off at the conclusion of this war, will remain on us long, will be made heavier and heavier, till our rights shall revive or expire in a convulsion.

QUERY XVIII.

The particular customs and manners that may happen to be received in that State?

It is difficult to determine on the standard by which the manners of a nation may be tried, whether *catholic* or *particular*. It is more difficult for a native to bring to that standard the manners of his own nation, familiarized to him by habit.   There must doubtless be an unhappy influence on the manners of our people produced by the existence of slavery among us.   The whole commerce between master and slave is a perpetual exercise of the most boisterous passions, the most unremitting despotism on the one part, and degrading submissions on the other.   Our children see this, and learn to imitate it; for man is an imitative animal.   This quality is the germ of all education in him.   From his cradle to his grave he is learning to do what he sees others do.   If a parent could find no motive either in his philanthropy or his self-love, for restraining the intemperance of passion towards his slave, it should always be a sufficient one that his child is present.   But generally it is not sufficient.   The parent storms, the child looks on, catches the lineaments of wrath, puts on the same airs in the circle of smaller slaves, gives a loose to the worst of passions, and thus nursed, educated, and daily exercised in tyranny, cannot but be stamped by it with odious peculiarities.   The man must be a prodigy who can retain his manners and morals undepraved by such circumstances.   And with what execration should the statesman be loaded, who, permitting one half the citizens thus to trample on the rights of the other, transforms those into despots, and these into enemies, destroys the morals of the one part, and the *amor patriæ* of the other. For if a slave can have a country in this world, it must be any other in preference to that in which he is born to live and labor for another ; in which he must lock up the faculties of his nature, contribute as far as depends on his individual endeavors to the evanishment of the human race, or entail his own miserable condition on the endless generations proceeding from him.   With the morals of the people, their industry also is destroyed. For in a warm climate, no man will labor for himself who can make another labor for him. This is so true, that of the proprietors of slaves a very small proportion indeed are ever seen to labor. And can the liberties of a nation be thought secure when we have removed their only firm basis, a conviction in the minds of the people that these liberties are of the gift of God? That they are not to be violated but with his wrath? Indeed I tremble for my country when I reflect that God is just; that his justice cannot sleep forever; that considering numbers, nature and natural means only, a revolution of the wheel of fortune, an exchange of situation is among possible events; that it may become probable by supernatural interference! The Almighty has no attribute which can take side with us in such a contest. But it is impossible to be temperate and to pursue this subject through the various considerations of policy, of morals, of history natural and civil. We must be contented to hope they will force their way into every one's mind. I think a change already perceptible, since the origin of the present revolution. The spirit of the master is abating, that of the slave rising from the dust, his condition mollifying, the way I hope preparing, under the auspices of heaven, for a total emancipation, and that this is disposed, in the order of events, to be with the consent of the masters, rather than by their extirpation.

QUERY XIX.

The present state of manufactures, commerce, interior and exterior trade?

We never had an interior trade of any importance. Our exterior commerce has suffered very much from the beginning of the present contest. During this time we have manufactured within our families the most necessary articles of clothing. Those of cotton will bear some comparison with the same kinds of manufacture in Europe; but those of wool, flax and hemp are very coarse, unsightly, and unpleasant ; and such is our attachment to agriculture, and such our preference for foreign manufactures, that be it wise or unwise, our people will certainly return as soon as they can, to the raising raw materials, and exchanging them for finer manufactures than they are able to execute themselves.

The political economists of Europe have established it as a principle, that every State should endeavor to manufacture for itself ; and this principle, like many others, we transfer to America, without calculating the difference of circumstance which should often produce a difference of result. In Europe the lands are either cultivated, or locked up against the cultivator. Manufacture must therefore be resorted to of necessity not of choice, to support the surplus of their people. But we have an immensity of land courting the industry of the husbandman. Is it best then that all our citizens should be employed in its improvement, or that one half should be called off from that to exercise manufactures and handicraft arts for the other? Those who labor in the earth are the chosen people of God, if ever He had a chosen people, whose breasts He has made His peculiar deposit for substantial and genuine virtue. It is the focus in which he keeps alive that sacred fire, which otherwise might escape from the face of the earth. Corruption of morals in the mass of cultivators is a phenomenon of which no age nor nation has furnished an example. It is the mark set on those, who, not looking up to heaven, to their own soil and industry, as does the husbandman, for their subsistence, depend for it on casualties and caprice of customers. Dependence begets subservience and venality, suffocates the germ of virtue, and prepares fit tools for the designs of ambition. This, the natural progress and consequence of the arts, has sometimes perhaps been retarded by accidental circumstances ; but, generally speaking, the proportion which the aggregate of the other classes of citizens bears in any State to that of its husbandmen, is the proportion of its unsound to its healthy parts, and is a good enough barometer whereby to measure its degree of corruption. While we have land to labor then, let us never wish to see our citizens occupied at a workbench, or twirling a distaff. Carpenters, masons, smiths, are wanting in husbandry; but, for the general operations of manufacture, let our workshops remain in Europe. It is better to carry provisions and materials to workmen there, than bring them to the provisions and materials, and with them their manners and principles. The loss by the transportation of commodities across the Atlantic will be made up in happiness and permanence of government. The mobs of great cities add just so much to the support of pure government, as sores do to the strength of the human body. It is the manners and spirit of a people which preserve a republic in vigor. A degeneracy in these is a canker which soon eats to the heart of its laws and constitution.

QUERY XX.

A notice of the commercial productions particular to the State, and of those objects which the inhabitants are obliged to get from Europe and from other parts of the world?

Before the present war we exported, *communibus annis*, according to the best information I can get, nearly as follows:

Articles.	Quantity.	Price in Dollars.	Amount in Dollars
Tobacco	55,000 hhds of 1,000 lbs.	at 30d. per hhd.	$1,650,000
Wheat	800,000 bushels.	at 5-6d. per bush.	666,666⅔
Indian corn	600,000 "	at ¼d. per bush.	200,000
Shipping	....	....	100,000
Masts, planks, scantling, shingles, staves	....	....	66,666⅔
Tar, pitch, turpentine	30,000 barrels.	at 1½d. per bbl.	40,000
Peltry, viz., skins of deer, beavers, otters, musk rats, raccoons, foxes	180 hhds. of 600 lbs.	at 5-12d. per lb.	42,000
Pork	4,000 barrels.	at 10d. per bbl.	40,000
Flax-seed, hemp, cotton	....	....	8,000
Pit coal, pig iron	....	....	6,666⅔
Peas	5,000 bushels.	at ⅜d. per bush.	3,333⅓
Beef	1,000 barrels.	at 3½d. per bbl.	3,333⅓
Sturgeon, white shad, herring	....	....	3,333⅓
Brandy from peaches and apples, and whiskey	....	....	1,666⅔
Horses	....	....	1,666⅔
	....	....	*$2,833,333⅓

* This sum is equal to £850,000; Virginia money, 607,142 guineas.

In the year 1758 we exported seventy thousand hogsheads of tobacco, which was the greatest quantity ever produced in this country in one year. But its culture was fast declining at the commencement of this war and that of wheat taken its place; and it must continue to decline on the return of peace. I suspect that the change in the temperature of our climate has become sensible to that plant, which to be good, requires an extraordinary degree of heat. But it requires still more indispensably an uncommon fertility of soil; and the price which it commands at market will not enable the planter to produce this by manure. Was the supply still to depend on Virginia and Maryland alone as its culture becomes more difficult, the price would rise so as to enable the planter to surmount those difficulties and to live. But the western country on the Mississippi, and the midlands of Georgia, having fresh and fertile lands in abundance, and a hotter sun, will be able to undersell these two States, and will oblige them to abandon the raising of tobacco altogether. And a happy obligation for them it will be. It is a culture productive of infinite wretchedness. Those employed in it are in a continual state of exertion beyond the power of nature to support. Little food of any kind is raised by them; so that the men and animals on these farms are badly fed, and the earth is rapidly impoverished. The cultivation of wheat is the reverse in every circumstance. Besides clothing the earth with herbage, and preserving its fertility, it feeds the laborers plentifully, requires from them only a moderate toil, except in the season of harvest, raises great numbers of animals for food and service, and diffuses plenty and happiness among the whole. We find it easier to make an hundred bushels of heat than a thousand weight of tobacco, and they are worth more when made. The weavil indeed is a formidable obstacle to the cultivation of this grain with us. But principles are already known which must lead to a remedy. Thus a certain degree of heat, to wit, that of the common air in summer, is necessary to hatch the eggs. If subterranean granaries, or others, therefore, can be contrived below that temperature, the evil will be cured by cold. A degree of heat beyond that which hatches the egg we know will kill it. But in aiming at this we easily run into that which produced putrefaction. To produce putrefaction, however, three agents are requisite, heat moisture, and the external air. If the absence of any one of these be secured, the other two may safely be admitted. Heat is the one we want. Moisture then, or external air, must be excluded. The former has been done by exposing the grain in kilns to the action of fire, which produces heat, and extracts moisture at the same time ; the latter, by putting the grain into hogsheads, covering it with a coating of lime, and heading it up. In this situation its bulk produced a heat sufficient to kill the eggs ; the moisture is suffered to remain indeed, but the external air is excluded. A nicer operation yet has been attempted ; that is, to produce an intermediate temperature of heat between that which kills the egg, and that which produces putrefaction. The threshing the grain as soon as it is cut, and laying it in its chaff in large heaps, has been found very nearly to hit this temperature, though not perfectly, nor always. The heap generates heat sufficient to kill most of the eggs, whilst the chaff commonly restrains it from rising into putrefaction. But all these methods abridge too much the quantity which the farmer can manage, and enable other countries to undersell him, which are not infested with this insect. There is still a desideratum then to give with us decisive triumph to this branch of agriculture over that of tobacco. The culture of wheat by enlarging our pasture, will render the Arabian horse an article of very considerable profit. Experience has shown that ours is the particular climate of America where he may be raised without degeneracy. Southwardly the heat of the sun occasions a deficiency of pasture, and northwardly the winters are too cold for the short and fine hair, the particular sensibility and constitution of that race. Animals transplanted into unfriendly climates, either change their nature and acquire new senses against the new difficulties in which they are placed, or they multiply poorly and become extinct. A good foundation is laid for their propagation here by our possessing already great numbers of horses of that blood, and by a decided taste and preference for them established among the people. Their patience of heat without injury, their superior wind, fit them better in this and the more southern climates even for the drudgeries of the plough and wagon. Northwardly they will become an object only to persons of taste and fortune, for the saddle and light carriages. To those, and for these uses, their fleetness and beauty will recommend them. Besides these there will be other valuable substitutes when the cultivation of tobacco shall be discontinued such as cotton in the eastern parts of the State, and hemp and flax in the western.

It is not easy to say what are the articles either of necessity, comfort, or luxury, which we cannot raise, and which we therefore shall be under a necessity of importing from abroad, as everything hardier than the olive, and as hardy as the fig, may be raised here in the open air. Sugar, coffee and tea, indeed, are not between these limits ; and habit having placed them among the necessaries of life with the wealthy part of our citizens, as long as these habits remain we must go for them to those countries which are able to furnish them.

———

QUERY XXI.

The weights, measures and the currency of the hard money ? Some details relating to exchange with Europe ?

Our weights and measures are the same which are fixed by acts of parliament in England. How it has happened that in this as well as the other American States the nominal value of coin was made to differ from what it was in the country we had left, and to differ among ourselves too, I am not able to say with certainty. I find that in 1631 our house of burgesses desired of the privy council in England, a coin debased to twenty-five per cent. ; that in 1645 they forbid dealing by barter for tobacco, and established the Spanish piece of eight at six shillings, as the standard of their currency ; that in 1655 they changed it to five shillings sterling. In 1680 they sent an address to the king, in consequence of which, by proclamation in 1683, he fixed the value of French crowns, rix dollars, and pieces of eight, at six

shillings, and the coin of New England at one shilling. That
in 1710, 1714, 1727, and 1762, other regulations were made,
which will be better presented to the eye stated in the form of a
table as follows:

	1710.	1714.	1727.	1762.
Guineas...................................	....	26s.		
British gold coin not milled, gold coin of Spain and France, chequins, Arabian gold, moidores of Portugal.............	....	5s. dwt.		
Coined gold of the empire	....	5s. dwt.	....	4s. 3d. dwt.
English milled silver money, in proportion to the crown, at..................	....	5s. 10d.	6s. 3d.	
Pieces of eight of Mexico, Seville & Pillar, ducatoons of Flanders, French ecus, or silver Louis, crusados of Portugal....................................	3¾d. dwt.	....	4d. dwt.	
Peru pieces, cross dollars, and old rix dollars of the empire..................	3½d. dwt.	....	3¾d. dwt.	
Old British silver coin not milled.........	....	3¾d. dwt.		

The first symptom of the depreciation of our present paper
money, was that of silver dollars selling at six shillings, which
had before been worth but five shilling and ninepence. The
assembly thereupon raised them by law to six shillings. As the
dollar is now likely to become the money-unit of America, as it
passes at this rate in some of our sister States, and as it facilitates
their computation in pounds and shillings, &c., converso, this
seems to be more convenient than its former denomination. But
as this particular coin now stands higher than any other in the
proportion of one hundred and thirty-three and a half to one
hundred and twenty-five, or sixteen to fifteen, it will be necessary to raise the others in proportion.

QUERY XXII.

The public Income and expenses?

The nominal amount of these varying constantly and rapidly,
with the constant and rapid depreciation of our paper money, it
becomes impracticable to say what they are. We find ourselves
cheated in every essay by the depreciation intervening between
the declaration of the tax and its actual receipt. It will therefore
be more satisfactory to consider what our income may be when

we shall find means of collecting what our people may spare. I should estimate the whole taxable property of this State at an hundred millions of dollars, or thirty millions of pounds, our money. One per cent. on this, compared with anything we ever yet paid, would be deemed a very heavy tax. Yet I think that those who manage well, and use reasonable economy, could pay one and a half per cent., and maintain their household comfortably in the meantime, without aliening any part of their principal, and that the people would submit to this willingly for the purpose of supporting their present contest. We may say, then, that we could raise, from one million to one million and a half of dollars annually, that is from three hundred to four hundred and fifty thousand pounds, Virginia money.

Of our expenses it is equally difficult to give an exact state, and for the same reason. They are mostly stated in paper money, which varying continually, the legislature endeavors at every session, by new corrections, to adapt the nominal sums to the value it is wished they would bear. I will state them, therefore, in real coin, at the point at which they endeavor to keep them:

	Dollars.
The annual expenses of the general assembly are about	20,000
The governor	3,333⅓
The council of state	10,666⅔
Their clerks	1,166⅔
Eleven judges	11,000
The clerk of the chancery	666⅔
The attorney general	1,000
Three auditors and a solicitor	5,333⅓
Their clerks	2,000
The treasurer	2,000
His clerks	2,000
The keeper of the public jail	1,000
The public printer	1,666⅔
Clerks of the inferior courts	43,333⅓
Public levy; this is chiefly for the expenses of criminal justice	40,000
County levy, for bridges, court-houses, prisons, &c.	40,000
Members of Congress	7,000
Quota of the federal civil list, supposed one-sixth of about $78,000	13,000
Expenses of collecting, six per cent. on the above	12,310
The clergy receive only voluntary contributions; suppose them on an average one-eighth of a dollar a tythe on 200,000 tythes	25,000
Contingencies, to make round numbers not far from truth	7,523⅓
	$250,000

or 53,571 guineas. This estimate is exclusive of the military expense. That varies with the force actually employed, and in time of peace will probably be little or nothing. It is exclusive also of the public debts, which are growing while I am writing, and cannot therefore be now fixed. So it is of the maintenance of the poor, which being merely a matter of charity cannot be deemed expended in the administration of government. And if we strike out the $25,000 for the services of the clergy, which neither makes part of that administration, more than what is paid to physicians, or lawyers, and being voluntary, is either much or nothing as every one pleases, it leaves $225,-000, equal to 48,208 guineas, the real cost of the apparatus of, government with us. This divided among the actual inhabitants of our country, comes to about two-fifths of a dollar, twenty-one pence sterling, or forty-two sols, the price which each pays annually for the protection of the residue of his property, and the other advantages of a free government. The public revenues of Great Britain divided in like manner on its inhabitants would be sixteen times greater. Deducting even the double of the expenses of government, as before estimated, from the million and a half of dollars which we before supposed might be annually paid without distress, we may conclude that this State can contribute one million of dollars annually towards supporting the federal army, paying the federal debt, building a federal navy, or opening roads, clearing rivers, forming safe ports, and other useful works.

To this estimate of our abilities, let me add a word as to the application of them. If, when cleared of the present contest, and of the debts with which that will charge us, we come to measure force hereafter with any European power. Such events are devoutly to be deprecated. Young as we are, and with such a country before us to fill with people and with happiness, we should point in that direction the whole generative force of nature, wasting none of it in efforts of mutual destruction. It should be our endeavor to cultivate the peace and friendship of every nation, even of that which has injured us most, when we shall have carried our point against her. Our interest will be to throw open the doors of commerce, and to knock off all its shackles, giving perfect freedom to all persons for the vent of whatever they may chose to bring into our ports, and asking the same in theirs.   Never was so much false arithmetic employed on any subject, as that which has been employed to persuade nations that it is their interest to go to war.   Were the money which it has cost to gain, at the close of a long war, a little town, or a little territory, the right to cut wood here, or to catch fish there, expended in improving what they already possess, in making roads, opening rivers, building ports, improving the arts, and finding employment for their idle poor, it would render them much stronger, much wealthier and happier.   This I hope will be our wisdom.   And, perhaps, to remove as much as possible the occasions of making war, it might be better for us to abandon the ocean altogether, that being the element whereon we shall be principally exposed to jostle with other nations ; to leave to others to bring what we shall want, and to carry what we can spare.   This would make us invulnerable to Europe, by offering none of our property to their prize, and would turn all our citizens to the cultivation of the earth ; and, I repeat it again, cultivators of the earth are the most virtuous and independent citizens.   It might be time enough to seek employment for them at sea, when the land no longer offers it.   But the actual habits of our countrymen attach them to commerce.   They will exercise it for themselves.   Wars then must sometimes be our lot ; and all the wise can do, will be to avoid that half of them which would be produced by our own follies and our own acts of injustice ; and to make for the other half the best preparations we can.   Of what nature should these be ?   A land army would be useless for offence, and not the best nor safest instrument of defence.   For either of these purposes, the sea is the field on which we should meet an European enemy.   On that element it is necessary we should possess some power.   To aim at such a navy as the greater nations of Europe possess, would be a foolish and wicked waste of the energies of our countrymen.   It would be to pull on our own heads that load of military expense which makes the European laborer go supperless to bed, and moistens his bread with the sweat of his brows. It will be enough if we enable ourselves to prevent insults from those nations of Europe which are weak on the sea, because circumstances exist, which render even the stronger ones weak as to us. Providence has placed their richest and most defenceless possessions at our door; has obliged their most precious commerce to pass, as it were, in review before us. To protect this, or to assail, a small part only of their naval force will ever be risked across the Atlantic. The dangers to which the elements expose them here are too well known, and the greater dangers to which they would be exposed at home were any general calamity to involve their whole fleet. They can attack us by detachment only; and it will suffice to make ourselves equal to what they may detach. Even a smaller force than they may detach will be rendered equal or superior by the quickness with which any check may be repaired with us, while losses with them will be irreparable till too late. A small naval force then is sufficient for us, and a small one is necessary. What this should be, I will not undertake to say. I will only say, it should by no means be so great as we are able to make it. Suppose the million of dollars, or three hundred thousand pounds, which Virginia could annually spare without distress, to be applied to the creating a navy. A single year's contribution would build, equip, man, and send to sea a force which should carry three hundred guns. The rest of the confederacy, exerting themselves in the same proportion, would equip in the same time fifteen hundred guns more. So that one year's contributions would set up a navy of eighteen hundred guns. The British ships of the line average seventy-six guns; their frigates thirty-eight. Eighteen hundred guns then would form a fleet of thirty ships, eighteen of which might be of the line, and twelve frigates. Allowing eight men, the British average, for every gun, their annual expense, including subsistence, clothing, pay, and ordinary repairs, would be about $1,280 for every gun, or $2,304,000 for the whole. I state this only as one year's possible exertion, without deciding whether more or less than a year's exertion should be thus applied.

The value of our lands and slaves, taken conjunctly, doubles in about twenty years. This arises from the multiplication of our slaves, from the extension of culture, and increased demand for lands. The amount of what may be raised will of course rise in the same proportion.

QUERY XXIII.

The histories of the State, the memorials published in its name in the time of its being a colony, and the pamphlets relating to its interior or exterior affairs present or ancient ?

Captain Smith, who next to Sir Walter Raleigh may be considered as the founder of our colony, has written its history, from the first adventures to it, till the year 1624. He was a member of the council, and afterwards president of the colony ; and to his efforts principally may be ascribed its support against the opposition of the natives. He was honest, sensible, and well informed ; but his style is barbarous and uncouth. His history, however, is almost the only source from which we derive any knowledge of the infancy of our State.

The reverend William Stith, a native of Virginia, and president of its college, has also written the history of the same period, in a large octavo volume of small print. He was a man of classical learning, and very exact, but of no taste in style. He is inelegant, therefore, and his details often too minute to be tolerable, even to a native of the country, whose history he writes.

Beverley, a native also, has run into the other extreme, he has comprised our history from the first propositions of Sir Walter Raleigh to the year 1700, in the hundredth part of the space which Stith employs for the fourth part of the period.

Sir Walter Keith has taken it up at its earliest period, and continued it to the year 1725. He is agreeable enough in style, and passes over events of little importance. Of course he is short and would be preferred by a foreigner.

During the regal government, some contest arose on the exaction of an illegal fee by governor Dinwiddie, and doubtless there were others on other occasions not at present recollected. It is supposed that these are not sufficiently interesting to a foreigner to merit a detail.

The petition of the council and burgesses of Virginia to the king, their memorials to the lords, and remonstrance to the commons in the year 1764, began the present contest; and these having proved ineffectual to prevent the passage of the stampact, the resolutions of the house of burgesses of 1765 were passed declaring the independence of the people of Virginia of the parliament of Great Britain, in matters of taxation. From that time till the declaration of independence by Congress in 1776, their journals are filled with assertions of the public rights.

The pamphets published in this State on the controverted question, were :

1766, An Inquiry into the rights of the British Colonies, by Richard Bland.

1769, The Monitor's Letters, by Dr. Arthur Lee.

1774, A summary View of the rights of British America.*

1774, Considerations, &c., by Robert Carter Nicholas.

Since the declaration of independence this State has had no controversy with any other, except with that of Pennsylvania, on their common boundary. Some papers on this subject passed between the executive and legislative bodies of the two States, the result of which was a happy accommodation of their rights.

To this account of our historians, memorials, and pamphlets, it may not be unuseful to add a chronological catalogue of American state-papers, as far as I have been able to collect their titles. It is far from being either complete or correct. Where the title alone, and not the paper itself, has come under my observation, I cannot answer for the exactness of the date. Sometimes I have not been able to find any date at all, and sometimes have not been satisfied that such a paper exists. An extensive collection of papers of this description has been for some time in a course of preparation by a gentleman† fully equal to the task,

---

* By the author of these notes.   † Mr. Hazard.

and from whom, therefore, we may hope ere long to receive it. In the meantime accept this as the result of my labors, and as closing the tedious detail which you have so undesignedly drawn upon yourself.

Pro Johanne Caboto et filiis suis super terra incognita investiganda. 12. Ry. 595. 3. Hakl. 4. 2. Mem. A. 409. — 1496, Mar. 5. 11. H. 7.

Billa signata anno 13. Henrici septimi. 3. Hakluyt's voiages 5. — 1498, Feb. 3. 13. H. 7.

De potestatibus ad terras incognitas investigandum. 13. Rymer. 37. — 1502, Dec. 19. 18. H. 7.

Commission de François I. à Jacques Catier pour l'establissement du Canada. L'Escarbot. 397. 2. Mem. Am. 416. — 1540, Oct. 17.

An act against the exaction of money, or any other thing, by any officer for license to traffique into Iseland and New-foundland, made in An. 2. Edwardi sexti. 3. Hakl. 131. — 1548, 2. E. 6.

The letters-patent granted by her Majestie to Sir Humphrey Gilbert, knight, for the inhabiting and planting of our people in America. 3. Hakl. 135. — 1578, June 11. 20. El.

Letetrs-patent of Queen Elizabeth to Adrian Gilbert and others, to discover the northwest passage to China. 3. Hakl. 96. — 1583, Feb. 6.

The letters-patent granted by the Queen's majestie to M. Walter Raleigh, now knight, for the discovering and planting of new lands and countries, to continue the space of six years and no more. 3. Hakl. 243. — 1584, Mar. 25. 26 El.

An assignment by Sir Walter Raleigh for continuing the action of inhabiting and planting his people in Virginia. Hakl. 1st. ed. publ. in 1589. p. 815. — Mar. 7. 31. El.

Lettres de Lieutenant General de l'Acadie et pays circonvoisins pour le Sieur de Monts. L'Escarbot. 417. — 1603, Nov. 8.

Letters-patent to Sir Thomas Gates, Sir George Somers and others of America. Stith. Apend. No. 1. — 1606, Apr. 10. 4. Jac. 1.

An ordinance and constitution enlarging the council of the two colonies in Virginia and America, and augmenting their authority, M. S. — 1607, Mar. 9. 4. Jac. 1.

The second charter to the treasurer and company for Virginia, erecting them into a body politick. Stith. Ap. 2. — 1609, May 23. 7. Jac. 1.

Letters-patents to the E. of Northampton, granting part of the island of Newfoundland. 1. Harris. 861. — 1610, April 10. Jac. 1.

A third charter to the treasurer and company for Virginia. Stith. Ap. 3. — 1611, Mar. 12. 9. Jac. 1.

A commission to Sir Walter Raleigh. Qu. — 1617. Jac. 1.

Commissio specialis concernens le garbling herbæ Nocotianæ. 17. Rym. 190. — 1620. Apr. 7. 18. Jac. 1.

A proclamation for restraint of the disordered trading of tobacco. 17. Rym. 233. — 1620. June 29. 18. Jac. 1.

A grant of New-England to the council of Plymouth. — 1620. Nov. 3. Jac. 1.

1621, July 24. Jac. 1.	An ordinance and constitution of the treasurer, council and company in England, for a council of state and general assembly in Virginia. Stith. Ap. 4.
1621, Sep. 10. 20 Jac. 1	A grant of Nova Scotia to Sir William Alexander. 2. Mem. de l'Amerique. 193.
1622, Nov. 6. 20 Jac. 1.	A proclamation prohibiting interloping and disorderly trading to New England in America. 17. Rym. 416.
1623, May 9. 21 Jac. 1.	De commissione speciali Willelmo Jones militi directa. 17. Rym. 490.
1623.	A grant to Sir Edmund Ployden, of New Albion. Mentioned in Smith's examination. 82.
1624, July 15. 22. Jac. 1,	De commissione Henrico vicecomiti Mandevill et aliis. 17. Rym. 609.
1624, Aug. 26. 22 Jac. 1.	De commissione speciali concernenti gubernationem in Virginia. 17. Rym. 618.
1624, Sep. 29. 22 Jac. 1.	A proclamation concerning tobacco. 17. Rym. 621.
1624, Nov. 9. 22 Jac. 1.	De concessione demiss, Edwardo Ditchfield et aliis. 17. Rym. 633.
1625, Mar. 2. 22 Jac. 1.	A proclamation for the utter prohibiting the importation and use of all tobacco which is not of the proper growth of the colony of Virginia and the Somer islands, or one of them. 17. Rym. 668.
1625, Mar. 4 1 Car. 1.	De commissione directa Georgio Yardeley militi et aliis. 18. Rym. 311.
1625, Apr. 9. 1 Car. 1.	Proclamatio de herba Nicotianâ. 18. Rym. 19.
1625, May 13. 1 Car. 1.	A proclamation for settlinge the plantation of Virginia. 18. Rym. 72.
1625, July 12.	A grant of the soil, barony, and domains of Nova Scotia to Sir Wm. Alexander of Minstrie. 2. Mem. Am. 226.
1626, Jan. 31. 2 Car. 1.	Commissio directa a Johanni Wolstenholme militi et aliis. 18. Rym. 831.
1626, Feb. 17. 2 Car. 1.	A proclamation touching tobacco. Rym. 848.
1627, Mar. 19. qu? 2 Car. 1.	A grant of Massachusetts bay by the council of Plymouth to Sir Henry Roswell and others.
1627, Mar. 26. 3 Car. 1.	De concessione commissionis specialis proconcilio in Virginia. 18. Rym. 980.
1627, Mar. 30. 3 Car. 1.	De proclamatione de signatione de tobacco. 18. Rym. 886.
1627, Aug. 9. 3 Car. 1.	De proclamatione pro ordinatione de tobacco. 18. Rym. 920.
1628, Mar. 4. 3 Car. 1.	A confirmation of the grant of Massachusetts bay by the crown.
1629, Aug. 19.	The capitulation of Quebec. Champlain pert. 2. 216. 2. Mem. Am. 489.
1630, Jan. 6. 5 Car. 1.	A proclamation concerning tobacco. 19. Rym. 235.
1630, April 30.	Conveyance of Nova Scotia (Port-royal excepted) by Sir William Alexander to Sir Claude St. Etienne Lord of la Tour and of Uarre and to his son Sir Charles de St. Etienne Lord of St. Denniscourt, on condition that they continue subjects to the king of Scotland under the great seal of Scotland.

A proclamation forbidding the disorderly trading with the savages in New England in America, especially the furnishing the natives in those and other parts of America by the English with weapons and habiliments of warre. 19. Ry. 210. 3. Rushw. 82.

1630-31, Nov. 24. 6 Car. 1.

A proclamation prohibiting the selling arms, &c. to the savages in America. Mentioned 3. Rushw. 75.

1630, Dec. 5. 6 Car. 1.

A grant of Connecticut by the council of Plymouth to the E. of Warwick.

1630, Car. 1.

A confirmation by the crown of the grant of Connecticut [said to be in the petty-bag office in England.]

1630, Car. 1.

A conveiance of Connecticut by the E. of Warwick to Lord Say, and Seal, and others. Smith's examination, Appendix No. 1.

1631, Mar. 19. 6 Car. 1.

A special commission to Edward, Earle of Dorsett, and others, for the better plantation of the colony of Virginia. 19. Ry. 301.

1631, June 27. 7 Car. 1.

Litere continentes promissionem regis ad tradenum castrum et habitationem de Kebec in Canada ad regem Francorum. 19. Ry. 303.

1632, June 29. 7 Car. 1.

Traité entre le roy Louis XIII. et Charles roi d'Angleterre pour la restitution de la nouvelle France, la Cadie et Canada et des navires et merchandises pris de part et d'autre. Fait a St. Germain. 19. Ry. 361. 2. Mem. Am. 5.

1632, Mar. 29. 8 Car. 1.

A grant of Maryland to Cæcilius Calvert, baron of Baltimore in Ireland.

1632, June 20. 8 Car. 1.

A petition of the planters of Virginia against the grant to lord Baltimore.

1633, July 3, 9 Car. 1.

Order of council upon the dispute between the Virginia planters and lord Baltimore, Votes of repres. Pennsylvania. V.

1633, July 3.

A proclamation to prevent abuses growing by the unordered retailing of tobacco. Mentioned 3. Rushw. 191,

1633, Aug. 13. 9 Car. 1.

A special commission to Thomas Young to search, discover and find out what ports are not yet inhabited in Virginia and America and other parts thereunto adjoining. 19. Ry. 472.

1633, Sept. 23. 9 Car. 1.

A proclamation for preventing of the abuses growing by the unordered retailing of tobacco. 19. Ry. 474.

1633, Oct. 13. 9 Car. 1.

A proclamation restraining the abusive venting of tobacco. 19. Rym. 522.

1633, Mar. 13. Cer. 1.

A proclamation concerning the landing of tobacco, and also forbidding the planting thereof in the king's dominions. 19. Ry. 553.

1634, May 19. 10 Car. 1.

A commission to the Archbishop of Canterbury and 11 others, for governing the American colonies.

1634, Car. 1.

A commission concerning tobacco. M. S.

1634, June 19. 10 Car. 1.

A commission from Lord Say, and Seal, and others, to John Winthrop to be governor of Connecticut. Smith's App.

1635, July 18. 11 Car. 1.

A grant to Duke Hamilton.

1635, Car. 1.

1636, Apr. 2. 12 Car. I.	De commissione speciali Johanni Harvey militi to pro meliori regimine coloniae in Virginia. 20. Ry. 3.
1637, Mar. 14. Car. 1.	A proclamation concerning tobacco. Title in 3. Rush. 617.
1636–7, Mar. 16. 12 Car. 1.	De commissione speciali Georgio domino Goring et aliis concessâ concernente venditionem de tobacco absque licentiâ regiâ. 20. Ry. 116.
1637, Apr. 30. 13 Car. 1.	A proclamation against disorderly transporting his Majesty's subjects to the plantations within the parts of America. 20. Ry. 143. 3. Rush. 409.
1637, May 1. 13 Car. 1.	An order of the privy council to stay 8 ships now in the Thames from going to New England. 3. Rush. 409.
1637, Car. 1.	A warrant of the Lord Admiral to stop unconformable ministers from going beyond the sea. 3. Rush. 410.
1638, Apr. 4. Car. 1.	Order of council upon Claiborne's petition against Lord Baltimore. Votes of representatives of Pennsylvania. vi.
1638, Apr. 6. 14 Car. 1.	An order of the king and council that the attorney general draw up a proclamation to prohibit transportation of passengers to New England without license. 3. Rush. 718.
1638, May 1. 14 Car. 1.	A proclamation to restrain the transporting of passengers and provisions to New England without license. 20. Ry. 223.
1639, Mar. 25. Car. 1.	A proclamation concerning tobacco. Title 4. Rush. 1060.
1639, Aug. 19. 15 Car. 1.	A proclamation declaring his majesty's pleasure to continue his commission and letters patents for licensing retailers of tobacco. 20. Ry. 348.
1639, Dec. 16. 15 Car. 1.	De commissione speciali Henrico Ashton armigero et aliis ad amovendum Henricum Hawley gubernatorem de Barbadoes. 20. Rym. 357.
1639, Car. 1.	A proclamation concerning retailers of tobacco. 4. Rush. 966.
1641, Aug. 9. 17 Car. 1.	De constitutione gubernatoris et concilii pro Virginia. 20. Ry. 484.
1643, Car. 1.	Articles of union and confederacy entered into by Massachusetts, Plymouth, Connecticut and New-haven. 1. Neale. 223.
1644, Car. 1.	Deed from George Fenwick to the old Connecticut jurisdiction. An ordinance of the lords and commons assembled in parliament, for exempting from custom and imposition all commodities exported for, or imported from New England, which has been very prosperous and without any public charge to this State, and is likely to prove very happy for the propagation of the gospel in those parts. Tit. in Amer. library 90. 5. No date. But seems by the neighbouring articles to have been in 1644.
1644, June 20. Car. 2.	An act for charging of tobacco brought from New England with custom and excise. Title in American library. 99. 8.
1644, Aug. 1. Car. 2.	An act for the advancing and regulating the trade of this commonwealth. Tit. in Amer. libr. 99. 9.
Sep. 18. 1 Car. 2.	Grant of the Northern neck of Virginia to Lord Hopton, Lord Jermyn, Lord Culpepper, Sir John Berkley, Sir William Moreton, Sir Dudley Wyatt, and Thomas Culpepper.

An act prohibiting trade with the Barbadoes, Virginia, Bermudas and Antego Scobell's Acts. 1027.	1650, Oct. 3. 2 Car. 2.
A declaration of Lord Willoughby, governor of Barbadoes, and of his council, against an act of parliament of 3d of October, 1650. 4. Polit. register. 2. cited from 4 Neal. hist. of the Puritans. App. No. 12 but not there.	1650, Car. 2.
A final settlement of boundaries between the Dutch New Netherlands and Connecticut.	1650, Car. 2.
Instructions for Captain Robert Dennis, Mr. Richard Bennet, Mr. Thomas Stagge, and Captain William Claibourn, appointed commissioners for the reducing of Virginia and the inhabitants thereof to their due obedience to the commonwealth of England. 1 Thurloe's state papers, 197.	1651, Sept. 26. 3 Car. 2.
An act for increase of shipping and encouragement of the navigation of this nation. Scobell's acts, 1449.	1651, Oct. 9. 8 Car. 2.
Articles agreed on and concluded at James citie in Virginia for the surrendering and settling of that plantation under the obedience and government of the commonwealth of England, by the commissioners of the council of state, by authoritie of the parliament of England, and by the grand assembly of the governor, council, and burgesse of that state. M. S. [Ante. p. 206.]	1651-2, Mar. 12. 4 Car. 2.
An act of indempnitie made at the surrender of the country [of Virginia.] [Ante p. 206.]	1651-2, Mar. 12. 4 Car. 1.
Capitulation de Port Royal. Mem. Am. 507.	1654, Aug. 16.
A proclamation of the protector relating to Jamaica. 3 Thurl. 75.	1655, Car. 2.
The protector to the commissioners of Maryland. A letter. 4 Thurl. 55.	1655, Sep. 26. 7 Car. 2.
An instrument made at the council of Jamaica, Oct. 8, 1655, for the better carrying on of affairs there. 4 Thurl. 17.	1655, Oct. 8. 7 Car. 2.
Treaty of Westminster between France and England. 6. corps diplom. part 2. p. 121. 2 Mem. Am. 10.	1655, Nov. 3.
The assembly at Barbadoes to the protector. 4 Thurl. 651.	1656, Mar. 27. 8 Car. 2.
A grant by Cromwell to Sir Charles de Saint Etienne, a baron of Scotland, Crowne and Temple. A French translation of it. 2 Mem. Am. 511.	1656, Aug. 9.
A paper concerning the advancement of trade, 5 Thurl. 80.	1656, Car. 2.
A brief narration of the English rights to the Northern parts of America. 5 Thurl. 81.	1656, Car. 2.
Mr. R. Bennet and Mr. S. Matthew to Secretary Thurlow. 5 Thurl. 482.	1656, Oct. 10. 8 Car. 2.
Objections against the Lord Baltimore's patent, and reasons why the government of Maryland should not be put into his hands. 5 Thurl. 482.	1656, Oct. 10. 8 Car. 2.
A paper relating to Maryland. 5 Thurl. 483.	1656, Oct. 10. 8 Car. 2.
A breviet of the proceedings of the lord Baltimore and his officers and compliers in Maryland, against the authority of the	1656, Oct. 10. 8 Car. 2.

parliament of the commonwealth of England and against his highness the lord protector's authority, laws and government 5 Thurl 486.

1656, Oct. 15. 8 Car. 2. The assembly of Virginia to secretary Thurlow. 5 Thurl. 497.

1657, Apr. 4. 9 Car. 2. The governor of Barbadoes to the protector. 6 Thurl. 69.

1661, Car. 2. Petition of the general court at Hartford upon Connecticut for charter. Smith's exam. App. 4.

1662, Apr. 23. 14 Car. 2. Charter of the colony of Connecticut. Smith's exam. App. 6.

1662-2, Mar. 24. Apr. 4. 15 C. 2. The first charter granted by Charles II. to the proprietaries of Carolina, to wit, to the Earl of Clarendon, Duke of Albemarle, Lord Craven, Lord Berkeley, Lord Ashley, Sir George Carteret, Sir William Berkeley, and Sir John Colleton. 4 Mem. Am. 554.

1664, Feb. 10. The concessions and agreement of the lords proprietors of the province of New Cæsarea, or New Jersey, to and with all and every of the adventurers and all such as shall settle or plant there. Smith's New Jersey. App. 1.

1664, Mar. 12. 20 Car. 2. A grant of the colony of New York to the Duke of York.

1664, Apr. 26. 16 Car. 2. A commission to Colonel Nichols and others to settle disputes in New England. Hutch. Hist. Mass. Bay, App. 537.

1664, Apr. 26. The commission to Sir Robert Carre and others to put the Duke of York in possession of New York, New Jersey, and all other lands thereunto appertaining.

Sir Robert Carre and others proclamation to the inhabitants of New York, New Jersey, &c. Smith's N. J. 36.

1664, June 23. 24. 16 Car. 2. Deeds of lease and release of New Jersey by the Duke of York to Lord Berkeley and Sir George Carteret.

A conveiance of the Delaware counties to William Penn.

1664, Aug. 19-29, 20-30, 24. Aug. 25. Sept. 4. Letters between Stuyvesant and Colonel Nichols on the English right. Smith's N. J. 37—42.

1664, Aug. 27. Treaty between the English and Dutch for the surrender of the New Netherlands. Sm. N. J. 42.

Sept. 3. Nicoll's commission to Sir Robert Carre to reduce the Dutch on Delaware bay. Sm. N. J. 47.

Instructions to Sir Robert Carre for reducing of Delaware bay and settling the people there under his majesty's obedience. Sm. N. J. 47.

1664, Oct. 1. Articles of capitulation between Sir Robert Carre and the Dutch and Swedes on Delaware bay and Delaware river. Sm. N. J. 49.

1664, Dec. 1. 16 Car. 2. The determination of the commissioners of the boundary between the Duke of York and Connecticut. Sm. Ex. Ap. 9.

1664. The New Haven case. Smith's Ex. Ap. 20.

1665, June 13. 24. 17 Car. 2. The second charter granted by Charles II. to the same proprietors of Carolina. 4. Mem. Am. 586.

1666, Jan. 26. Declaration de guerre par la France contre l'Angleterre. 3 Mem. Am. 123.

Declaration of war by the king of England against the king of France.	1666, Feb. 9. 17 Car. 2.
The treaty of peace between France and England made at Breda. 7 Corps, Dipl. part 1. p. 51 2. Mem. Am. 32.	1667, July 31.
The treaty of peace and alliance between England and the United Provinces made at Breda. 7. Cor. Dip. p. 1. d. 44. 2. Mem. Am. 40.	1667, July 31.
Acte de la cession de l'Acadie au roi de France. 2. Mem. Am. 40.	1667-8, Feb. 17.
Directions from the governor and council of New York for a better settlement of the government on Delaware. Sm. N. J. 51.	1668, April 21.
Lovelace's order for customs at the Hoarkills. Sm. N. J. 55.	1668.
A confirmation of the grant of the northern neck of Virginia to the Earl of St. Albans, Lord Berkeley, Sir William Moreton and John Tretheway.	16– May 8. 21 Car. 2.
Incorporation of the town of Newcastle or Amstell.	1672,
A demise of the colony of Virginia to the Earl of Arlington and Lord Culpepper for 31 years. M. S.	1673, Feb. 25. 25 Car. 2.
Treaty at London between king Charles II. and the Dutch. Article VI.	1673-4.
Remonstrance against the two grants of Charles II. of Northern and Southern Virginia. Ment⁴. Beverley 65.	
Sir George Carteret's instructions to Governor Carteret.	1674, July 13.
Governor Andros's proclamation on taking possession of Newcastle for the Duke of York. Sm. N. J. 78.	1674, Nov. 9.
A proclamation for prohibiting the importation of commodities of Europe into any of his majesty's plantations in Africa, Asia, or America, which were not laden in England; and for putting all other laws relating to the trade of the plantations in effectual execution.	1675, Oct. 1 27 Car. 2.
The concessions and agreements of the proprietors, freeholders and inhabitants of the province of West New Jersey in America. Sm. N. J. App. 2.	1676, Mai. 3.
A deed quintipartite for the division of New Jersey.	1676, July 1.
Letter from the proprietors of New Jersey to Richard Hartshorne. Sm. N. J. 80.	1676, Aug. 18
Proprietors instructions to James Wasse and Richard Hartshorne. Sm. N. J. 83.	
The charter of king Charles II. to his subjects of Virginia. M.S.	1676, Oct. 10. 28 Car. 2.
Cautionary epistle from the trustees of Byllinge's part of New Jersey. Sm. N. J. 84.	1676.
Indian deed for the lands between Rankokas creek and Timber creek, in New Jersey.	1677, Sept. 10.
Indian deed for lands from Oldman's creek to Timber creek, in New Jersey.	1677, Sept. 27.
Indian deed for the lands from Rankokos creek to Assunpink creek, in New Jersey.	1677, Oct. 10.

1678, Dec. 5.   The will of Sir George Carteret, sole proprieter of East Jersey ordering the same to be sold.

1680, Feb. 16.   An order of the king in council for the better encouragement of all his majesty's subjects in their trade to his majesty's plantations, and for the better information of all his majesty's loving subjects in these matters—Lond. Gaz. No. 1596. Title in Amer. library. 134. 6.

1680.   Arguments against the customs demanded in New West Jersey by the governor of New York, addressed to the Duke's commissioners. Sm. N. J. 117.

1680, June 14. 23. 25. Oct. 16. Nov. 4. 8. 11. 18. 20. 23. Dec. 16. 1680-1, Jan. 15. 22. Feb. 24.   Extracts of proceedings of the committee of trade and plantations; copies of letters, reports, &c., between the board of trade, Mr. Penn, Lord Baltimore and Sir John Werden, in the behalf of the Duke of York and the settlement of the Pennsylvania boundaries by the L. C. J. North. Votes of Repr. Pennsyl. vii.–xiii.

1631, Mar. 4. Car. 2.   A grant of Pennsylvania to William Penn. Votes of Represen. Pennsyl. xviii.

1681, Apr. 2.   The king's declaration to the inhabitants and planters of the province of Pennsylvania. Vo. Repr. Penn. xxiv.

1681, July 11.   Certain conditions or concessions agreed upon by William Penn, proprietary and governor of Pennsylvania, and those who are the adventurers and purchasers in the same province. Votes of Rep. Pennsyl. xxiv.

1681, Nov. 9.   Fundamental laws of the province of West New Jersey. Sm. N. J. 126.

1681-2, Jan. 14.   The methods of the commissioners for settling and regulation of lands in New Jersey. Sm. N. J. 130.

1681-2, F. 1. 2.   Indentures of lease and release by the executors of Sir George Carteret to William Penn and 11 others, conveying East Jersey.

1682, Mar. 14.   The Duke of York's fresh grant of East New Jersey to the 24 proprietors.

1682, Apr. 25.   The frame of the government of the province of Pennsylania, in America. Votes of Repr. Penn. xxvii.

1682, Aug. 21.   The Duke of York's deed for Pennsylvania. Vo. Repr. Penn. xxxv.

1682, Aug. 24.   The Duke of York's deed for the feoffment of Newcastle and twelve miles circle to William Penn. Vo. Repr. Penn.

1682, Aug. 24.   The Duke of York's deed of feoffment of a tract of land 12 miles south from Newcastle to the Whorekills, to William Penn. Vo. Repr. Penn. xxxvii.

1682, Nov. 27. 34 Car. 2.   A commission to Thomas Lord Culpepper to be lieutenant and governor-general of Virginia. M. S.

1682, 10th mon. 6th day.   An act of union for annexing and uniting of the counties of Newcastle, Jones's and Whorekill's, alias Deal, to the province of Pennsylvania, and of naturalization of all foreigners in the province and counties aforesaid.

An act of settlement.

1682, Dec. 6.

The frame of the government of the province of Pennsylvania and territories thereunto annexed in America.

1683, Apr. 2.

Proceedings of the committee of trade and Plantations in the dispute between Lord Baltimore and Mr. Penn. Vo. R. P. xiii—xviii.

1683, Apr. 17. '27. May 30. June 12.

1684, Feb. 12. July 2, 16, 23, Sept. 30. Dec. 9.

1685, Mar. 17. Aug. 18. 26. Sept. 2. Oct. 8, 17, 31. Nov. 7.

A commission by the proprietors of East New Jersey to Robert Barclay to be governor. Sm. N. J. 166.

1683, July 17.

An order of council for issuing a quo warranto against the charter of the colony of the Massachusetts bay in New England, with his majesty's declaration that in case the said corporation of Massachusetts bay shall before prosecution had upon the same quo warranto make a full submission and entire resignation to his royal pleasure, he will then regulate their charter in such a manner as shall be for his service and the good of that colony. Title in American library. 139, 6.

1683, July 26. 35 Car. 2.

A commission to Lord Howard of Effingham to be lieutenant and governor general of Virginia. M. S.

1683, Sept. 28. 35 Car. 2.

The humble address of the chief governor, council and representatives of the island of Nevis, in the West Indies, presented to his majesty by Colonel Netheway and Captain Jefferson, at Windsor, May 3, 1684. Title in Amer. libr. 142. 3. cites Lond. Gaz. No. 1927.

1684, May 3.

A treaty with the Indians at Albany.

1684, Aug. 2.

A treaty of neutrality for America between France and England. 7 Corps Dipl. part 2, p. 44. 2. Mem. Am. 40.

1686, Nov. 16.

By the king, a proclamation for the more effectual reducing and suppressing of pirates and privateers in America, as well on the sea as on the land in great numbers, committing frequent robberies and piracies, which hath occasioned a great prejudice and obstruction to trade and commerce, and given a great scandal and disturbance to our government in those parts. Title Amer. libr. 147. 2. cites Lond. Gaz. No. 2315.

1687, Jan. 20.

Constitution of the council of proprietors of West Jersey. Smith's N. Jersey. 199.

1687, Feb. 12.

A confirmation of the grant of the Northern neck of Virginia to Lord Culpepper.

1687, qu. Sept. 27. 4. Jac. 2.

Governor Coxe's declaration to the council of proprietors of West Jersey. Sm. N. J. 190.

1687, Sept. 5.

Provisional treaty of Whitehall concerning America between France and England. 2 Mem. de l'Am. 89.

1687, Dec. 16

Governor Coxe's narrative relating to the division line, directed to the council of proprietors of West Jersey. Sm. App. No. 4.

1687.

The representation of the council of proprietors of West Jersey to Governor Burnet. Smith. App. No. 5.

1687.

The remonstrance and petition of the inhabitants of East New Jersey to the king. Sm. App. No. 8.

The memorial of the proprietors of East New Jersey to the Lords of trade. Sm. App. No. 9.

1778, Sept. 5.   Agreement of the line of partition between East and West New Jersey. Smith's N. J. 196.

1691.   Conveyance of the government of West Jersey and territories, by Dr. Coxe, to the West Jersey society.

1691, Oct. 7.   A charter granted by King William and Queen Mary to the inhabitants of the province of Massachusetts bay, in New England. 2 Mem. de l'Am. 593.

1696, Nov. 7.   The frame of government of the province of Pennsylvania and the territories thereunto belonging, passed by Gov. Markham. Nov. 7, 1696.

1697, Sept. 20.   The treaty of peace between France and England, made at Ryswick. 7 Corps Dipl. part 2. p. 399. 2 Mem. Am. 89.

1699, July 5.   The opinion and answer of the Lords of trade to the memorial of the proprietors of East N. Jersey. Sm. App. No. 10.

1700, Jan. 15.   The memorial of the proprietors of East New Jersey to the Lords of trade. Sm. App. No. 11.

The petition of the proprietors of East and West New Jersey to the Lords justices of England. Sm. App. No. 12.

1700, W. 3.   A confirmation of the boundary between the colonies of New York and Connecticut, by the crown.

1701, Aug. 12.   The memorial of the proprietors of East and West New Jersey to the king. Sm. App. No. 14.

1701, Oct. 2.   Representation of the Lords of trade to the Lords justices. Sm. App. No. 18.

1701.   A treaty with the Indians.

1701-2, Jan. 6.   Report of Lords of trade to king William, of draughts of a commission and instructions for a governor of N. Jersey. Sm. N. J. 262.

1702, Apr. 15.   Surrender from the proprietors of E. and W. N. Jersey, of their pretended right of government to her majesty Queen Anne. Sm. N. J. 211.

1702, Apr. 17.   The Queen's acceptance of the surrender of government of East and West Jersey. Sm. N. J. 219.

1702, Nov. 16.   Instructions to lord Cornbury. Sm. N. J. 230.

1702, Dec. 5.   A commission from Queen Anne to Lord Cornbury, to be captain general and governor in chief of New Jersey. Sm. N. J. 220.

1703, June 27   Recognition by the council of proprietors of the true boundary of the deeds of Sept. 10, and Oct. 10, 1677, (New Jersey.) Sm. N. J. 96.

1703.   Indian deeds for the lands above the falls of the Delaware in West Jersey.

Indian deed for the lands at the head of Rankokus river, in West Jersey.

1733.	Petition of Lord Fairfax, that a commission might issue for running and marking the dividing line between his district and the province of Virginia.
1733, Nov. 29.	Order of the king in council for commissioners to survey and settle the said dividing line between the proprietary and royal territory.
1736, Aug. 5.	Report of the Lords of trade relating to the separating the government of the province of New Jersey from New York. Sm. N. J. 423.
1737, Aug. 10.	Survey and report of the commissioners appointed on the part of the crown to settle the line between the crown and Lord Fairfax.
1737, Aug. 11.	Survey and report of the commissioners appointed on the part of Lord Fairfax to settle the line between the crown and him.
1738, Dec. 21.	Order of reference of the surveys between the crown and Lord Fairfax to the council for plantation affairs.
1744, June.	Treaty with the Indians of the six nations at Lancaster.
1745, Apr. 6.	Report of the council for plantation affairs, fixing the head springs of Rappahanoc and Potomac, and a commission to extend the line.
1745, Apr. 11.	Order of the king in council confirming the said report of the council for plantation affairs.
1748, Apr. 30.	Articles préliminaires pour parvenir à la paix, signés à Aix-la-Chapelle entre les ministres de France, de la Grande-Bretagne, et des Provinces-Unies des Pays-Bas. 2 Mem. de l'Am. 159.
1748, May 21.	Declaration des ministres de France, de la Grande-Bretagne, et des Provinces-Unies des Pays-Bas, pour rectifier les articles I. et II. des préliminaires. 2. Mem. Am. 165.
1748, Oct. 7-18. 22. G. 2.	The general and definitive treaty of peace concluded at Aix-la-Chapelle. Lon. Mag. 1748. 503. French 2. Mem. Am. 169.
1754.	A treaty with the Indians.
1758, Aug. 7.	A conference between governor Bernard and Indian nations at Burlington. Sm. N. J. 449.
1758, Oct. 8.	A conference between governor Denny, governor Bernard, and others, and Indian nations at Easton. Sm. N. J. 455.
1759, July 25. 33. G. 2.	The capitulation of Niagara.
175-.	The king's proclamation proming lands to soldiers.
1763, Feb. 10. 3. G. 3.	The definitive treaty concluded at Paris. Lon. Mag. 1763. 149.
1763, Oct. 7. G. 3.	A proclamation for regulating the cessions made by the last treaty of peace. Guth. Geogr. Gram. 623.
1763.	The king's proclamation against settling on any lands on the waters westward of the Alleghany.
1768, Nov. 3.	Deed from the six nations of Indians to William Trent, and others, for lands betwixt the Ohio and Monongahela. View of the title to Indiana. Phil. Steiner and Cist. 1776.
1768, Nov. 5	Deed from the six nations of Indians to the crown for certain lands and settling a boundary. M.S.

APPENDIXES

No. I.

The preceding sheets have been submitted to my friend **Mr.** Charles Thompson, Secretary of Congress; he has furnished me with the following observations, which have too much merit not to be communicated:

(A.) p. 262.   Besides the three channels of communication mentioned between the western waters and the Atlantic, there are two others to which the Pennsylvanians are turning their attention; one from Presque Isle, on Lake Erie, to Le Bœuf, down the Alleghany to Kiskiminitas, then up the Kiskiminitas, and from thence, by a small portage, to Juniata, which falls into the Susquehanna; the other from Lake Ontario to the East Branch of the Delaware, and down that to Philadelphia.   Both these are said to be very practicable; and, considering the enterprising temper of the Pennsylvanians, and particularly of the merchants of Philadelphia, whose object is concentred in promoting the commerce and trade of one city, it is not improbable but one or both of these communications will be opened and improved.

(B.) p. 265.   The reflections I was led into on viewing this passage of the Potomac through the Blue Ridge were, that this country must have suffered some violent convulsion, and that the face of it must have been changed from what it probably was some centuries ago; that the broken and ragged faces of the mountain on each side the river; the tremendous rocks, which are left with one end fixed in the precipice, and the other jutting out, and seemingly ready to fall for want of support, the bed of the river for several miles below obstructed, and filled with the loose stones carried from this mound; in short, everything on which you cast your eye evidently demonstrates a disrupture and breach in the mountain, and that, before this happened, what is now a fruitful vale, was formerly a great lake or collection of water, which possibly might have here formed a mighty cascade, or had its vent to the ocean by the Susquehanna, where the Blue Ridge seems to terminate. Besides this, there are other parts of this country which bear evident traces of a like convulsion. From the best accounts I have been able to obtain, the place where the Delaware now flows through the Kittatinney mountain, which is a continuation of what is called the North Ridge, or mountain, was not its original course, but that it passed through what is now called " the Wind-gap," a place several miles to the westward, and about a hundred feet higher than the present bed of the river. This Wind-gap is about a mile broad, and the stones in it such as seem to have been washed for ages by water running over them. Should this have been the case, there must have been a large lake behind that mountain, and by some uncommon swell in the waters, or by some convulsion of nature, the river must have opened its way through a different part of the mountain, and meeting there with less obstruction, carried away with it the opposing mounds of earth, and deluged the country below with the immense collection of waters to which this new passage gave vent. There are still remaining, and daily discovered, innumerable instances of such a deluge on both sides of the river, after it passed the hills above the falls of Trenton, and reached the Champaign. On the New Jersey side, which is flatter than the Pennsylvania side, all the country below Croswick hills seems to have been overflowed to the distance of from ten to fifteen miles back from the river, and to have acquired a new soil by the earth and clay brought down and mixed with the native sand. The spot on which Philadelphia stands evidently appears to be made ground. The different strata through which they pass in digging to water, the acorns, leaves, and sometimes branches, which are found above twenty feet below the surface, all seem to demonstrate this. I am informed that at Yorktown in Virginia, in the bank of York river, there are different strata of shells and earth, one above another, which seem to point out that the country there has undergone several changes; that the sea has, for a succession of ages.

occupied the place where dry land now appears; and that the ground has been suddenly raised at various periods. What a change would it make in the country below, should the mountains at Niagara, by any accident, be cleft asunder, and a passage suddenly opened to drain off the waters of Erie and the upper lakes! While ruminating on these subjects, I have often been hurried away by fancy, and led to imagine, that what is now the bay of Mexico, was once a champaign country; and that from the point or cape of Florida, there was a continued range of mountains through Cuba, Hispaniola, Porto Rico, Martinique, Guadaloupe, Barbadoes, and Trinidad, till it reached the coast of America, and formed the shores which bounded the ocean, and guarded the country behind; that by some convulsion or shock of nature, the sea had broken through these mounds, and deluged that vast plain, till it reached the foot of the Andes; that being there heaped up by the trade winds, always blowing from one quarter, it had found its way back, as it continues to do, through the Gulf between Florida and Cuba, carrying with it the loom and sand it may have scooped from the country it had occupied, part of which it may have deposited on the shores of North America, and with part formed the banks of Newfoundland. But these are only the visions of fancy.

(3.) p. 283. There is a plant, or weed, called the Jamestown weed,* of a very singular quality. The late Dr. Bond informed me, that he had under his care a patient, a young girl, who had put the seeds of this plant into her eye, which dilated the pupil to such a degree, that she could see in the dark, but in the light was almost blind. The effect that the leaves had when eaten by a ship's crew that arrived at Jamestown, are well known.†

(4.) p. 312. Monsieur Buffon has indeed given an afflicting picture of human nature in his description of the man of America. But sure I am there never was a picture more unlike the original. He grants indeed that his stature is the same as that of the man of Europe. He might have admitted, that the Iro-

---

* Datura pericarpiis erectis ovatis. Linn.

† An instance of temporary imbecility produced by them is mentioned, Beverl. H. of Virg. b 2, c. 4.

quois were larger, and the Lenopi, or Delawares, taller than people in Europe generally are. But he says their organs of generation are smaller and weaker than those of Europeans. Is this a fact? I believe not; at least it is an observation I never heard before.—"They have no beard." Had he known the pains and trouble it costs the men to pluck out by the roots the hair that grows on their faces, he would have seen that nature had not been deficient in that respect. Every nation has its customs. I have seen an Indian beau, with a looking-glass in his hand, examining his face for hours together, and plucking out by the roots every hair he could discover, with a kind of tweezer made of a piece of fine brass wire, that had been twisted round a stick, and which he used with great dexterity.—"They have no ardor for their females." It is true they do not indulge those excesses, nor discover that fondness which is customary in Europe; but this is not owing to a defect in nature but to manners. Their soul is wholly bent upon war. This is what procures them glory among the men, and makes them the admiration of the women. To this they are educated from their earliest youth. When they pursue game with ardor, when they bear the fatigues of the chase, when they sustain and suffer patiently hunger and cold; it is not so much for the sake of the game they pursue, as to convince their parents and the council of the nation that they are fit to be enrolled in the number of the warriors. The songs of the women, the dance of the warriors, the sage counsel of the chiefs, the tales of the old, the triumphal entry of the warriors returning with success from battle, and the respect paid to those who distinguish themselves in war, and in subduing their enemies; in short, everything they see or hear tends to inspire them with an ardent desire for military fame. If a young man were to discover a fondness for women before he has been to war, he would become the contempt of the men, and the scorn and ridicule of the women. Or were he to indulge himself with a captive taken in war, and much more were he to offer violence in order to gratify his lust, he would incur indelible disgrace. The seeming frigidity of the men, therefore, is the effect of manners, and not a defect of nature. Besides, a celebrated warrior is oftener courted by the females, than he has occasion to court ; and this is a point of honor which the men aim at.   Instances similar to that of Ruth and Boaz* are not uncommon among them.   For though the women are modest and diffident, and so bashful that they seldom lift up their eyes, and scarce ever look a man full in the face, yet, being brought up in great subjection, custom and manners reconcile them to modes of acting, which, judged of by Europeans, would be deemed inconsistent with the rules of female decorum and propriety.   I once saw a young widow, whose husband, a warrior, had died about eight days before, hastening to finish her grief, and who, by tearing her hair, beating her breast, and drinking spirits, made the tears flow in great abundance, in order that she might grieve much in a short space of time, and be married that evening to another young warrior.   The manner in which this was viewed by the men and women of the tribe, who stood round, silent and solemn spectators of the scene, and the indifference with which they answered my question respecting it, convinced me that it was no unusual custom.   I have known men advanced in years, whose wives were old and past child-bearing, take young wives, and have children, though the practice of polygamy is not common.   Does this savor of frigidity, or want of ardor for the female ?   Neither do they seem to be deficient in natural affection.   I have seen both fathers and mothers in the deepest affliction, when their children have been dangerously ill ; though I believe the affection is stronger in the descending than the ascending scale, and though custom forbids a father to grieve immoderately for a son slain in battle.   " That they are timorous and cowardly," is a character with which there is little reason to charge them, when we recollect the manner in which the Iroquois met Monsieur ———, who marched into their country ; in which the old men, who scorned to fly, or to survive the capture of their town, braved death, like the old Romans in the time of the Gauls, and in which they soon after revenged them-

* When Boaz had eaten and drank, and his heart was merry, he went to lie down at the end of the heap of corn; and Ruth came softly, and uncovered his feet, and laid her down. Ruth, iii. 7.

selves by sacking and destroying Montreal. But above all, the unshaken fortitude with which they bear the most excruciating tortures and death when taken prisoners, ought to exempt them from that character. Much less are they to be characterized as a people of no vivacity, and who are excited to action or motion only by the calls of hunger and thirst. Their dances in which they so much delight, and which to an European would be the most severe exercise, fully contradict this, not to mention their fatiguing marches, and the toil they voluntarily and cheerfully undergo in their military expeditions. It is true, that when at home, they do not employ themselves in labor or the culture of the soil; but this again is the effect of customs and manners, which have assigned that to the province of the women. But it is said, they are averse to society and a social life. Can anything be more inapplicable than this to a people who always live in towns or clans? Or can they be said to have no "republic," who conduct all their affairs in national councils, who pride themselves in their national character, who consider an insult or injury done to an individual by a stranger as done to the whole, and resent it accordingly? In short, this picture is not applicable to any nation of Indians I have ever known or heard of in North America.

(5.) p. 340. As far as I have been able to learn, the country from the sea coast to the Alleghany, and from the most southern waters of James river up to Patuxen river, now in the State of Maryland, was occupied by three different nations of Indians, each of which spoke a different language, and were under separate and distinct governments. What the original or real names of those nations were, I have not been able to learn with certainty; but by us they are distinguished by the names of Powhatans, Mannahoacs, and Monacans, now commonly called Tuscaroras. The Powhatans, who occupied the country from the sea shore up to the falls of the rivers, were a powerful nation, and seem to have consisted of seven tribes, five on the western and two on the eastern shore. Each of these tribes was subdivided into towns, families, or clans, who lived together. All the nations of Indians in North America lived in the hunter state, and depended for subsistence on hunting, fishing, and the spontaneous fruits of the earth, and a kind of grain which was planted and gathered by the women, and is now known by the name of Indian corn.   Long potatoes, pumpkins of various kinds, and squashes, were also found in use among them.   They had no flocks, herds, or tamed animals of any kind.   Their government is a kind of patriarchal confederacy.   Every town or family has a chief, who is distinguished by a particular title, and whom we commonly call " Sachem."   The several towns or families that compose a tribe, have a chief who presides over it, and the several tribes composing a nation have a chief who presides over the whole nation.   These chiefs are generally men advanced in years, and distinguished by their prudence and abilities in council.   The matters which merely regard a town or family are settled by the chief and principal men of the town ; those which regard a tribe, such as the appointment of head warriors or captains, and settling differences between different towns and families, are regulated at a meeting or council of the chiefs from the several towns ; and those which regard the whole nation, such as the making war, concluding peace, or forming alliances with the neighboring nations, are deliberated on and determined in a national council composed of the chiefs of the tribe, attended by the head warriors and a number of the chiefs from the towns, who are his counsellors.   In every town there is a council house, where the chief and old men of the town assemble, when occasion requires, and consult what is proper to be done.   Every tribe has a fixed place for the chiefs of the towns to meet and consult on the business of the tribe ; and in every nation there is what they call the central council house, or central council fire, where the chiefs of the several tribes, with the principal warriors, convene to consult and determine on their national affairs.   When any matter is proposed in the national council, it is common for the chiefs of the several tribes to consult thereon apart with their counsellors, and when they have agreed, to deliver the opinion of the tribe at the national council ; and, as their government seems to rest wholly on persuasion, they endeavor, by mutual concessions, to obtain unanimity.   Such is the government that still subsists among the Indian nations bordering upon the United States. Some historians seem to think, that the dignity of office of Sachem was hereditary. But that opinion does not appear to be well founded. The sachem or chief of the tribe seems to be by election. And sometimes persons who are strangers, and adopted into the tribe, are promoted to this dignity, on account of their abilities. Thus on the arrival of Captain Smith, the first founder of the colony of Virginia, Opechancanough, who was Sachem or chief of the Chickahominies, one of the tribes of the Powhatans, is said to have been of another tribe, and even of another nation, so that no certain account could be obtained of his origin or descent. The chiefs of the nation seem to have been by a rotation among the tribes. Thus when Captain Smith, in the year 1609, questioned Powhatan (who was the chief of the nation, and whose proper name is said to have been Wahunsonacock) respecting the succession, the old chief informed him, " that he was very old, and had seen the death of all his people thrice ;* that not one of these generations were then living except himself ; that he must soon die, and the succession descend in order to his brother Opichapan, Opechancanough, and Catataugh, and then to his two sisters, and their two daughters." But these were appellations designating the tribes in the confederacy. For the persons named are not his real brothers, but the chiefs of different tribes. Accordingly in 1618, when Powhatan died, he was succeeded by Opichapan, and after his decease, Opechancanough became chief of the nation. I need only mention another instance to show that the chiefs of the tribes claimed this kindred with the head of the nation. In 1622, when Raleigh Crashaw was with Japa-

---

* This is one generation more than the poet ascribes to the life of Nestor :

Tö d' ede duo men geneai meropö anthröpön
Ephthiath oi oi prosthen ama traphen ed' egneonto
En Pulö egathee, meta de tritatoisin anassen.

II. Hom. II. 250.

Two generations now had passed away,
Wise by his rules, and happy by his sway ;
Two ages o'er his native realm he reign'd,
And now th' example of the third remained.   POPE

zaw, the Sachem or chief of the Potomacs, Opechancanough, who had great power and influence, being the second man in the nation, and next in succession to Opichapan, and who was a bitter but secret enemy to the English, and wanted to engage his nation in a war with them, sent two baskets of beads to the Potomac chief, and desired him to kill the Englishman that was with him. Japazaw replied, that the English were his friends, and Opichapan his *brother*, and that therefore there should be no blood shed between them by his means. It is also to be observed, that when the English first came over, in all their conferences with any of the chiefs, they constantly heard him make mention of his *brother*, with whom he must consult, or to whom he referred them, meaning thereby either the chief of the nation, or the tribes in confederacy. The Manahoacks are said to have been a confederacy of four tribes, and in alliance with the Monacans, in the war which they were carrying on against the Powhatans.

To the northward of these there was another powerful nation which occupied the country from the head of the Chesapeake bay up to the Kittatinney mountain, and as far eastward as Connecticut river, comprehending that part of New York which lies between the Highlands and the ocean, all the State of New Jersey, that part of Pennsylvania which is watered, below the range of the Kittatinney mountains, by the rivers or streams falling into the Delaware, and the county of Newcastle in the State of Delaware, as far as Duck creek. It is to be observed, that the nations of Indians distinguished their countries one from another by natural boundaries, such as ranges of mountains or streams of water. But as the heads of rivers frequently interlock, or approach near to each other, as those who live upon a stream claim the country watered by it, they often encroached on each other, and this is a constant source of war between the different nations. The nation occupying the tract of country last described, called themselves Lenopi. The French writers call them Loups ; and among the English they are now commonly called Delawares. This nation or confederacy consisted of five tribes, who all spoke one language. 1. The Chihohocki.

who dwelt on the west side of the river now called Delaware, a name which it took from Lord De la War, who put into it on his passage from Virginia in the year ———, but which by the Indians was called Chihohocki. 2. The Wanami, who inhabit the country called New Jersey, from the Rariton to the sea. 3. The Munsey, who dwelt on the upper streams of the Delaware, from the Kittatinney mountains down to the Lehigh or western branch of the Delaware. 4. The Wabinga, who are sometimes called River Indians, sometimes Mohickanders, and who had their dwelling between the west branch of Delaware and Hudson's river, from the Kittatinney Ridge down to the Rariton; and 5. The Mahiccon, or Manhattan, who occupied Staten Island, York Island (which from its being the principal seat of their residence was formerly called Manhattan), Long Island, and that part of New York and Connecticut which lies between Hudson and Connecticut rivers, from the highland, which is a continuation of the Kittatinney Ridge down to the Sound. This nation had a close alliance with the Shawanese, who lived on the Susquehanna and to the westward of that river, as far as the Alleghany mountains, and carried on a long war with another powerful nation or confederacy of Indians, which lived to the north of them between the Kittatinney mountains or highlands, and the Lake Ontario, and who call themselves Mingoes, and are called by the French writers Iroquois, by the English the Five Nations, and by the Indians to the southward, with whom they were at war, Massawomacs. This war was carrying on in its greatest fury, when Captain Smith first arrived in Virginia. The Mingo warriors had penetrated down the Susquehannah to the mouth of it. In one of his excursions up the bay, at the mouth of Susquehannah, in 1608, Captain Smith met with six or seven of their canoes full of warriors, who were coming to attack their enemies in the rear. In an excursion which he had made a few weeks before, up the Rappahannock, and in which he had a skirmish with a party of the Manahoacs, and taken a brother of one of their chiefs prisoner, he first heard of this nation. For when he asked the prisoner why his nation attacked the English? the prisoner said, because his nation had heard that the

English came from under the world to take their world from them. Being asked, how many worlds he knew? he said, he knew but one, which was under the sky that covered him, and which consisted of Powhatans, the Manakins, and the Massawomacs. Being questioned concerning the latter, he said, they dwelt on a great water to the North, that they had many boats, and so many men, that they waged war with all the rest of the world. The Mingo confederacy then consisted of five tribes; three who are the elder, to wit, the Senecas, who live to the West, the Mohawks to the East, and the Onondagas between them; and two who are called the younger tribes, namely, the Cayugas and Oneidas. All these tribes speak one language, and were then united in a close confederacy, and occupied the tract of country from the east end of Lake Erie to Lake Champlain, and from the Kittatinney and Highlands to the Lake Ontario and the river Cadaraqui, or St. Lawrence. They had some time before that, carried on a war with a nation, who lived beyond the lakes, and were called Adirondacks. In this war they were worsted; but having made a peace with them, through the intercession of the French who were then settling Canada, they turned their arms against the Lenopi; and as this war was long and doubtful, they, in the course of it, not only exerted their whole force, but put in practice every measure which prudence or policy could devise to bring it to a successful issue. For this purpose they bent their course down the Susquehannah, and warring with the Indians in their way, and having penetrated as far as the mouth of it, they, by the terror of their arms, engaged a nation, now known by the name of Nanticocks, Conoys, and Tuteloes, and who lived between Chesapeake and Delaware bays, and bordering on the tribe of Chihohocki, to enter into an alliance with them. They also formed an alliance with the Monicans, and stimulated them to a war with the Lenopi and their confederates. At the same time the Mohawks carried on a furious war down the Hudson against the Mohiccons and River Indians, and compelled them to purchase a temporary and precarious peace, by acknowledging them to be their superiors, and paying an annual tribute. The Lenopi being surrounded with enemies, and hard pressed, and having lost many of their warriors, were at last compelled to sue for peace, which was granted to them on the condition that they should put themselves under the protection of the Mingoes, confine themselves to raising corn, hunting for the subsistence of their families, and no longer have the power of making war. This is what the Indians call making them women. And in this condition the Lenopi were when William Penn first arrived and began the settlement of Pennsylvania in 1682.

(6.) p. 342. From the figurative language of the Indians, as well as from the practice of those we are still acquainted with, it is evident that it was and still continues to be, a constant custom among the Indians to gather up the bones of the dead, and deposit them in a particular place. Thus, when they make peace with any nation with whom they have been at war, after burying the hatchet, they take up the belt of wampum, and say, " We now gather up all the bones of those who have been slain, and bury them," &c. See all the treaties of peace. Besides, it is customary when any of them die at a distance from home, to bury them, and afterwards to come and take up the bones and carry them home. At a treaty which was held at Lancaster with the Six Nations, one of them died, and was buried in the woods a little distance from the town. Some time after a party came and took up the body, separated the flesh from the bones by boiling and scraping them clean, and carried them to be deposited in the sepulchres of their ancestors. The operation was so offensive and disagreeable, that nobody could come near them while they were performing it.

(7.) p. 350. The Osweàtchies, Connosedàgoes and Cohunnegagoes, or, as they are commonly called, Caghnewàgos, are of the Mingo or Six Nation Indians, who, by the influence of the French missionaries, have been separated from their nation, and induced to settle there.

I do not know of what nation the Augquàgahs are, but suspect they are a family of the Senecas.

The Nanticocks and Conòies were formerly of a nation that lived at the head of Chesapeake bay, and who, of late years, have been adopted into the Mingo or Iroquois confederacy, and make a seventh nation. The Monacans or Tuscaroras, who were taken into the confederacy in 1712, making the sixth.

The Saponies are families of the Wanamies, who removed from New Jersey, and with the Mohiccons, Munsies, and Delawares, belonging to the Lenopi nation. The Mingos are a war colony from the Six Nations; so are the Cohunnewagos.

Of the rest of the Northern tribes I never have been able to learn anything certain. But all accounts seem to agree in this, that there is a very powerful nation, distinguished by a variety of names taken from the several towns or families, but commonly called Tawas or Ottawas, who speak one language, and live round and on the waters that fall into the western lakes, and extend from the waters of the Ohio quite to the waters falling into Hudson's bay.

No. II.

In the summer of the year 1783, it was expected that the assembly of Virginia would call a Convention for the establishment of a Constitution. The following draught of a fundamental Constitution for the Commonwealth of Virginia was then prepared, with a design of being proposed in such Convention had it taken place.

To the citizens of the commonwealth of Virginia, and all others whom it may concern, the delegates for the said commonwealth in Convention assembled, send greeting:

It is known to you and to the world, that the government of Great Britain, with which the American States were not long since connected, assumed over them an authority unwarrantable and oppressive; that they endeavored to enforce this authority by arms, and that the States of New Hampshire, Massachusetts, Rhode Island, Connecticut, New York, New Jersey, Pennsylvania, Delaware, Maryland, Virginia, North Carolina, South Carolina, and Georgia, considering resistance, with all its train of horrors, as a lesser evil than abject submission, closed in the appeal to arms. It hath pleased the Sovereign Disposer of all human events to give to this appeal an issue favorab e to the rights of the States ; to enable them to reject forever all dependence on a government which had shown itself so capable of abusing the trusts reposed in it ; and to obtain from that government a solemn and explicit acknowledgment that they are free, sovereign, and independent States. During the progress of that war, through which we had to labor for the establishment of our rights, the legislature of the commonwealth of Virginia found it necessary to make a temporary organization of government for preventing anarchy, and pointing our efforts to the two important objects of war against our invaders, and peace and happiness among ourselves. But this, like all other acts of legislation, being subject to change by subsequent legislatures, possessing equal powers with themselves ; it has been thought expedient, that it should receive those amendments which time and trial have suggested, and be rendered permanent by a power superior to that of the ordinary legislature. The general assembly therefore of this State recommend it to the good people thereof, to choose delegates to meet in general convention, with powers to form a constitution of government for them, and to declare those fundamentals to which all our laws present and future shall be subordinate ; and, in compliance with this recommendation, they have thought proper to make choice of us, and to vest us with powers for this purpose.

We, therefore, the delegates, chosen by the said good people of this State for the purpose aforesaid, and now assembled in general convention, do in execution of the authority with which we are invested, establish the following constitution and fundamentals of government for the said State of Virginia :

The said State shall forever hereafter be governed as a commonwealth.

The powers of government shall be divided into three distinct departments, each of them to be confided to a separate body of magistracy ; to wit, those which are legislative to one, those which are judiciary to another, and those which are executive to another. No person, or collection of persons, being of one of these departments, shall exercise any power properly belonging to either of the others, except in the instances hereinafter expressly permitted.

The legislature shall consist of two branches, the one to be called the House of Delegates, the other the Senate, and both together the General Assembly. The concurrence of both of these, expressed on three several readings, shall be necessary to the passage of a law.

Delegates for the general assembly shall be chosen on the last Monday of November in every year. But if an election cannot be concluded on that day, it may be adjourned from day to day till it can be concluded.

The number of delegates which each county may send shall be in proportion to the number of its qualified electors; and the whole number of delegates for the State shall be so proportioned to the whole number of qualified electors in it, that they shall never exceed three hundred, nor be fewer than one hundred. Whenever such excess or deficiency shall take place, the House of Delegates so deficient or excessive shall, notwithstanding this, continue in being during its legal term; but they shall, during that term, re-adjust the proportion, so as to bring their number within the limits before mentioned at the ensuing election. If any county be reduced in its qualified electors below the number authorized to send one delegate, let it be annexed to some adjoining county.

For the election of senators, let the several counties be allotted by the senate, from time to time, into such and so many districts as they shall find best; and let each county at the time of electing its delegates, choose senatorial electors, qualified as themselves are, and four in number for each delegate their county is entitled to send, who shall convene, and conduct themselves, in such manner as the legislature shall direct, with the senatorial electors from the other counties of their district, and then choose, by ballot, one senator for every six delegates which their district is entitled to choose. Let the senatorial districts be divided into two classes, and let the members elected for one of them be dissolved at the first ensuing general election of delegates, the other at the next, and so on alternately forever.

All free male citizens, of full age, and sane mind, who for one year before shall have been resident in the county, or shall through the whole of that time have possessed therein real property of the value of —————————; or shall for the same time have been enrolled in the militia, and no others, shall have a right to vote for delegates for the said county, and for senatorial electors for the district. They shall give their votes personally, and *viva voce*.

The general assembly shall meet at the place to which the last adjournment was, on the forty-second day after the day of election of delegates, and thencefoward at any other time or place on their own adjournment, till their office expires, which shall be on the day preceding that appointed for the meeting of the next general assembly. But if they shall at any time adjourn for more than one year, it shall be as if they had adjourned for one year precisely. Neither house, without the concurrence of the other, shall adjourn for more than one week, nor to any other place than the one at which they are sitting. The governor shall also have power, with the advice of the council of State, to call them at any other time to the same place, or to a different one, if that shall have become, since the last adjournment, dangerous from an enemy, or from infection.

A majority of either house shall be a quorum, and shall be requisite for doing business; but any smaller proportion which from time to time shall be thought expedient by the respective houses, shall be sufficient to call for, and to punish, their non-attending members, and to adjourn themselves for any time not exceeding one week.

The members, during their attendance on the general assembly, and for so long a time before and after as shall be necessary for travelling to and from the same, shall be privileged from all personal restraint and assault, and shall have no other privilege whatsoever. They shall receive during the same time, daily wages in gold or silver, equal to the value of two bushels of wheat. This value shall be deemed one dollar by the bushel till the year 1790, in which, and in every tenth year thereafter, the general court, at their first sessions in the year, shall cause a special jury, of the most respectable merchants and farmers, to be summoned, to declare what shall have been the averaged value of wheat during the last ten years ; which averaged value shall be the measure of wages for the ten subsequent years.

Of this general assembly, the treasurer, attorney general, register, ministers of the gospel, officers of the regular armies of this State, or of the United States, persons receiving salaries or emoluments from any power foreign to our confederacy, those who are not resident in the county for which they are chosen delegates, or districts for which they are chosen senators, those who are not qualified as electors, persons who shall have committed treason, felony, or such other crime as would subject them to infamous punishment, or who shall have been convicted by due course of law of bribery or corruption, in endeavoring to procure an election to the said assembly, shall be incapable of being members. All others, not herein elsewhere excluded, who may elect, shall be capable of being elected thereto.

Any member of the said assembly accepting any office of profit under this State, or the United States, or any of them, shall thereby vacate his seat, but shall be capable of being re-elected.

Vacancies occasioned by such disqualifications, by death, or otherwise, shall be supplied by the electors, on a writ from the speaker of the respective house.

The general assembly shall not have power to infringe this constitution ; to abridge the civil rights of any person on account of his religious belief ; to restrain him from professing and supporting that belief, or to compel him to contributions, other than those he shall have personally stipulated for the support of that or any other ; to ordain death for any crime but treason or murder, or military offences ; to pardon, or give a power of pardoning persons duly convicted of treason or felony, but instead thereof they may substitute one or two new trials, and no more ; to pass laws for punishing actions done before the existence of such laws ; to pass any bill of attainder of treason or felony ; to prescribe torture in any case whatever ; nor to permit the introduction of any more slaves to reside in this State, or the continuance of slavery beyond the generation which shall be living on the thirty-first day of December, one thousand eight hundred; all persons born after that day being hereby declared free.

The general assembly shall have power to sever from this State all or any parts of its territory westward of the Ohio, or of the meridian of the mouth of the Great Kanhaway, and to cede to Congress one hundred square miles of territory in any other part of this State, exempted from the jurisdiction and government of this State so long as Congress shall hold their sessions therein, or in any territory adjacent thereto, which may be tendered to them by any other State.

They shall have power to appoint the speakers of their respective houses, treasurer, auditors, attorney general, register, all general officers of the military, their own clerks and serjeants, and no other officers, except where, in other parts of this constitution, such appointment is expressly given them.

The executive powers shall be exercised by a *Governor*, who shall be chosen by joint ballot of both houses of assembly, and when chosen shall remain in office five years, and be ineligible a second time. During his term he shall hold no other office or emolument under this State, or any other State or power whatsoever. By executive powers, we mean no reference to those powers exercised under our former government by the crown as of its prerogative, nor that these shall be the standard of what may or may not be deemed the rightful powers of the governor. We give him those powers only, which are necessary to execute the laws (and administer the government), and which are not in their nature either legislative or judiciary. The application of this idea must be left to reason. We do however expressly deny him the prerogative powers of erecting courts, offices, boroughs, corporations, fairs, markets, ports, beacons, light-houses, and seamarks; of laying embargoes, of establishing precedence, of retaining within the State, or recalling to it any citizen thereof, and of making denizens, except so far as he may be authorized from time to time by the legislature to exercise any of those powers. The power of declaring war and concluding peace, of contracting alliances, of issuing letters of marque and reprisal, of raising and introducing armed forces, of building armed ves-seis, forts, or strongholds, of coining money or regulating its value, of regulating weights and measures, we leave to be exercised under the authority of the confederation; but in all cases respecting them which are out of the said confederation, they shall be exercised by the governor, under the regulation of such laws as the legislature may think it expedient to pass.

The whole military of the State, whether regular, or of militia, shall be subject to his directions; but he shall leave the execution of those directions to the general officers appointed by the legislature.

His salary shall be fixed by the legislature at the session of the assembly in which he shall be appointed, and before such appointment be made; or if it be not then fixed, it shall be the same which his next predecessor in office was entitled to. In either case he may demand it quarterly out of any money which shall be in the public treasury; and it shall not be in the power of the legislature to give him less or more, either during his continuance in office, or after he shall have gone out of it. The lands, houses, and other things appropriated to the use of the governor, shall remain to his use during his continuance in office.

A *Council of State* shall be chosen by joint ballot of both houses of assembly, who shall hold their offices seven years, and be ineligible a second time, and who, while they shall be of the said council, shall hold no other office or emolument under this State, or any other State or power whatsoever. Their duty shall be to attend and advise the governor when called on by him, and their advice in any case shall be a sanction to him. They shall also have power, and it shall be their duty, to meet at their own will, and to give their advice, though not required by the governor, in cases where they shall think the public good calls for it. Their advice and proceedings shall be entered in books to be kept for that purpose, and shall be signed as approved or disapproved by the members present. These books shall be laid before either house of assembly when called for by them. The said council shall consist of eight members for the present; but their numbers may be increased or reduced by the legislature, whenever they shall think it necessary; provided such reduction be made only as the appointments become vacant by death, resignation, disqualification, or regular deprivation. A majority of their actual number, and not fewer, shall be a quorum. They shall be allowed for the present —— each by the year, payable quarterly out of any money which shall be in the public treasury. Their salary, however, may be increased or abated from time to time, at the discretion of the legislature; provided such increase or abatement shall not, by any ways or means, be made to affect either then, or at any future time, any one of those then actually in office. At the end of each quarter their salary shall be divided into equal portions by the number of days on which, during that quarter, a council has been held, or required by the governor, or by their own adjournment, and one of those portions shall be withheld from each member for every of the said days which, without cause allowed good by the board, he failed to attend, or departed before adjournment without their leave. If no board should have been held during that quarter, there shall be no deduction.

They shall annually choose a *President*, who shall preside in council in the absence of the governor, and who, in case of his office becoming vacant by death or otherwise, shall have authority to exercise all his functions, till a new appointment be made, as he shall also in any interval during which the governor shall declare himself unable to attend to the duties of his office.

The *Judiciary* powers shall be exercised by county courts and such other inferior courts as the legislature shall think proper to continue or to erect, by three superior courts, to wit, a Court of Admiralty, a general Court of Common Law, and a High Court of Chancery ; and by one Supreme Court, to be called the Court of Appeals.

The judges of the high court of chancery, general court, and court of admiralty, shall be four in number each, to be appointed by joint ballot of both houses of assembly, and to hold their offices during good behavior. While they continue judges, they shall hold no other office or emolument, under this State, or any other State or power whatsoever, except that they may be delegated to Congress, receiving no additional allowance.

These judges, assembled together, shall constitute the Court of Appeals, whose business shall be to receive and determine appeals from the three superior courts, but to receive no original causes, except in the cases expressly permitted herein.

A majority of the members of either of these courts, and not fewer, shall be a quorum. But in the Court of Appeals nine members shall be necessary to do business. Any smaller numbers however may be authorized by the legislature to adjourn their respective courts.

They shall be allowed for the present —— each by the year, payable quarterly out of any money which shall be in the public treasury. Their salaries, however, may be increased or abated, from time to time, at the discretion of the legislature, provided such increase or abatement shall not by any ways or means, be made to affect, either then, or at any future time, any one of those then actually in office. At the end of each quarter their salary shall be divided into equal portions by the number of days on which, during that quarter, their respective courts sat, or should have sat, and one of these portions shall be withheld from each member for every of the said days which, without cause allowed good by his court, he failed to attend, or departed before adjournment without their leave. If no court should have been held during the quarter, there shall be no deduction.

There shall, moreover, be a *Court of Impeachments*, to consist of three members of the Council of State, one of each of the superior courts of Chancery, Common Law, and Admiralty, two members of the house of delegates and one of the Senate, to be chosen by the body respectively of which they are. Before this court any member of the three branches of government, that is to say, the governor, any member of the council, of the two houses of legislature, or of the superior courts, may be impeached by the governor, the council, or either of the said houses or courts, and by no other, for such misbehavior in office as would be sufficient to remove him therefrom; and the only sentence they shall have authority to pass shall be that of deprivation and future incapacity of office. Seven members shall be requisite to make a court, and two-thirds of those present must concur in the sentence. The offences cognizable by this court shall be cognizable by no other, and they shall be triers of the fact as well as judges of the law.

The justices or judges of the inferior courts already erected, or hereafter to be erected, shall be appointed by the governor, on advice of the council of State, and shall hold their offices during good behavior, or the existence of their courts. For breach of the good behavior, they shall be tried according to the laws of the land, before the Court of Appeals, who shall be judges of the fact as well as of the law. The only sentence they shall have authority to pass shall be that of deprivation and future incapacity of office, and two-thirds of the members present must concur in this sentence.

All courts shall appoint their own clerks, who shall hold their offices during good behavior, or the existence of their court; they shall also appoint all other attending officers to continue during their pleasure. Clerks appointed by the supreme or superior courts shall be removable by their respective courts. Those to be appointed by other courts shall have been previously examined, and certified to be duly qualified, by some two members of the general court, and shall be removable for breach of the good behavior by the Court of Appeals only, who shall be judges of the fact as well as of the law. Two-thirds of the members present must concur in the sentence.

The justices or judges of the inferior courts may be members of the legislature.

The judgment of no inferior court shall be final, in any civil case, of greater value than fifty bushels of wheat, as last rated in the general court for setting the allowance to the members of the general assembly, nor in any case of treason, felony, or other crime which should subject the party to infamous punishment.

In all causes depending before any court, other than those of impeachments, of appeals, and military courts, facts put in issue shall be tried by jury, and in all courts whatever witnesses shall give testimony *viva voce* in open court, wherever their attendance can be procured; and all parties shall be allowed counsel and cumpulsory process for their witnesses.

Fines, amercements, and terms of imprisonment left indefinite by the law, other than for contempts, shall be fixed by the jury, triers of the offence.

The governor, two councillors of State, and a judge from each of the superior Courts of Chancery, Common Law, and Admiralty, shall be a council to revise all bills which shall have passed both houses of assembly, in which council the governor, when present, shall preside. Every bill, before it becomes a law, shall be represented to this council, who shall have a right to advise its rejection, returning the bill, with their advice and reasons in writing, to the house in which it originated, who shall proceed to reconsider the said bill. But if after such reconsideration, two-thirds of the house shall be of opinion that the bill should pass finally, they shall pass and send it, with the advice and written reasons of the said Council of Revision, to the other house, wherein if two-thirds also shall be of opinion it should pass finally, it shall thereupon become law ; otherwise it shall not.

If any bill, presented to the said council, be not, within one week (exclusive of the day of presenting it) returned by them, with their advice of rejection and reasons, to the house wherein it originated, or to the clerk of the said house, in case of its adjournment over the expiration of the week, it shall be law from the expiration of the week, and shall then be demandable by the clerk of the House of Delegates, to be filed of record in his office.

The bills which they approve shall become law from the time of such approbation, and shall then be returned to, or demandable by, the clerk of the House of Delegates, to be filed of record in his office.

A bill rejected on advice of the Council of Revision may again be proposed, during the same session of assembly, with such alterations as will render it conformable to their advice.

The members of the said Council of Revision shall be appointed from time to time by the board or court of which they respectively are. Two of the executive and two of the judiciary members shall be requisite to do business ; and to prevent the evils of non-attendance, the board and courts may at any time name all, or so many as they will, of their members, in the particular order in which they would choose the duty of attendance to devolve from preceding to subsequent members, the preceding failing to attend. They shall have additionally for their services in this council the same allowance as members of assembly have.

The confederation is made a part of this constitution, subject to such future alterations as shall be agreed to by the legislature of this State, and by all the other confederating States.

The delegates to Congress shall be five in number; any three of whom, and no fewer, may be a representation. They shall be appointed by joint ballot of both houses of assembly for any term not exceeding one year, subject to be recalled, within the term, by joint vote of both the said houses. They may at the same time be members of the legislative or judiciary departments, but not of the executive.

The benefits of the writ of Habeas Corpus shall be extended, by the legislature, to every person within this State, and without fee, and shall be so facilitated that no person may be detained in prison more than ten days after he shall have demanded and been refused such writ by the judge appointed by law, or if none be appointed, then by any judge of a superior court, nor more than ten days after such writ shall have been served on the person detaining him, and no order given, on due examination, for his remandment or discharge.

The military shall be subordinate to the civil power.

Printing presses shall be subject to no other restraint than liableness to legal prosecution for false facts printed and published.

Any two of the three branches of government concurring in opinion, each by the voice of two-thirds of their whole existing number, that a convention is necessary for altering this constitution, or correcting breaches of it, they shall be authorized to issue writs to every county for the election of so many delegates as they are authorized to send to the general assembly, which elections shall be held, and writs returned, as the laws shall have provided in the case of elections of delegates of assembly, *mu-*

tatis mutandis, and the said delegates shall meet at the usual place of holding assemblies, three months after date of such writs, and shall be acknowledged to have equal powers with this present convention. The said writs shall be signed by all the members approving the same.

To introduce this government, the following special and temporary provision is made.

This convention being authorized only to amend those laws which constituted the form of government, no general dissolution of the whole system of laws can be supposed to have taken place ; but all laws in force at the meeting of this convention, and not inconsistent with this constitution, remain in full force, subject to alterations by the ordinary legislature.

The present general assembly shall continue till the forty-second day after the last Monday of November in this present year. On the said last Monday of November in this present year, the several counties shall by their electors qualified as provided by this constitution, elect delegates, which for the present shall be, in number, one for every ———— militia of the said county, according to the latest returns in possession of the governor, and shall also choose senatorial electors in proportion thereto, which senatorial electors shall meet on the fourteenth day after the day of their election, at the court house of that county of their present district which would stand first in an alphabetical arrangement of their counties, and shall choose senators in the proportion fixed by this constitution. The elections and returns shall be conducted, in all circumstances not hereby particularly prescribed, by the same persons and under the same forms as prescribed by the present laws in elections of senators and delegates of assembly. The said senators and delegates shall constitute the first general assembly of the new government, and shall specially apply themselves to the procuring an exact return from every county of the number of its qualified electors, and to the settlement of the number of delegates to be elected for the ensuing general assembly.

The present governor shall continue in office to the end of the term for which he was elected.

All other officers of every kind shall continue in office as they would have done had their appointment been under this constitution, and new ones, where new are hereby called for, shall be appointed by the authority to which such appointment is referred. One of the present judges of the general court, he consenting thereto, shall by joint ballot of both houses of assembly, at their first meeting, be transferred to the High Court of Chancery.

No. III.

An Act for establishing Religious Freedom, passed in the Assembly of Virginia in the beginning of the year 1786.

Well aware that Almighty God hath created the mind free ; that all attempts to influence it by temporal punishments or burdens, or by civil incapacitations, tend only to beget habits of hypocrisy and meanness, and are a departure from the plan of the Holy Author of our religion, who being Lord both of body and mind, yet chose not to propagate it by coercions on either, as was in his Almighty power to do ; that the impious presumption of legislators and rulers, civil as well as ecclesiastical, who, being themselves but fallible and uninspired men have assumed dominion over the faith of others, setting up their own opinions and modes of thinking as the only true and infallible, and as such endeavoring to impose them on others, hath established and maintained false religions over the greatest part of the world, and through all time ; that to compel a man to furnish contributions of money for the propagation of opinions which he disbelieves, is sinful and tyrannical ; that even the forcing him to support this or that teacher of his own religious persuasion, is depriving him of the comfortable liberty of giving his contributions to the particular pastor whose morals he would make his pattern, and whose powers he feels most persuasive to righteousness, and is withdrawing from the ministry those temporal rewards, which proceeding from an approbation of their personal

conduct, are an additional incitement to earnest and unremitting
labors for the instruction of mankind ; that our civil rights
have no dependence on our religious opinions, more than our
opinions in physics or geometry ; that, therefore, the proscrib-
ing any citizen as unworthy the public confidence by laying
upon him an incapacity of being called to the offices of trust
and emolument, unless he profess or renounce this or that religious opinion, is depriving him injuriously of those privileges
and advantages to which in common with his fellow citizens he
has a natural right ; that it tends also to corrupt the principles
of that very religion it is meant to encourage, by bribing, with a
monopoly of worldly honors and emoluments, those who will
externally profess and conform to it ; that though indeed these
are criminal who do not withstand such temptation, yet neither
are those innocent who lay the bait in their way ; that to suffer
the civil magistrate to intrude his powers into the field of opinion and to restrain the profession or propagation of principles, on
the supposition of their ill tendency, is a dangerous fallacy, which
at once destroys all religious liberty, because he being of course
judge of that tendency, will make his opinions the rule of judgment, and approve or condemn the sentiments of others only as
they shall square with or differ from his own ; that it is time
enough for the rightful purposes of civil government, for its officers to interfere when principles break out into overt acts
against peace and good order; and finally, that truth is great and
will prevail if left to herself, that she is the proper and sufficient
antagonist to error, and has nothing to fear from the conflict,
unless by human interposition disarmed of her natural weapons,
free argument and debate, errors ceasing to be dangerous when
it is permitted freely to contradict them.

Be it therefore enacted by the General Assembly, That no
man shall be compelled to frequent or support any religious worship, place or ministry whatsoever, nor shall be enforced, restrained, molested, or burthened in his body or goods, nor shall
otherwise suffer on account of his religious opinions or belief;
but that all men shall be free to profess, and by argument to
maintain, their opinions in matters of religion, and that the

same shall in nowise diminish, enlarge, or affect their civil capacities.

And though we well know this Assembly, elected by the people for the ordinary purposes of legislation only, have no power to restrain the acts of succeeding assemblies, constituted with the powers equal to our own, and that therefore to declare this act irrevocable, would be of no effect in law, yet we are free to declare, and do declare, that the rights hereby asserted are of the natural rights of mankind, and that if any act shall be hereafter passed to repeal the present or to narrow its operation, such act will be an infringement of natural right.

No. IV.

The "Notes on Virginia" were written, in Virginia, in the years 1781 and 1782, in answer to certain queries proposed to me by Monsieur de Marbois, then secretary of the French legation in the United States; and a manuscript copy was delivered to him. A few copies, with some additions, were afterwards, in 1784, printed in Paris, and given to particular friends. In speaking of the animals of America, the theory of M. de Buffon, the Abbe Raynal, and others presented itself to consideration. They have supposed there is something in the soil, climate, and other circumstances of America, which occasions animal nature to degenerate, not excepting even the man, native or adoptive, physical or moral. This theory, so unfounded and degrading to one-third of the globe, was called to the bar of fact and reason. Among other proofs adduced in contradiction of this hypothesis, the speech of Logan, an Indian chief, delivered to Lord Dunmore in 1774, was produced, as a specimen of the talents of the aboriginals of this country, and particularly of their eloquence; and it was believed that Europe had never produced anything superior to this morsel of eloquence. In order to make it intelligible to the reader, the transaction, on which it was founded, was stated, as it had been generally related in America at the time, and as I had heard it myself, in the circle of Lord Dunmore, and the officers who accompanied him; and the speech itself was given as it had, ten years before the printing of that book, circulated in the newspapers through all the then colonies,

* In connection with this appendix see letter to Governor Henry, printed as Note in p. 61.

through the magazines of Great Britain, and periodical publications of Europe. For three and twenty years it passed uncontradicted; nor was it ever suspected that it even admitted contradiction. In 1797, however, for the first time, not only the whole transaction respecting Logan was affirmed in the public papers to be false, but the speech itself suggested to be a forgery, and even a forgery of mine, to aid me in proving that the man of America was equal in body and in mind, to the man of Europe. But wherefore the forgery; whether Logan's or mine, it would still have been American. I should indeed consult my own fame if the suggestion, that this speech is mine, were suffered to be believed. He would have just right to be proud who could with truth claim that composition. But it is none of mine; and I yield it to whom it is due.

On seeing then that this transaction was brought into question, I thought it my duty to make particular inquiry into its foundation. It was the more my duty, as it was alleged that, by ascribing to an individual therein named, a participation in the murder of Logan's family, I had done an injury to his character, which it had not deserved. I had no knowledge personally of that individual. I had no reason to aim an injury at him. I only repeated what I had heard from others, and what thousands had heard and believed as well as myself; and which no one indeed, till then, had been known to question. Twenty-three years had now elapsed, since the transaction took place. Many of those acquainted with it were dead, and the living dispersed to very distant parts of the earth. Few of them were even known to me. To those however of whom I knew, I made application by letter; and some others, moved by a regard for truth and justice, were kind enough to come forward, of themselves, with their testimony. These fragments of evidence, the small remains of a mighty mass which time has consumed, are here presented to the public, in the form of letters, certificates, or affidavits, as they came to me. I have rejected none of these forms, nor required other solemnities from those whose motives and characters were pledges of their truth. Historical transactions are deemed to be well vouched by the simple declarations of those who have borne a part in them ; and especially of persons having no interest to falsify or disfigure them. The world will now see whether they, or I, have injured Cresap, by believing Logan's charge against him ; and they will decide between Logan and Cresap, whether Cresap was innocent, and Logan a calumniator ?

In order that the reader may have a clear conception of the transactions, to which the different parts of the following declarations refer, he must take notice that they establish four different murders. 1. Of two Indians, a little above Wheeling. 2. Of others at Grave Creek, among whom were some of Logan's relations. 3. The massacre at Baker's bottom, on the Ohio, opposite the mouth of Yellow Creek, where were other relations of Logan. 4. Of those killed at the same place, coming in canoes to the relief of their friends. I place the numbers 1, 2, 3, 4, against certain paragraphs of the evidence, to indicate the particular murder to which the paragraph relates, and present also a small sketch or map of the principal scenes of these butcheries, for their more ready comprehension.

Extract of a letter from the Honorable Judge Innes, of Frankfort in Kentucky, to Thomas Jefferson, dated Kentucky, near Frankfort, March 2d, 1799

I recollect to have seen Logan's speech in 1775, in one of the public prints. That Logan conceived Cresap to be the author of the murder at Yellow Creek, it is in my power to give, perhaps, a more particular information, than any other person you can apply to.

In 1774 I lived in Fincastle county, now divided into Washington, Montgomery and part of Wythe. Being intimate in Col. Preston's family, I happened in July to be at his house, when an express was sent to him as County Lieut. requesting a guard of the militia to be ordered out for the protection of the inhabitants residing low down on the north fork of Holston river. The express brought with him a War Club, and a note which was left tied to it at the house of one Robertson, whose family were cut off by the Indians, and gave rise for the application to Col. Preston, of which the following is a copy, then taken by me in my memorandum book.

" Captain Cresap,—What did you kill my people on Yellow Creek for ? The white people killed my kin at Conestoga, a great while ago ; and I thought nothing of that. But you killed my kin again, on Yellow Creek, and took my Cousin Prisoner. Then I thought I must kill too; and I have been three times to war since; but the Indians are not angry; only myself.

"July 21st, 1774.   Captain JOHN LOGAN."

With great respect, I am, Dear Sir, your most obedient servant,

HARRY INNES.

<hr>

Alleghany County, ss.)
State of Pennsylvania.)

Before me, the subscriber, a justice of the peace in and for said county, personally appeared John Gibson, Esquire, an associate Judge of same county, who being duly sworn, deposeth and saith that he traded with the Shawanese and other tribes of Indians then settled on the Siota in the year 1773, and in the beginning of the year 1774, and that in the month of April of the same year, he left the same Indian towns, and came to this place, in order to procure some goods and provisions, that he remained here only a few days, and then set out in company with a certain Alexander Blaine and M. Elliot by water to return to the towns on the Siota, and that one evening as they were drifting in their canoes near the Long Reach on the Ohio, they were hailed by a number of white men on the South West shore, who requested them to put ashore, as they had disagreeable news to inform them of; that we then landed on shore; and found amongst the party, a Major Angus M'Donald from West Chester, a Doctor Woods from same place, and a party as they said of one hundred and fifty men. We then asked the news. They informed us that some of the party who had been taken up, and improving lands near the Big Kanhawa river, had seen another party of white men, who informed them that they and some others had fell in with a party of Shawanese, who had been hunting on the South West side of the Ohio, that they had killed the whole of the Indian party, and that the others had gone across the country to Cheat river with the horses and plunder, the consequence of which they apprehended would be an Indian war, and that they were flying away. On making inquiry of them when this murder should have happened, we found that it must have been some considerable time before we left the Indian towns, and that there was not the smallest foundation for the report, as there was not a single man of the Shawanese, but what returned from hunting long before this should have happened.

We then informed them that if they would agree to remain at the place we then were, one of us would go to Hock Hocking river with some of their party, where we should find some of our people making canoes, and that if we did not find them there, we might conclude that everything was not right. Doctor Wood and another person then proposed going with me; the rest of the party seemed to agree, but said they would send and consult Captain Cresap, who was about two miles from that place. They sent off for him, and during the greatest part of the night they behaved in the most disorderly manner, threatening to kill us, and saying the damned traders were worse than the Indians and ought to be killed. In the morning Captain Michael Cresap came to the camp. I then gave him the information as above related. They then met in council, and after an hour or more Captain Cresap returned to me, and informed that he could not prevail on them to adopt the proposal I had made to them, that as he had a great regard for Captain R. Callender, a brother-in-law of mine with whom I was connected in trade, he advised me by no means to think of proceeding any further, as he was convinced the present party would fall on and kill every Indian they met on the river, that for his part he should not continue with them, but go right across the country to Red-Stone to avoid the consequences. That we then proceeded to Hocking and went up the same to the canoe place where we found our people at work, and after some days we proceeded to the towns on Siota by land. On our arrival there, we heard of the different murders committed by the party on their way up the Ohio.

This Deponent further saith that in the year 1774, he accompanied Lord Dunmore on the expedition against the Shawanese and other Indians on the Siota, that on their arrival within fifteen miles of the towns, they were met by a flag, and a white man of the name of Elliot, who informed Lord Dunmore that the Chiefs of the Shawanese had sent to request his Lordship to halt his army and send in some person, who understood their language; that this Deponent, at the request of Lord Dunmore and the whole of the officers with him, went in; that on his arrival at the towns, Logan, the Indian, came to where the deponent was sitting with the Corn-Stalk, and the other chiefs of the Shawanese, and asked him to walk out with him; that they went into a copse of wood, where they sat down, when Logan, after shedding abundance of tears, delivered to him the speech, nearly as related by Mr. Jefferson in his notes on the State of Virginia; that he the deponent told him that it was not Col. Cresap who had murdered his relations, and that although his son Captain Michael Cresap was with the party who killed a Shawanese chief and other Indians, yet he was not present when his relations were killed at Baker's, near the mouth of Yellow Creek on the Ohio; that this Deponent on his return to camp delivered the speech to Lord Dunmore; and that the murders perpetrated as above were considered as ultimately the cause of the war of 1774, commonly called Cresap's war.   JOHN GIBSON.

Sworn and subscribed the 4th April, 1800, at Pittsburg, before me,

JER. BARKER.

———

Extract of a letter from Col. Ebenezer Zane, to the honorable John Brown, one of the senators in Congress from Kentucky; dated Wheeling, Feb. 4th, 1800.

I was myself, with many others, in the practice of making improvements on lands upon the Ohio, for the purpose of acquiring rights to the same. Being on the Ohio at the mouth of Sandy Creek, in company with many others, news circulated that the Indians had robbed some of the Land jobbers. This news induced the people generally to ascend the Ohio. I was among the number. I On our arrival at the Wheeling, being informed that there were two Indians with some traders near and above Wheeling, a proposition was made by the then Captain Michael Cresap to waylay and kill the Indians upon the river. This measure I opposed with much violence, alleging that the killing of those Indians might involve the country in a war. But the opposite party prevailed, and proceeded up the Ohio with Captain Cresap at their head.

In a short time the party returned, and also the traders, in a canoe; but there were no Indians in the company. I inquired what had become of the Indians, and was informed by the traders and Cresap's party that they had fallen overboard. I examined the canoe, and saw much fresh blood and some bullet holes in the canoe. This fully convinced me that the party had killed the two Indians, and thrown them into the river.

On the afternoon of the day this action happened, a report prevailed that 2 there was a camp, or party of Indians on the Ohio below and near the Wheeling. In consequence of this information, Captain Cresap with his party, joined by a number of recruits, proceeded immediately down the Ohio for the purpose, as was then generally understood, of destroying the Indians above mentioned. On the succeeding day, Captain Cresap and his party returned to Wheeling, and it was generally reported by the party that they had killed a number of Indians. Of the truth of this report I had no doubt, as one of Cresap's party was badly wounded, and the party had a fresh scalp, and a quantity of property, which they called Indian plunder. At the time of the last-mentioned transaction, it was generally reported that the party of Indians down the Ohio were Logan and his family; but I have reason to believe that this report was unfounded.

Within a few days after the transaction above mentioned, a party of Indians 3 were killed at Yellow Creek. But I must do the memory of Captain Cresap the justice to say that I do not believe that he was present at the killing of the Indians at Yellow Creek. But there is not the least doubt in my mind, that the massacre at Yellow Creek was brought on by the two transactions first stated.

All the transactions, which I have related happened in the latter end of April 1774; and there can scarcely be a doubt that they were the cause of the war which immediately followed, commonly called Dunmore's War.

I am with much esteem, yours, &c,

EBENEZER ZANE.

The certificate of William Huston of Washington county, in the State of Pennsylvania, communicated by David Riddick, Esquire, Prothonotary of Washington county, Pennsylvania; who in the letter enclosing it says "Mr. William Huston is a man of established reputation in point of integrity."

I William Huston of Washington county, in the State of Pennsylvania, do hereby certify to whom it may concern, that in the year 1774, I resided at Catfishes camp, on the main path from Wheeling to Redstone; that Michael Cresap, who resided on or near the Potomac river, on his way up from the river Ohio, at the head of a party of armed men, lay some time at my cabin.

2   I had previously heard the report of Mr. Cresap having killed some Indians, said to be the relations of "Logan" an Indian Chief. In a variety of conversations with several of Cresap's party, they boasted of the deed; and that

ın the presence of their chief. They acknowledged they had fired first on the Indians. They had with them one man on a litter, who was in the skirmish.

I do further certify that, from what I learned from the party themselves, I then formed the opinion, and have not had any reason to change the opinion since, that the killing, on the part of the whites, was what I deem the grossest murder. I further certify that some of the party, who afterwards killed some 3 women and other Indians at Baker's bottom, also lay at my cabin, on their march to the interior part of the country; they had with them a little girl, whose life had been spared by the interference of some more humane than the rest. If necessary I will make affidavit to the above to be true. Certified at Washington, this 18th day of April, Anno Domini, 1798.

WILLIAM HUSTON.

The certificate of Jacob Newland, of Shelby County, Kentucky, communicated by the Honorable Judge Innes, of Kentucky.

In the year 1774, I lived on the waters of Short Creek, a branch of the Ohio, twelve miles above Wheeling. Some time in June or in July of that year, Capt. Michael Cresap raised a party of men, and came out under Col. M'Daniel, of Hampshire County, Virginia, who commanded a detachment against the Wappotommaka towns on the Muskinghum. I met with Capt. Cresap, at Redstone fort, and entered his company. Being very well acquainted with him, we conversed freely; and he, among other conversations, informed me several times of falling in with some Indians on the Ohio some distance below the mouth 2 of Yellow Creek, and killed two or three of them; and that this murder was before that of the Indians by Great-house and others, at Yellow Creek. I do 3 not recollect the reason which Capt. Cresap assigned for committing the act, but never understood that the Indians gave any offence. Certified under my hand this 15th day of November, 1799, being an inhabitant of Shelby county, and State of Kentucky.

JACOB NEWLAND.

The Certificate of John Anderson, a merchant in Fredericksburg, Virginia; communicated by Mann Page, Esquire, of Mansfield, near Fredericksburg, who in the letter accompanying it, says, " Mr. John Anderson has for many years past been settled in Fredericksburg, in the mercantile line. I have known him in prosperous and adverse situations. He has always shown the greatest degree of Equanimity, his honesty and veracity are unimpeachable. These things can be attested by all the respectable part of the town and neighborhood of Fredericksburg."

Mr. John Anderson, a merchant in Fredericksburg, says, that in the year 1774, being a trader in the Indian country, he was at Pittsburg, to which place he

had a cargo brought up the river in a boat navigated by a Delaware Indian
1 and a white man.   That on their return down the river, with a cargo, belonging to Messrs. Butler, Michael Cresap fired on the boat, and killed the Indian,
after which two men of the name of Gatewood, and others of the name of
3 Tumblestone,* who lived on the opposite side of the river from the Indians,
with whom they were on the most friendly terms, invited a party of them to
come over and drink with them; and that, when the Indians were drunk, they
murdered them to the number of six, among whom was Logan's mother.
4 That five other Indians uneasy at the absence of their friends, came over the
river to inquire after them; when they were fired upon, and two were killed.
and the others wounded.   This was the origin of the war.

I certify the above to be true to the best of my recollection.

Attest DAVID BLAIR, 30th June, 1798.   JOHN ANDERSON.

---

*The Deposition of James Chambers, communicated by David Riddick, Esquire, Pro-
thonotary of Washington county, Pennsylvania, who, in the letter enclosing it,
shows that he entertains the most perfect confidence in the truth of Mr. Chambers.*

WASHINGTON County, ss.

Personally came before me Samuel Shannon, Esquire, one of the Commonwealth
Justices for the County of Washington in the State of Pennsylvania, James Chambers, who, being sworn according to law, deposeth and saith that in the spring
of the year 1774, he resided on the frontier near Baker's bottom on the Ohio; that
he had an intimate companion, with whom he sometimes lived, named Edward
2 King; that a report reached them that Michael Cresap had killed some Indians
3 near Grave Creek, friends to an Indian, known by the name of "Logan;" that
other of his friends, following down the river, having received intelligence, and
fearing to proceed, lest Cresap might fall in with them, encamped near the mouth of
Yellow Creek, opposite Baker's bottom; that Daniel Great-house had determined
to kill them; had made the secret known to the deponent's companion, King;
that the deponent was earnestly solicited to be of the party, and, as an induce-
ment, was told that they would get a great deal of plunder; and further, that
the Indians would be made drunk by Baker, and that little danger would follow
the expedition.   The deponent refused having any hand in killing unoffending people.   His companion, King, went with Great-house, with divers others, some of
whom had been collected at a considerable distance under an idea that Joshua Baker's family was in danger from the Indians, as war had been commenced between
Cresap and them already; that Edward King, as well as others of the party, did not
conceal from the deponent the most minute circumstances of this affair; they informed him that Great-house, concealing his people, went over to the Indian en-
campments and counted their number, and found that they were too large a party
to attack with his strength; that he then requested Joshua Baker, when any of
them came to his house, (which they had been in the habit of,) to give them what
rum they could drink, and to let him know when they were in a proper train,

* The popular pronunciation of Tomlinson, which was the real name.

and that he would then fall on them; that accordingly they found several men and women at Baker's house; that one of these women had cautioned Great-house, when over in the Indian camp, that he had better return home, as the Indian men were drinking, and that having heard of Cresap's attack on their relations down the river, they were angry, and, in a friendly manner, told him to go home. Great-house, with his party, fell on them, and killed all except a little girl, which the deponent saw with the party after the slaughter; that the Indians 4 in the camp hearing the firing, manned two canoes, supposing their friends at Baker's to be attacked, as was supposed; the party under Great-house prevented their landing by a well-directed fire, which did execution in the canoes : that Edward King showed the deponent one of the scalps. The deponent further saith, that the settlements near the river broke up, and he the deponent immediately repaired to Catfish's camp, and lived some time with Mr. William Huston; that not long after his arrival, Cresap, with his party, returning from the Ohio, came to Mr. Huston's and tarried some time; that in various conversations with the party, and in particular with a Mr. Smith, who had one arm 2 only, he was told that the Indians were acknowledged and known to be Logan's friends which they had killed, and that he heard the party say, that Logan would probably avenge their deaths.

They acknowledged that the Indians passed Cresap's encampment on the bank of the river in a peaceable manner, and encamped below him; that they went down and fired on the Indians and killed several; that the survivors flew to their arms and fired on Cresap, and wounded one man, whom the deponent saw carried on a litter by the party; that the Indians killed by Cresap were not 2 only Logan's relations, but of the women killed at Baker's one was said 3 and generally believed to be Logan's sister. The deponent further saith, that on the relation of the attack by Cresap on the unoffending Indians, he exclaimed in their hearing, that it was an atrocious murder; on which Mr. Smith threatened the deponent with the tomahawk; so that he was obliged to be cautious, fearing an injury, as the party appeared to have lost, in a great degree, sentiments of humanity as well as the effects of civilization. Sworn and subscribed at Washington, the 20th day of April, Anno Domini 1798.

Before Samuel Shannon.   JAMES CHAMBERS.

Washington County, ss.

Seal.   I, David Reddick, prothonotary of the court of common pleas, for the county of Washington in the State of Pennsylvania, do certify that Samuel Shannon, Esq., before whom the within affidavit was made, was, at the time thereof, and still is, a justice of the peace in and for the county of Washington aforesaid; and that full credit is due to all his judicial acts as such as well in courts of justice as thereout.

In testimony whereof I have hereunto set my hand and affixed the seal of my office at Washington, the 26th day of April, Anno Dom. 1798.

                                                                 DAVID REDDICK.

The certificate of Charles Polke, of Shelby County, in Kentucky, communicated by the Hon. Judge Innes, of Kentucky, who in the letter enclosing it, together with Newland's certificate, and his own declaration of the information given him by Baker, says, "I am well acquainted with John Newland, he is a man of integrity. Charles Polke and Joshua Baker both support respectable characters."

About the latter end of April or beginning of May 1774, I lived on the waters of Cross creek, about sixteen miles from Joshua Baker, who lived on the Ohio, opposite the mouth of Yellow Creek. A number of persons collected at my 3 house, and proceeded to the said Baker's and murdered several Indians, among whom was a woman said to be the sister of the Indian chief, Logan. The principal leader of the party was Daniel Great-house. To the best of my recollection the cause which gave rise to the murder was a general idea that the Indians were meditating an attack on the frontiers. Capt. Michael Cresap was not of the party; but I recollect that some time before the perpetration of the 2 above fact it was currently reported that Capt. Cresap had murdered some Indians on the Ohio, one or two, some distance below Wheeling.

Certified by me, an inhabitant of Shelby county and State of Kentucky, this 15th day of November, 1799. CHARLES POLKE.

———

The Declaration of the Hon. Judge Innes, of Frankfort, in Kentucky.

On the 14th of November, 1799, I accidentally met upon the road Joshua Baker, the person referred to in the certificate signed by Polke, who in- 3 formed me that the murder of the Indians in 1774, opposite the mouth of Yellow Creek, was perpetrated at his house by thirty-two men, led on by Daniel Great-house; that twelve were killed and six or eight wounded; among the slain was a sister and other relations of the Indian chief, Logan. Baker says, Captain Michael Cresap was not of the party; that some days preceding 1 the murder at his house two Indians left him and were on their way home; that they fell in with Capt. Cresap and a party of land improvers on the Ohio, and were murdered, if not by Cresap himself, with his approbation; he being the leader of the party, and that he had this information from Cresap.

HARRY INNES.

———

The Declaration of William Robinson.

William Robinson, of Clarksburg, in the county of Harrison, and State of Virginia, subscriber to these presents, declares that he was, in the year 1774, a resident on the west fork of Monongahela river, in the county then called West Augusta, and being in his field on the 12th of July, with two other men, they were surprised by a party of eight Indians, who shot down one of the others and made himself and the remaining one prisoners; this subscriber's wife and four children having been previously conveyed by him for safety to a fort about twenty-four miles off; that the principal Indian of the party which took them was Captain Logan; that Logan spoke English well, and very soon manifested a friendly disposition to this subscriber, and told him to be of good heart, that he would not be killed, but must go with him to his town, where he would probably be adopted in some of their families; but above all things, that he must not attempt to run away; that in the course of the journey to the Indian town he generally endeavored to keep close to Logan, who had a great deal of conversation with him, always encouraging him to be cheerful and without fear; for that he would not be killed, but should become one of them; and constantly impressing on him not to attempt to run away; that in these conversations he always charged Capt. Michael Cresap with the murder of his family; that on his arrival in the town, which was on the 18th of July, he was tied to a stake and a great debate arose whether he should not be burnt; Logan insisted on having him adopted, while others contended to burn him; that at length Logan prevailed, tied a belt of wampum round him as the mark of adoption, loosed him from the post and carried him to the cabin of an old squaw, where Logan pointed out a person who he said was this subscriber's cousin; and he afterwards understood that the old woman was his aunt, and two others his brothers, and that he now stood in the place of a warrior of the family who had been killed at Yellow Creek; that about three days after this Logan brought him a piece of paper, and told him he must write a letter for him, which he meant to carry and leave in some house where he should kill somebody; that he made ink with gun powder, and the subscriber proceeded to write the letter by his direction, addressing Captain Michael Cresap in it, and that the purport of it was, to ask "why he had killed his people? That some time before they had killed his people at some place, (the name of which the subscriber forgets,) which he had forgiven; but since that he had killed his people again at Yellow Creek, and taken his cousin, a little girl, prisoner; that therefore he must war against the whites; but that he would exchange the subscriber for his cousin." And signed it with Logan's name, which letter Logan took and set out again to war; and the contents of this letter, as recited by the subscriber, calling to mind that stated by Judge Innes to have been left, tied to a war club, in a house where a family was murdered, and that being read to the subscriber, he recognizes it, and declares he verily believes it to have been the identical letter which he wrote, and supposes he was mistaken in stating as he has done before from memory, that the offer of exchange was proposed in the letter; that it is probable that it was only promised him by Logan, but not put in the letter; while he was with the old woman, she repeatedly endeavored to make him sensible that she had been of the party at Yellow Creek, and, by signs, showed him how they decoyed her friends over the river to drink, and when they were reeling and tumbling about, tomahawked them all, and that whenever she entered on this subject she was thrown into the most violent agitations, and that he afterwards understood that, amongst the Indians killed at Yellow Creek, was a sister of Logan, very big with child, whom they ripped open, and stuck on a pole; that he continued with the Indians till the month of November, when he was released in consequence of the peace made by them with Lord Dunmore; that, while he remained with them, the Indians in general were very kind to him; and especially those who were his adopted relations; but above all, the old woman and family in which he lived, who served him with everything in their power, and never asked, or even suffered him to do any labor, seeming in truth to consider and respect him as the friend they had lost. All which several matters and things, so far as they are stated to be of his own knowledge, this subscriber solemnly declares to be true, and so far as they are stated on information from others, he believes them to be true. Given and declared under his hand at Philadelphia, this 28th day of February, 1800.

WILLIAM ROBINSON.

The deposition of Colonel William M'Kee, of Lincoln County, Kentucky, communicated by the Hon. John Brown, one of the Senators in Congress from Kentucky.

Colonel William M'Kee of Lincoln county, declareth, that in autumn, 1774, he commanded as a captain in the Bottetourt Regiment under Colonel Andrew Lewis, afterwards General Lewis; and fought in the battle at the mouth of Kanhaway, on the 10th of October in that year. That after the battle, Colonel Lewis marched the militia across the Ohio, and proceeded towards the Shawnee towns on Sciota; but before they reached the towns, Lord Dunmore, who was Commander-in-Chief of the army, and had, with a large part thereof, been up the Ohio about Hockhockin, when the battle was fought, overtook the militia, and informed them of his having since the battle concluded a treaty with the Indians; upon which the whole army returned.

And the said William declareth that, on the evening of that day on which the junction of the troops took place, he was in company with Lord Dunmore and several of his officers, and also conversed with several who had been with Lord Dunmore at the treaty; said William, on that evening, heard repeated conversations concerning an extraordinary speech at the treaty, or sent there by a chieftain of the Indians named Logan, and heard several attempts at a rehearsal of it. The speech as rehearsed excited the particular attention of said William, and the most striking members of it were impressed on his memory.

And he declares that when Thomas Jefferson's "Notes on Virginia" were published, and he came to peruse the same, he was struck with the speech of Logan as there set forth, as being substantially the same, and accordant with the speech he heard rehearsed in the camp as aforesaid.

Signed, WILLIAM M'KEE.

DANVILLE, December 18th, 1799.

We certify that Colonel William M'Kee this day signed the original certificate, of which the foregoing is a true copy, in our presence.

JAMES SPEED, Junior.

J. H. DEWEES.

The Certificate of the Honorable Stevens Thompson Mason, one of the Senators in Congress from the State of Virginia.

"Logan's Speech, delivered at the Treaty, after the battle in which Colonel Lewis was killed in 1774."

[Here follows a copy of the speech agreeing verbatim with that printed in Dixon and Hunter's Virginia Gazette of February 4, 1775, under the Williamsburg head. At the foot is this certificate.]

"The foregoing is a copy taken by me, when a boy, at school, in the year 1775, or at farthest in 1776, and lately found in an old pocket-book, containing papers and manuscripts of that period.   STEVENS THOMPSON MASON.

"January 20th, 1798."

A copy of Logan's speech, given by the late General Mercer, who fell in the battle of Trenton, January 1776, to Lewis Willis, Esquire, of Fredericksburg, in Virginia, upwards of twenty years ago, (from the date of February 1798,) communicated through Mann Page, Esquire.

"The speech of Logan, a Shawanese chief, to Lord Dunmore."

[Here follows a copy of the speech, agreeing verbatim with that in the Notes on Virginia.]

A copy of Logan's speech from the Notes on Virginia having been sent to Captain Andrew Rodgers, of Kentucky, he subjoined the following certificate:

In the year 1774 I was out with the Virginia Volunteers, and was in the battle at the mouth of Canhawee, and afterwards proceeded over the Ohio to the Indian towns. I did not hear Logan make the above speech; but from the unanimous accounts of those in camp, I have reason to think that said speech was delivered to Dunmore. I remember to have heard the very things contained in the above speech, related by some of our people in camp at that time.

ANDREW RODGERS.

The declaration of Mr. John Heckewelder, for several years a missionary from the society of Moravians, among the western Indians.

In the spring of the year 1774, at a time when the interior part of the Indian country all seemed peace and tranquil, the villagers on the Muskingum were suddenly alarmed by two runners (Indians), who reported "that the Big Knife (Virginians) had attacked the Mingo settlement, on the Ohio, and butchered even the women with their children in their arms, and that Logan's family were among the slain." A day or two after this several Mingoes made their appearance; among whom were one or two wounded, who had in this manner effected their escape. Exasperated to a high degree, after relating the particulars of this transaction, (which for humanity's sake I forbear to mention,) after resting some time on the treachery of the Big Knives, of their barbarity to those who are their friends, they gave a figurative description of the perpetrators; named Cresap as having been at the head of this murderous act. They made mention of nine being killed, and two wounded; and were prone to take revenge on any person of a white color; for which reason the missionaries had to shut themselves up during their stay. From this time terror daily increased. The exasperated friends and relations of these murdered women and children, with the nations to whom they belonged, passed and repassed through the villages of the quiet Delaware towns, in search of white people, making use of the most abusive language to these (the Delawares), since they would not join in taking revenge. Traders had either to hide themselves, or try to get out of the country the best way they could. And even at this time, they yet found such true friends among the Indians, who, at the risk of their own lives, conducted them, with the best part of their property, to Pittsburg; although, (shameful to relate!) these benefactors were, on their return from this mission, waylaid, and fired upon by whites, while crossing Big Beaver in a canoe, and had one man, a Shawanese, named Silverheels, (a man of note in his nation,) wounded in the body. This exasperated the Shawanese so much, that they, or at least a great part of them, immediately took an active part in the cause; and the Mingoes, (nearest connected with the former,) became unbounded in their rage. A Mr. Jones, son to a respectable family of this neighborhood (Bethlehem), who was then on his passage up Muskinghum, with two other men, was fortunately espied by a friendly Indian woman, at the falls of Muskinghum; who through motives of humanity alone, informed Jones of the nature of the times, and that he was running right in the hands of the enraged; and put him on the way, where he might perhaps escape the vengeance of the strolling parties. One of Jones's men, fatigued by travelling in the woods, declared he would rather die than remain longer in this situation; and hitting accidentally on a path, he determined to follow the same. A few hundred yards decided his fate. He was met by a party of about fifteen Mingoes, (and as it happened, almost within sight of White Eyes town,) murdered, and cut to pieces; and his limbs and flesh stuck up on the bushes. White Eyes, on hearing the scalp halloo, ran immediately out with his men, to see what the matter was; and finding the mangled body in this condition, gathered the whole and buried it. But next day when some of the above party found on their return the body interred, they instantly tore up the ground, and endeavored to destroy or scatter about, the parts at a greater distance. White Eyes, with the Delawares, watching their motions, gathered and interred the same a second time. The war party finding this out, ran furiously into the Delaware village, exclaiming against the conduct of these people, setting forth the cruelty of Cresap towards women and children, and declaring at the same time, that they would, in consequence of this cruelty, serve every white man they should meet with in the same manner. Times grew worse and worse, war parties went out and took scalps and prisoners, and the latter, in hopes it might be of service in saving their lives, exclaimed against the barbarous act which gave rise to these troubles and against the perpetrators. The name of Great-house was mentioned as having been accomplice to Cresap. So detestable became the latter name among the Indians, that I have frequently heard them apply it to the worst of things; also in quieting or stilling their children, I have heard them say, hush! Cresap will fetch you; whereas otherwise, they name the Owl. The warriors having afterwards bent their course more toward the Ohio, and down the same, peace seemed with us already on the return; and this became the case soon after the decided battle fought on the Kanhaway. Traders, returning now into the Indian country again, related the story of the above-mentioned massacre, *after the same manner, and with the same words*, we have heard it related hitherto. So the report remained, and was believed by all who resided in the Indian country. So it was represented numbers of times, in the peaceable Delaware towns, by the enemy. So the christian Indians were continually told they would one day be served. With this impression, a petty chief hurried all the way from Wabash in 1779, to take his relations (who were living with the peaceable Delawares near Coshachking) out of the reach of the Big Knives, in whose friendship he never more would place any confidence. And when this man found that his numerous relations would not break friendship with the Americans, nor be removed, he took two of his relations (women) off by force, saying, "The whole crop should not be destroyed; I will have seed out of it for a new crop;" alluding to, and repeatedly reminding those of the family of Logan, who he said had been real friends to the whites, and yet were cruelly murdered by them.

In Detroit, where I arrived the same Spring, the report respecting the murder of the Indians on the Ohio (amongst whom was Logan's family) was the same as related above; and on my return to the United States in the fall of 1786, and from that time, whenever and wherever in my presence, this subject was the topic of conversation, I found the report still the same; viz. that a person, bearing the name of Cresap, was the author, or perpetrator of this deed.

Logan was the second son of Shikellemus, a celebrated chief of the Cayuga nation. This chief, on account of his attachment to the English government, was of great service to the country, having the confidence of all the Six Nations, as well as that of the English, he was very useful in settling disputes, &c., &c. He was highly esteemed by Conrad Weisser, Esq., (an officer for government in the Indian department), with whom he acted conjunctly, and was faithful unto his death. His residence was at Shamokin, where he took great delight in acts of hospitality to such of the white people whose business led them that way.* His name and fame were so high on record, that Count Zinzendorf, when in this country in 1742, became desirous of seeing him, and actually visited him at his house in Shamokin.† About the year 1772, Logan was introduced to me by an Indian friend, as son to the late reputable chief Shikellemus, and as a friend to the white people. In the course of conversation I thought him a man of superior talents than Indians generally were. The subject turning on vice and immorality, he confessed his too great share of this, especially his fondness for liquor. He exclaimed against the white people for imposing liquors upon the Indians; he otherwise admired their ingenuity; spoke of gentlemen, but observed the Indians unfortunately had but few of these as their neighbors, &c. He spoke of his friendship to the white people, wished always to be a neighbor to them, intended to settle on the Ohio, below Big Beaver; was (to the best of my recollection) then encamped at the mouth of this river, (Beaver,) urged me to pay him a visit, &c. Note. I was then living at the Moravian town on this river, in the neighborhood of Cuskuskee. In April 1773, while on my passage down the Ohio for Muskinghum, I called at Logan's settlement; where I received every civility I could expect from such of the family as were at home.

Indian reports concerning Logan, after the death of his family, ran to this; that he exerted himself during the Shawanese war, (then so called,) to take all the

---

* The preceding account of Shikellemus, (Logan's father,) is copied from manuscripts of the Rev. C. Pyrlœus, written between the years 1741 and 1748.

† See G. H. Hoskiel's history of the Mission of the United Brethren, &c. Part II. Chap. 11, Page 31.

revenge he could, declaring he had lost all confidence in the white people. At the time of negotiation, he declared his reluctance in laying down the hatchet, not having (in his opinion) yet taken ample satisfaction ; yet, for the sake of the nation, he would do it. His expressions, from time to time, denoted a deep melancholy. Life (said he) had become a torment to him: he knew no more what pleasure was: he thought it had been better if he had never existed, &c., &c. Report further states, that he became in some measure delirious, declared he would kill himself, went to Detroit, drank very freely, and did not seem to care what he did, and what became of himself. In this condition he left Detroit, and on his way between that place and Miami was murdered. In October, 1781, (while as prisoner on my way to Detroit,) I was shown the spot where this should have happened. Having had an opportunity since last June of seeing the Rev. David Zeisberger, senior, missionary to the Delaware nation of Indians, who had resided among the same on Muskinghum, at the time when the murder was committed on the family of Logan, I put the following questions to him; first, who he had understood it was that had committed the murder on Logan's family? and secondly, whether he had any knowledge of a speech sent to Lord Dunmore by Logan, in consequence of this affair, &c. To which Mr. Zeisberger's answer was: That he had, from that time when this murder was committed to the present day, firmly believed the common report (which he had never heard contradicted) viz., that one Cresap was the author of the massacre ; or that it was committed by his orders ; and that he had known Logan as a boy, had frequently seen him from that time, and doubted not in the least, that Logan had sent such a speech to Lord Dunmore on this occasion, as he understood from me had been published ; that expressions of that kind from Indians were familiar to him ; that Logan in particular was a man of quick comprehension, good judgment and talents. Mr. Zeisberger has been a missionary upwards of fifty years; his age is about eighty ; speaks both the language of the Onondagoes and the Delawares ; resides at present on the Muskinghum, with his Indian congregation ; and is beloved and respected by all who are acquainted with him. JOHN HECKEWELDER.

From this testimony the following historical statement results:

In April or May, 1774, a number of people being engaged in looking out for settlements on the Ohio, information was spread among them, that the Indians had robbed some of the land-jobbers, as those adventurers were called. Alarmed for their safety, they collected together at Wheeling Creek. *Hearing there that there were two Indians and some traders a little above Wheeling, Captain Michael Cresap, one of the party, proposed to waylay and kill them. The proposition, though opposed, was adopted. A party went up the river, with Cresap at their head, and killed the two Indians.

† The same afternoon it was reported that there was a party of Indians on the Ohio, a little below Wheeling. Cresap and his party immediately proceeded down the river, and encamped on the bank. The Indians passed him peaceably,

* First murder of the two Indians by Cresap.
† Second murder on Grave Creek.

and encamped at the mouth of Grave Creek, a little below. Cresap and his party attacked them, and killed several. The Indians returned the fire, and wounded one of Cresap's party. Among the slain of the Indians were some of Logan's family. Colonel Zane indeed expresses a doubt of it; but it is affirmed by Huston and Chambers. Smith, one of the murderers, said they were known and acknowledged to be Logan's friends, and the party themselves generally said so; boasted of it in presence of Cresap; pretended no provocation; and expressed their expectations that Logan would probably avenge their deaths.

Pursuing these examples, *Daniel Great-house, and one Tomlinson, who lived on the opposite side of the river from the Indians, and were in habits of friendship with them, collected, at the house of Polke, on Cross Creek, about 16 miles from Baker's Bottom, a party of 32 men. Their object was to attack a hunting encampment of Indians, consisting of men, women, and children, at the mouth of Yellow Creek, some distance above Wheeling. They proceeded, and when arrived near Baker's Bottom, they concealed themselves, and Great-house crossed the river to the Indian camp. Being among them as a friend, he counted them, and found them too strong for an open attack with his force. While here, he was cautioned by one of the women not to stay, for that the Indian men were drinking, and having heard of Cresap's murder of *their relations* at Grave Creek, were angry, and she pressed him in a friendly manner, to go home; whereupon, after inviting them to come over and drink, he returned to Baker's, which was a tavern, and desired that when any of them should come to his house he would give them as much rum as they would drink. When his plot was ripe, and a sufficient number of them were collected at Baker's, and intoxicated, he and his party fell on them and massacred the whole, except a little girl, whom they preserved as a prisoner. Among these was the very woman who had saved his life, by pressing him to retire from the drunken wrath of her friends, when he was spying their camp at Yellow Creek. Either she herself, or some other of the murdered women, was the sister of Logan, very big with child, and inhumanly and indecently butchered; and there were others of his relations who fell here.

The party on the other side of the river,* alarmed for their friends at Baker's, on hearing the report of the guns, manned two canoes and sent them over. They were received, as they approached the shore, by a well-directed fire from Great-house's party, which killed some, wounded others, and obliged the rest to put back. Baker tells us there were twelve killed, and six or eight wounded.

This commenced the war, of which Logan's war-club and note left in the house of a murdered family, was the notification. In the course of it, during the ensuing summer, a great number of innocent men, women, and children, fell victims to the tomahawk and scalping knife of the Indians, till it was arrested in the autumn following by the battle at Point Pleasant, and the pacification with Lord Dunmore, at which the speech of Logan was delivered.

Of the genuineness of that speech nothing need be said. It was known to the camp where it was delivered; it was given out by Lord Dunmore and his officers; it ran through the public papers of these States; was rehearsed as an exercise at schools; published in the papers and periodical works of Europe; and all this, a dozen years before it was copied into the Notes on Virginia. In fine, General Gibson concludes the question for ever, by declaring that he received it from

* Massacre at Baker's Bottom, opposite Yellow Creek, by Great-house.

Logan's hand, delivered it to Lord Dunmore, translated it for him, and that the copy in the Notes on Virginia is a faithful copy.

The popular account of these transactions, as stated in the Notes on Virginia, appears, on collecting exact information, imperfect and erroneous in its details. It was the belief of the day; but how far its errors were to the prejudice of Cresap, the reader will now judge. That he, and those under him, murdered two Indians above Wheeling; that they murdered a large number at Grave Creek, among whom were a part of the family and relations of Logan, cannot be questioned; and as little that this led to the massacre of the rest of the family at Yellow Creek. Logan imputed the whole to Cresap, in his war-note and peace-speech: the Indians generally imputed it to Cresap: Lord Dunmore and his officers imputed it to Cresap: the country, with one accord, imputed it to him: and whether he were innocent, let the universal verdict now declare.

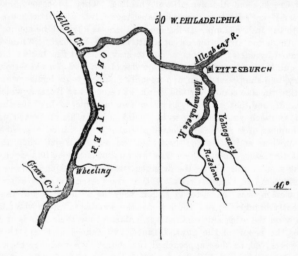

The declaration of John Sappington, received after the publication of the preceding Appendix.

I, JOHN SAPPINGTON, declare myself to be intimately acquainted with all the circumstances respecting the destruction of Logan's family, and do give in the following narrative, a true statement of that affair:

"Logan's family (if it was his family) was not killed by Cresap, nor with his knowledge, nor by his consent, but by the Great-houses and their associates. They were killed 30 miles above Wheeling, near the mouth of Yellow Creek. Logan's camp was on one side of the river Ohio, and the house, where the murder was committed, opposite to it on the other side. They had encamped

* Fourth murder, by Great-house.

there only four or five days, and during that time had lived peaceably and neighbourly with the whites on the opposite side, until the very day the affair happened. A little before the period alluded to, letters had been received by the inhabitants from a man of great influence in that country, and who was then, I believe, at Capteener, informing them that war was at hand, and desiring them to be on their guard. In consequence of those letters and other rumors of the same import, almost all the inhabitants fled for safety into the settlements. It was at the house of one Baker the murder was committed. Baker was a man who sold rum, and the Indians had made frequent visits at his house, induced, probably, by their fondness for that liquor. He had been particularly desired by Cresap to remove and take away his rum, and he was actually preparing to move at the time of the murder. The evening before, a squaw came over to Baker's house, and by her crying seemed to be in great distress. The cause of her uneasiness being asked, she refused to tell; but getting Baker's wife alone, she told her that the Indians were going to kill her and all her family the next day, that she loved her, did not wish her to be killed, and therefore told her what was intended, that she might save herself. In consequence of this information, Baker got a number of men, to the amount of twenty-one, to come to his house, and they were all there before morning. A council was held, and it was determined that the men should lie concealed in the back apartment; that if the Indians did come, and behaved themselves peaceably, they should not be molested; but if not, the men were to show themselves, and act accordingly. Early in the morning, seven Indians, four men and three squaws, came over. Logan's brother was one of them. They immediately got rum, and all, except Logan's brother, became very much intoxicated. At this time all the men were concealed, except the man of the house, Baker, and two others who staid out with him. Those Indians came unarmed. After some time Logan's brother took down a coat and hat, belonging to Baker's brother-in-law, who lived with him, and put them on, and setting his arms a-kimbo, began to strut about, till at length coming up to one of the men, he attempted to strike him, saying, "White man, son of a bitch." The white man, whom he treated thus, kept out of his way for some time; but growing irritated, he jumped to his gun, and shot the Indian as he was making to the door with the coat and hat on him. The men who lay concealed then rushed out, and killed the whole of them, excepting one child, which I believe is alive yet. But before this happened, one with two, the other with five Indians, all naked, painted, and armed completely for war, were discovered to start from the shore on which Logan's camp was. Had it not been for this circumstance, the white men would not have acted as they did; but this confirmed what the squaw had told before. The white men, having killed, as aforesaid, the Indians in the house, ranged themselves along the bank of the river, to receive the canoes. The canoe with the two Indians came near, being the foremost. Our men fired upon them and killed them both. The other canoe then went back. After this, two other canoes started, the one containing eleven, the other seven, Indians, painted and armed as the first. They attempted to land below our men, but were fired upon; had one killed, and retreated, at the same time firing back. To the best of my recollection there were three of the Great-houses engaged in this business. This is a true representation of the affair from beginning to end. I was intimately acquainted with Cresap, and know he had no hand in that transaction. He told me himself afterwards, at Redstone Old Fort, that the day before Logan's people were killed, he, with a small party, had an engagement with a party of Indians on Capteener, about forty-four miles lower down. Logan's people were killed at the mouth of Yellow Creek, on the 24th of May, 1774 and the 23d, the day before, Cresap was engaged as already stated. I know, likewise, that he was generally blamed for it, and believed by all who were not acquainted with the circumstances to have been the perpetrator of it. I know that he despised and hated the Great-houses ever afterwards on account of it. I was intimately acquainted with General Gibson, and served under him during the late war, and I have a discharge from him now lying in the land-office at Richmond, to which I refer any person for my character, who might be disposed to scruple my veracity. I was likewise at the treaty held by Lord Dunmore with the Indians, at Chelicothe. As for the speech said to have been delivered by Logan on that occasion, it might have been, or might not, for anything I know, as I never heard of it till long afterwards. I do not believe that Logan had any relations killed, except his brother. Neither of the squaws who were killed was his wife. Two of them were old women, and the third, with her child, which was saved, I have the best reason in the world to believe was the wife and child of General Gibson. I know he educated the child, and took care of it, as if it had been his own. Whether Logan had a wife or not, I can't say; but it is probable that as he was a chief, he considered them all as his people. All this I am ready to be qualified to at any time.   JOHN SAPPINGTON.

Attest, SAMUEL M‘KEE, Junr.

Madison County, Feb. 13th, 1800.

I do certify further, that the above-named John Sappington told me, at the same time and place at which he gave me the above narrative, that he himself was the man who shot the brother of Logan in the house, as above-related, and that he likewise killed one of the Indians in one of the canoes, which came over from the opposite shore.

He likewise told me, that Cresap never said an angry word to him about the matter, although he was frequently in company with Cresap, and indeed had been, and continued to be, in habits of intimacy with that gentleman, and was always befriended by him on every occasion. He further told me, that after they had perpetrated the murder, and were flying into the settlement, he met with Cresap (if I recollect right, at Redstone Old Fort); and gave him a scalp, a very large fine one, as he expressed it, and adorned with silver. This scalp, I think he told me, was the scalp of Logan's brother; though as to this I am not absolutely certain.   Certified by   SAMUEL M‘KEE, Junr.

hɑRpER ✦ ϹoRϲhbooϗs

HUMANITIES AND SOCIAL SCIENCES

American Studies

JOHN R. ALDEN: The American Revolution, 1775-1783.† *Illus.* TB/3011

RAY STANNARD BAKER: Following the Color Line: An Account of Negro Citizenship in the American Democracy.‡ *Illus. Introduction by Dewey Grantham, Jr.* TB/3053

RAY A. BILLINGTON: The Far Western Frontier, 1830-1860.† *Illus.* TB/3012

JOSEPH L. BLAU, Ed.: Cornerstones of Religious Freedom in America. *Selected Basic Documents, Court Decisions and Public Statements. Enlarged and revised edition with new Intro. by Editor* TB/118

RANDOLPH S. BOURNE: War and the Intellectuals: Collected Essays, 1915-1919.‡ *Edited with an Introduction by Carl Resek* TB/3043

A. RUSSELL BUCHANAN: The United States and World War II. † *Illus.* Volume I TB/3044
Volume II TB/3045

ABRAHAM CAHAN: The Rise of David Levinsky: *a novel. Introduction by John Higham* TB/1028

JOSEPH CHARLES: The Origins of the American Party System TB/1049

T. C. COCHRAN & WILLIAM MILLER: The Age of Enterprise: *A Social History of Industrial America* TB/1054

FOSTER RHEA DULLES: America's Rise to World Power, 1898-1954.† *Illus.* TB/3021

W. A. DUNNING: Reconstruction, Political and Economic, 1865-1877 TB/1073

CLEMENT EATON: The Growth of Southern Civilization, 1790-1860.† *Illus.* TB/3040

HAROLD U. FAULKNER: Politics, Reform and Expansion, 1890-1900.† *Illus.* TB/3020

LOUIS FILLER: The Crusade against Slavery, 1830-1860.† *Illus.* TB/3029

EDITORS OF FORTUNE: America in the Sixties: *the Economy and the Society. Two-color charts* TB/1015

LAWRENCE HENRY GIPSON: The Coming of the Revolution, 1763-1775.† *Illus.* TB/3007

FRANCIS J. GRUND: Aristocracy in America: *Jacksonian Democracy* TB/1001

OSCAR HANDLIN, Editor: This Was America: *As Recorded by European Travelers to the Western Shore in the Eighteenth, Nineteenth, and Twentieth Centuries. Illus.* TB/1119

MARCUS LEE HANSEN: The Atlantic Migration: 1607-1860. *Edited by Arthur M. Schlesinger; Introduction by Oscar Handlin* TB/1052

MARCUS LEE HANSEN: The Immigrant in American History. *Edited with a Foreword by Arthur Schlesinger, Sr.* TB/1120

JOHN D. HICKS: Republican Ascendancy, 1921-1933.† *Illus.* TB/3041

JOHN HIGHAM, Ed.: The Reconstruction of American History TB/1068

ROBERT H. JACKSON: The Supreme Court in the American System of Government TB/1106

THOMAS JEFFERSON: Notes on the State of Virginia.‡ *Introduction by Thomas Perkins Abernethy* TB/3052

WILLIAM E. LEUCHTENBURG: Franklin D. Roosevelt and the New Deal, 1932-1940.† *Illus.* TB/3025

LEONARD W. LEVY: Freedom of Speech and Press in Early American History: *Legacy of Suppression* TB/1109

ARTHUR S. LINK: Woodrow Wilson and the Progressive Era, 1910-1917.† *Illus.* TB/3023

BERNARD MAYO: Myths and Men: *Patrick Henry, George Washington, Thomas Jefferson* TB/1108

JOHN C. MILLER: The Federalist Era, 1789-1801.† *Illus.* TB/3027

PERRY MILLER & T. H. JOHNSON, Editors: The Puritans: *A Sourcebook of Their Writings*
Volume I TB/1093
Volume II TB/1094

GEORGE E. MOWRY: The Era of Theodore Roosevelt and the Birth of Modern America, 1900-1912.† *Illus.* TB/3022

WALLACE NOTESTEIN: The English People on the Eve of Colonization, 1603-1630.† *Illus.* TB/3006

RUSSEL BLAINE NYE: The Cultural Life of the New Nation, 1776-1801.† *Illus.* TB/3026

GEORGE E. PROBST, Ed.: The Happy Republic: *A Reader in Tocqueville's America* TB/1060

FRANK THISTLETHWAITE: America and the Atlantic Community: *Anglo-American Aspects, 1790-1850* TB/1107

---

† The New American Nation Series, edited by Henry Steele Commager and Richard B. Morris.

‡ American Perspectives series, edited by Bernard Wishy and William E. Leuchtenburg.

* The Rise of Modern Europe series, edited by William L. Langer.

** Researches in the Social, Cultural, and Behavioral Sciences, edited by Benjamin Nelson

§ The Library of Religion and Culture, edited by Benjamin Nelson.

Σ Harper Modern Science Series, edited by James R. Newman.

º Not for sale in Canada.

Anthropology & Sociology

Art and Art History

Business, Economics & Economic History

3

Intellectual History

Literature, Poetry, The Novel & Criticism

Myth, Symbol & Folklore

Philosophy

29547

A LETTER TO THE READER

Overseas, there is considerable belief that we are a country of extreme conservatism and that we cannot accommodate to social change.

Books about America in the hands of readers abroad can help change those ideas.

The U. S. Information Agency cannot, by itself, meet the vast need for books about the United States.

You can help.

Harper Torchbooks provides three packets of books on American history, economics, sociology, literature and politics to help meet the need.

To send a packet of Torchbooks [*] overseas, all you need do is send your check for $7 (which includes cost of shipping) to Harper & Row. The U. S. Information Agency will distribute the books to libraries, schools, and other centers all over the world.

I ask every American to support this program, part of a worldwide BOOKS USA campaign.

I ask you to share in the opportunity to help tell others about America.

EDWARD R. MURROW
Director,
U. S. Information Agency

[*retailing at $10.85 to $12.00]

PACKET I: *Twentieth Century America*

Dulles/America's Rise to World Power, 1898-1954
Cochran/The American Business System, 1900-1955
Zabel, Editor/Literary Opinion in America (two volumes)
Drucker/The New Society: *The Anatomy of Industrial Order*
Fortune Editors/America in the Sixties: *The Economy and the Society*

PACKET II: *American History*

Billington/The Far Western Frontier, 1830-1860
Mowry/The Era of Theodore Roosevelt and the
   Birth of Modern America, 1900-1912
Faulkner/Politics, Reform, and Expansion, 1890-1900
Cochran & Miller/The Age of Enterprise: *A Social History of
   Industrial America*
Tyler/Freedom's Ferment: *American Social History from the
   Revolution to the Civil War*

PACKET III: *American History*

Hansen/The Atlantic Migration, 1607-1860
Degler/Out of Our Past: *The Forces that Shaped Modern America*
Probst, Editor/The Happy Republic: *A Reader in Tocqueville's America*
Alden/The American Revolution, 1775-1783
Wright/The Cultural Life of the American Colonies, 1607-1763

*Your gift will be acknowledged directly to you by the overseas recipient.
Simply fill out the coupon, detach and mail with your check or money order.*

HARPER & ROW, PUBLISHERS · BOOKS USA DEPT.
49 East 33rd Street, New York 16, N. Y.

Packet I ☐   Packet II ☐   Packet III ☐

Please send the BOOKS USA library packet(s) indicated above, in my
name, to the area checked below. Enclosed is my remittance in the
amount of _____ for _____ packet(s) at $7.00 each.

_____ Africa   _____ Latin America
_____ Far East   1 9 4 2 3 Near East

Name_____

Address_____

_____

NOTE: This offer expires December 31, 1966.